In this radical and subversive book Brad Je............... ....
whole understanding of God in the light of the supreme divine self-revelation in Christ: if God is like Jesus then what must God be like? The results of exploring that simple question are far-reaching, surprising, and transformative. This clearly written volume with its theological sophistication and grace-infused vision of God will certainly provoke fresh perspectives, and even those who disagree with parts of it will find plenty to enrich their minds and hearts. Warmly recommended.

— **ROBIN A. PARRY, PhD**
Author of *The Evangelical Universalist* and *The Biblical Cosmos*

'Good souls many will one day be horrified at the things they now believe of God.' This prophecy of George MacDonald has found its fulfillment in Brad Jersak's journey from the 'volatile moral monster' to the face of Jesus' Father. *A More Christlike God* is a priceless treasure, worthy of serious reflection. Here the ancient song of light sings us new eyes: "Behold the Lamb, just like his Father." Here we are invited to take sides with Jesus against the way we see, expanding our minds, as St. Hilary said, until they are worthy of the theme, that we may live in Jesus' world.

— **C. BAXTER KRUGER, PhD**
Author of *The Shack Revisited* and *Patmos*

I sometimes hear Christians express their faith and think, "The God you are talking about needs to accept Jesus into his heart!" This book is an altar call to all our images of God that fall short of the beauty of the Risen Jesus. Let these pages invite you to contemplate again the Creator who hears the cries of the oppressed—who was in Christ, on a cross, reconciling the world to himself.

As the beauty of ancient Christianity rearticulates orthodoxy for tomorrow, we have yet to know what shape it must take, but like this book, you can be assured it will be more like the beauty of Jesus."

— **JARROD McKENNA**
Co-Founder of *First Home Project*
National Director of *CommonGrace.org.au*

Do yourself a favor and make this the last book besides the Gospels you read on Jesus. This is Brad Jersak's bold attempt to save Christianity from Christians. He writes, "In the flesh and blood person of Jesus, we have the only life ever lived that perfectly reveals the true nature of God." Jersak shows us how to restore the ruined image of God.

Bluntly, he makes belief in God a little less stupid. These days that's saying a lot. Or as Jersak writes: "May we be willing to revisit and reform our assumptions about the meaning of the Cross, and thereby make fresh and beautiful discoveries about Christ's glorious gospel."

— FRANK SCHAEFFER
Author of *Why I Am an Atheist Who Believes in God*

It has been said that the truth will set you free, but that it sometimes annoys you first. That's why I so value Brad Jersak's books. He just tells it like it is and leaves the results between the Teacher and the reader. Brad is a voice, not an echo. Honoring the centrality of Christ, he systematically and lovingly but boldly brings conservative minds forward toward the more Christlike God Jesus came to reveal.

Like his other books, *A More Christlike God* will provoke thought and study from the reader. It will make you think and might even make you repent, but the one thing it will assuredly do is cause you to see and to love this God of grace in a greater way.

— STEVE McVEY
Grace Walk Ministries
Author of *Grace Walk* and *Beyond an Angry God*

Written with the wisdom of a pastor's heart, familiar with the reality of people's real trauma and grief, Brad Jersak lovingly helps us to face the pain and darkness of our suffering head on. This is no mere apologetic that attempts to explain away the problem of evil, but a theodicy of the cross that faces it head on with brutal honesty, showing us that it is precisely there in that brokenness that we encounter God in Christ. A deeply needed and important book.

— DEREK FLOOD
Author of *Healing the Gospel*
and *Disarming Scripture*

Endorsements

The centerpiece of Christian theology is the incarnation of God in Jesus Christ. The Scriptures as a whole and the witness of Jesus himself, corroborated by those who knew him best, is unrelenting in insisting on this. So why is there so much hate, so much contentiousness, so much ill feeling among those who claim to be his followers? And especially among Evangelicals who take pride in having it "right"?

Brad Jersak has spent his life among Evangelicals as a pastor, evangelist and writer. Mostly he has immersed himself in the company of the poor, the addicted, the outsiders. He is determined to recover the essence of the "beautiful" gospel for all of us. The conspicuous mark that characterizes every page of this winsome witness is that this is a "lived theology." He has given attentive detail to what is in the theological libraries, but is not content with that. He has worked it out on the streets and in the lives of those with whom he has chosen to share his life and Christlike God witness, a convincingly beautiful Gospel.

— **EUGENE H. PETERSON, PhD**
Emeritus Professor of Spiritual Theology
Regent College, Vancouver, BC

This excellent and much-needed book confronts with both open heart and very good mind the major obstacles that we have created for people in their journey toward God! "Why didn't people teach us this many years ago?" so many of us are saying. I am so very grateful that Brad Jersak is re-opening the door that Jesus had already opened 2000 years ago. It is so terribly sad that it was ever closed.

— **Fr. RICHARD ROHR, O.F.M.**
Center for Action and Contemplation
Albuquerque, New Mexico

With theological integrity and open-hearted compassion, Brad Jersak creates a beautiful space for Jesus to challenge our views of God. A breath of clean and clarifying air.

— **WILLIAM PAUL YOUNG**
Author of *The Shack*

Brad Jersak has given us a gift of greatest value: a fresh vision of God, Christ, the cross, Scripture ... and ourselves. He demonstrates the rare ability to take deep theological issues and make them understandable to everyone. He represents a new generation of Christian theologians whose work, I believe, is both desperately needed and wonderfully liberating.

— **BRIAN D. McLAREN**
Author of *We Make the Road by Walking*

In our increasingly polarized 21st century, those who believe and follow the "wrong God" are routinely condemned and castigated. Some who worship the "wrong God" are in danger of being brutalized and/ or beheaded. In the midst of religiously inspired hatred, bigotry and violence in the name of God, Brad Jersak carefully and compassionately answers the urgent question: "Who is God?" We don't need more indoctrination. We don't need more dogma written by those who insist they uniquely speak for God. Our greatest need is to see and know God as he is. Jersak is a Christ-follower who opens our eyes and helps heal our hearts as he explains that God is exactly like Jesus. You will be enthralled by Brad Jersak's rendition of the "Gospel in Chairs" as he leads readers to the love and grace of God by repeating the query, "And what does God do?" A must read.

— **GREG ALBRECHT**
President, *Plain Truth Ministries*
Author of *A Taste of Grace: Christianity Without the Religion*

Brad Jersak's book is a much-needed corrective for those needing to hear again, or perhaps for the first time, of a God who is always for us and never against us. Written through the lens of pastor-theologian, Brad combines a deep compassion with a love of the church fathers to draw out fresh and powerful insights into the reality of the nature of God revealed as overwhelming love and mercy through the cross.

— **LUCY PEPPIATT, PhD**
Principal of *Westminster Theological Centre*, Cheltenham, UK
Author of *Women and Worship at Corinth*

In a single volume, Brad Jersak perfectly articulates the heart-cry of a generation who longs to believe in a more compassionate God. But he doesn't stop there: he deftly and expertly cuts away the brush—clearing every conceivable obstacle—and lays bare the path that leads to this God. A life-changing book by the most gifted of teacher-guides.

— **AMY HOLLINGSWORTH**
Author of *Runaway Radical*

This is a courageous, honest, and passionate book about how to understand and converse with the Christian God. Brad Jersak speaks from his heart about his own relationship with God, who is revealed in the person of Jesus Christ through the grace of the Holy Spirit. Brad explores the pitfalls that confront each of us as we grow in our spiritual lives; he pulls no punches in exposing these errors for what they are. The book conveys, however, a spirit of joyous discovery, reflecting the author's own confidence in God's infinite mercy and love for every human being.

— **MARY B. CUNNINGHAM, PhD**
Professor of Historical Theology
The University of Nottingham

Brad Jersak's book *A More Christlike God* reveals with stunning clarity the ways that the modern church has distorted our image of who God is and forgotten the Gospel of Jesus Christ. Jersak then calls the reader back to the heart of God and the true Good News as revealed in and proclaimed by Christ.

This timely book has the potential to fundamentally change the way we speak about God, understand the Bible, and live out our faith. It is my hope that this book will be read widely by Christians of all theological backgrounds as well as those who have been turned off to religion because of the perverse image of God that they have been exposed to.

In these pages you will encounter the true and living Christ and the extraordinary message of grace and love that he proclaimed. Prepare to be transformed.

— **BRANDAN ROBERTSON**
Founder of *The Revangelical Movement*

Through a remarkable mix of compassionate pastoral sensitivity and perceptive, crisp analysis, Brad Jersak reintroduces his readers in *A More Christlike God* to the ancient yet living voices that have parsed a crucial theological issue: what God is like. Routinely overlooked and taken for granted—often to our peril—discerning what God is truly like among the cacophony of available theistic representations requires space for honest, unsanitized inquiry.

In his colloquial writing style, Jersak provides this space, writing a book not simply to push his views on others or listen to himself talk, but to sincerely engage a myriad of legitimate objections and misgivings over the seemingly schizophrenic deity portrayed in the Scriptures.

Befitting the moniker of "Christianity," Jersak eventually concludes that God is like Christ—the image of the invisible God whose humanity reveals his divinity, whose self-emptying is an expression of the divine virtues of humility, patience, mercy, compassion, and love.

— **ANDREW P. KLAGER, PhD**
Adjunct Professor of History
Trinity Western University

A More Christlike God

A More Beautiful Gospel

Bradley Jersak

Published by Plain Truth Ministries
Pasadena, CA | www.ptm.org

Bible translation permissions:

Unless otherwise noted, all Scripture quotations are cited from the NIV:

NIV: The Holy Bible, New International Version®, NIV® Copyright © 1973,
1978, 1984, 2011 by Biblica, Inc.® UBP. All rights reserved worldwide.

KJV: The King James Version (Authorised): Public Domain.

NASB: The New American Standard Bible®, Copyright © 1960,1962,1963,1968,
1971,1972,1973,1975,1977,1995 by The Lockman Foundation. UBP.

NKJV: The New King James Version®. Copyright © 1982 by Thomas Nelson,
Inc. UBP. All rights reserved.

NLT: The Holy Bible, New Living Translation, copyright © 1996, 2004, 2007
by Tyndale House Foundation. UBP of Tyndale House Publishers, Inc., Carol
Stream, Illinois 60188. All rights reserved.

THE MESSAGE: Copyright © by Eugene H. Peterson 1993, 1994, 1995, 1996,
2000, 2001, 2002. Used by permission of Tyndale House Publishers, Inc.

Emphases: All emphases throughout the book are the author's, including
those in Scripture texts and cited material, unless otherwise indicated.

Library of Congress Control Number: 2015933662
Createspace ISBN 10: 150-8528373 / ISBN 13: 978-1508528371

Jersak, Bradley Mark, 1964 –
A More Christlike God : a more beautiful gospel / Bradley Jersak
1. Religion – Christianity – Theology
Cover Image: Pink Sky Design (www.pinkskydesign.com).

CWRpress
An imprint of Plain Truth Ministries

For Vladika Lazar Puhalo

For showing me Christ,
'the good and merciful and man-befriending God.'

Contents

Foreword

by Brian Zahnd

What is God like? What an enormous question. For those of us who believe that God is somehow at the foundation of existence, meaning and self-understanding, it's an all-important question. So how shall we answer? Our options are endless. Human inquiry into the divine has produced a vast pantheon of gods—from Ares to Zeus. Of course, the Christian will instinctively look to the Bible for the definition of God. I understand this instinct and in one sense it is correct; but it may not yield as clear an answer as we think. Even while speaking of the 'God of the Bible' we can cobble together whatever vision of God we choose from its disparate images. That we do this mostly unconsciously doesn't help matters.

Even if we restrict our inquiry into the nature of God to the Bible, we are likely to find just the kind of God that we want to find. If we want a God of peace, he's there. If we want a God of war, he's there. If we want a compassionate God, he's there. If we want a vindictive God, he's there. If we want an egalitarian God, he's there. If we want an ethnocentric God, he's there. If we want a God demanding blood sacrifice, he's there. If we want a God abolishing blood sacrifice, he's there. Sometimes the Bible is like a Rorschach test—it reveals more about the reader than the eternal I AM.

What are we to do? How are we to discover God as God is? As a Christian, pastor and preacher, I would like to recommend we look to Jesus for our answer to the question. Or let me say it this way: What if God is like Jesus? What if the personality of God is identical to the personality of the man called Jesus of Nazareth portrayed in the Gospels? Jesus audaciously made this claim: "Anyone who has seen me has seen the Father." What if that claim is true? Wouldn't that be good news? Ah, that *is* the good news! God *is* like Jesus!

This is Christianity, which is not to be confused with 'biblicism.' As Christians we worship Christ, not the Bible. The Bible is the inspired witness to the true Word of God who is Jesus. What the Bible does infallibly is take us on a journey that culminates with Christ—but it is Christ who fully reveals God. Or we can say it this way: The Scriptures ultimately bear witness to Christ, and Christ perfectly bears witness to God. While we are searching the Bible to find out what God is like, the Bible is all the while resolutely pointing us to Jesus. The revelation of God could not be contained in a book, but it could be contained in a human life—the life of Jesus Christ.

God is like Jesus. Jesus is the Message of God. Jesus is what God has to say. Jesus is the full and faithful witness to how God is to be understood. Jesus didn't come to save us from God (as some deplorable theories would lead us to believe)—Jesus came to reveal God as Savior. Jesus didn't come to enable God to love us—Jesus came to reveal God as love. Jesus didn't come to reconcile God to the world—Jesus came to reconcile the world to God. If Jesus' life is the definition of God, the defining moment of Jesus' life is the Cross. As John Cihak observed, "being disguised under the disfigurement of an ugly crucifixion and death, the Christform upon the Cross is the clearest revelation of who God is." As an evangelist I can do no better work than to point to Jesus on the Cross and say, "Right there! *That* is what God is like." God is not like Caiaphas needing a scapegoat to take the blame. God is not like Pilate requiring an execution to satisfy justice. God is like Jesus, absorbing, forgiving and taking away the sins of the world.

A return to the revelation that God is revealed in Christ could not be more timely. Western Christianity is in a crisis. It can no longer retain credibility and be transmitted to succeeding generations on the authority of tradition alone. Critical questions are being asked and Christianity must gain its adherents based on its own merits. Fortunately Christianity is up to the task. But not just any Christianity; the Christianity up to the task is the Christianity grounded in the confession that Jesus is the icon of the invisible God. I am in full sympathy with those who find "Sinners In the Hands of An Angry God" Christianity repellent and in need of being jettisoned. I too have pitched the theologies of an angry, retributive deity back into the dark sea of paganism. The good news is that buried under centuries of misconstrued Christianity there is a beautiful gospel just waiting to be discovered.

Brad Jersak knows this good news. In *A More Christlike God* Brad is a wise and patient guide, walking us toward the beautiful gospel while never shirking the hard questions. With the keen mind of a theologian and the tender heart of a pastor, Brad converses with seekers who want to believe in a more Christlike God, but don't want to arrive there by cheap clichés or wishful thinking. Brad Jersak is no purveyor of pop Christianity. He has done the hard work of real theology. He has gone down into the Patristic mines and brought back gold. He has become conversant with our best contemporary theologians and made their work accessible. He has struggled with his own dark night of the soul and comes to us holding a lantern. I am happy to have Brad Jersak as a guide. He knows the way beyond the ugly parodies of Christianity into the beautiful gospel of a Christlike God. Let the journey begin.

Brian Zahnd
Pastor of Word of Life Church, St. Joseph, Missouri
Author of *Beauty Will Save the World* and *A Farewell To Mars*

Preface
The Purpose of This Book

"Anyone who has seen me has seen the Father."
— Jesus (John 14:9) —

The purpose of this brief work is to introduce in simple terms a more Christlike image of God.

To do this, I will raise some of the heart-cry, faith-and-doubt questions I've heard as a minister from regular people in the pews and in coffee shops. And I will also share fresh (but ancient) insights that some of our best theologians are offering to our bewilderment about God and life and how the two come together in Christ. Unfortunately, their helpful ideas are often buried in thick textbooks, suffocated by complicated language or withheld by nervous ministers. Contrary to their reputation, not all seminaries are 'cemeteries' where scholars sit in ivory towers disputing how many angels can dance on the head of a pin. In truth, God's thinkers are real people who wrestle with God and care enough to do the spadework for answers to our heartfelt questions. You deserve a share in the treasures they are digging up!

In the following chapters, I will surface some of the gold nuggets that profs and prophets have unearthed in the deep mines of prayerful and careful meditation. I hope this book serves as a humble kiosk, where those riches are easily accessible to the average, but mindful, truth-seeker (Christian or not). For that reason I will be sharing as one shares over coffee, without a ton of supporting footnotes, carefully crafted arguments or mysterious terms. If I use a technical word, I'll try to define it simply and carefully in the text, in the 'call-out' boxes and in the glossary. The embarrassing truth is that authors can hide behind big words while we're still sifting through the raw ore of our first insights and finite perceptions. My hope is that you'll be able to track with me easily.

Of course, the answers I suggest may leave many 'What about this?' questions unanswered. There will be no pretense of neat bows on tidy, gift-wrapped packages. I'd rather be suggestive and provocative than pose as the latest expert who wants to indoctrinate you. I'm speaking as a witness to what I've seen and heard—not as a judge with a final verdict; or as a lawyer trying to make his case; or as a defendant taking the stand. For the reader who wants to go deeper—to test and weigh the truth of these proposals—the points I'll raise do appear in more thorough academic studies elsewhere. Solid, Christ-centered theologians are addressing the array of dilemmas we'll look at. I'll occasionally direct readers to their works. But for those whose lives don't allow time to wade through molasses-thick masterpieces, this summary snapshot says, "We hear your questions. No, you're not crazy. You're not a heretic for asking. We're working on it." This is an update on what that labor is producing.

I confess I've had one real downer in reporting our immensely encouraging findings. When we hear the very best news that we've all been hoping for—when our wildest hopes of God are confirmed—something odd happens. Instead of bringing relief and deliverance from old assumptions that made us afraid of God, a wall of resistance arises from certain quarters of American **Christendom.*** Why? The possibility that God is *that* good—as kind and loving and gracious as Jesus—may create panic because *that* God is unfamiliar to us. Through their own fears or stiff resistance from their peers or leaders, the very folks asking for hope may retreat back to the oppressive god they've known for many years. Perhaps they imagine their old certitude gives them a measure of control. When you 'know' something, questions become bad. Those who question doctrinal certitudes are considered dangerous. The watchdogs, mistaking themselves for watchmen, start barking and blogging.

I get it. After all, who wants to be deceived? Not me! But the fear of deception is not wisdom or discernment. In fact, fear only *opens* the door to deception. The fruit of such fear is rancid. Charges of heresy and liberalism start flying around. One elder statesman in the faith, respected by multitudes for his long-term faithfulness, recently called me and expressed that even he was surprised. "Brad," he asked, "why are they so mean?" Indeed.

But frankly, pursuing God is too important to us to simply let the discussion go. God has led us into a spacious place and we can't go back. Nor will God. He won't submit to confinement in our doctrinal ken-

'Christendom' refers to the sum total of Christian culture, especially where Christianity or the church as an institution forms its own kingdom of sorts. Christendom has historically included actual geopolitical kingdoms, but can also be any cultural dominance Christians enjoy or impose when they are strong enough to hold sway as a majority or powerful minority.

nels. The neo-Sanhedrin may bare their teeth as they did in Jesus' day. Once again, the Spirit of Jesus is being slandered rather badly, but these are the days when he's setting the record straight. The real God, the one true God, wants you to know what he's really like. Whatever you remember of this book, I hope this mantra will echo in your heart:

God is Good. God is Love. Life happens but redemption is coming. "The darkness is passing and the true light is already shining" (1 John 2:8).

Part I

What is God?

Competing Images of Will and Love

- In which we see competing images and projections of God.
- Is the image of God you hold accurate?
- Is it adequate?
- Or do worn and tired perceptions obscure God with your own reflection?
- Is God free to do whatever God pleases?
- Or does God's goodness direct God's freedom?
- Is God primarily willful or actually willing?
- What does the Incarnation show us about God?
- What if God is Christlike?

What is God Really Like? 1

"I am enough of a romantic to believe that,
if something is worth being rude about,
it is worth understanding well."

– David Bentley Hart (The Experience of God) –

If there is a God . . .

If there is a God—a *faith statement*[1] for sure—we don't get
to make him up. A *real* God should not and cannot merely be a
reflection of my imagination. A God who is real and alive must exist
beyond my own puny understanding, bigger than any box in which
I try to contain him or her or whatever pronoun we use for this
Being. Even using the simple pronoun 'he' for God is awkward and
inaccurate. I will use it, but when I do, I tend to cringe. God is *not*
a 'him' or a 'her.' Jesus said "God is Spirit" (John 4:24). But God is
far more personal than an 'it.' Thus, we lean to the language of 'him'
historically because when God showed up in the flesh, 'he' came as a
man, Jesus (his 'son'). Furthermore, Scripture mainly speaks of God
as Father and describes God with male metaphors, such as 'King.'
On the other hand, the Hebrew pronoun for the Spirit is 'she.' In
fact, God's caring and nurturing attributes, such as compassion and
mercy, are most often associated with feminine traits.

Some thinkers say that even calling God a 'being' falls short,
or claiming that God 'exists' says too little. Rather, God is the very
ground of being; God is *existence itself*, whatever that means. Those
who talk this way assert that nearly anything we claim about God
already belies our hidden desire to stand over, box in and control

him. Language, words, doctrine, theology—aren't these less than God? And yet don't they frequently function to shrink the Creator of all into a manageable doctrinal specimen we can pin down and dissect? Isn't it more convenient to cage him within our tiny, over-confident minds, where he must parrot our own lofty thoughts? The stubborn fact is that whatever we say about God or for God with great certitude is sifted through the thick veils of our religious tradi-tions, cultural assumptions and personal interpretations. Skeptics and agnostics ask, "What can we really *say* for sure about this God?" Rightly so.

There seem to be as many versions of God as there are people, even within a particular faith, no matter how diligently religion attempts to indoctrinate us. Never mind comparing Hindus to Buddhists or Moslems to Jews. Among Christians, we'll see later how John Wesley would say John Calvin's God was worse than the devil! Even today, among North America's most downloaded Protestant preachers, Mark Driscoll and John Piper's grasp of God stands poles apart from that of Gregory Boyd or Brian McLaren. I like to think we're all still serving the same Lord, and yet sometimes I wonder if we have two (or more) diverse religions competing for the same 'Christian' label! The Apostle Paul spoke about different gospels and other christs in his day (Gal. 1:6-8).

Much closer to home, unbeknownst to us, even our closest loved ones probably hold drastically different notions of God than what we imagine. And closer still, as my own spiritual journey progresses, I may continue to pray to the same God, never realizing how much 'the God of my understanding' (to use 12-step recovery lingo) has morphed. While God doesn't change, my image of God may progress (or regress) so much over time that I am virtually worshiping another god under the same name. Moreover, this may be both good and necessary.

My point here is that those of us who claim to believe in 'the

God of the Bible' must become more aware of how we read the text through thick lenses of our own unconscious biases. From these distorting filters we are prone to construct idols of God in our own image. And so, we hear the controversial German preacher, Meister Eckhart, cry out in exasperation, "God! Deliver me from 'god'!"[2] That is, save me from every shadowy *conception* of God that I've created and worshiped, deceiving myself into believing it is the one true God! So I say no—if there is a God, I *don't* just get to fashion him from the clay of my own image. I *need* him to reveal himself in a way that can be known.

What God is not . . .

One stream of Christian thought called *'negative theology'** suggests the best we can do is describe what God is *not*. You can name any attribute of God—any image of God you can find, even in the Bible—and then ask, "Okay, God is a father, but how is he *not* a father? God is a king, but how is he *not* a king? God is a shepherd, but how is he *not* a shepherd?" This is a good exercise as far as it goes, because it cautions us against taking these human metaphors too far. It reminds us that our image of God is just that: an image, an icon, a picture. We have these pictures, but God is bigger than any of them. God is *far more* than fire or light or water, even though these elements are used to describe to him. The hen, the eagle, the lion and the lamb signify some aspect of God's character, yet God is obviously *not* a bird or animal. Negative

'Negative Theology'

Also known as *via negativa* (negative way) or *apophatic* theology. 'Apophatic' comes from the word for 'deny.' It defines God by denying our definitions of God.

theology warns us against totalizing any of these symbols into an idol with which to displace God.

For example, in Numbers 21, we have the wilderness story in which a plague of venomous snakes attacked the Israelites. God told Moses to fashion a 'fiery serpent' made of bronze and erect it on a pole. All those bitten who turned their gaze toward the bronze serpent were immediately healed. The image represented the healing love of God and is used to this day as a logo in the medical world.

Unfortunately, the statue of the bronze serpent was later repurposed for idolatry. By the time of King Hezekiah, the people had named the bronze serpent 'Nehushtan' and begun to worship it. Thus, the king had to destroy it as part of his anti-idolatry reforms (2 Kings 18:4). Even so, the lesson is *not* simply to abandon all imagery of God, but to cleanse it and refocus it on Christ. Jesus himself modeled the use of divine imagery by recalling the bronze serpent during his moonlit chat with Nicodemus: "Just as Moses lifted up the snake in the wilderness, so the Son of Man must be lifted up, that everyone who believes may have eternal life in him" (John 3:14-15).

And so a negative theology urges us to keep asking the both/and questions. We say God is present. We pray that we may experience this presence, "Make your face shine on me!" But we also ask, "Why is he absent?" And we pray through genuine crises of absence, "Do not hide your face from me!" Using 'face' as an image of God, we reflect, "How is each statement true and how is it not true?"

Or again, we proclaim, "God is close," and then follow up with, "How is God far?" Paul says God dwells in *unapproachable* light, but Hebrews invites us to enter the Holy of Holies boldly and *draw near* to God's throne with confidence! How can God be near and far at the same time? If we can rise above either/or assumptions and assertions that would box God in, we'll be able to remember and recount our personal both/and experiences of God.

Basically, for every quality of God's self that we uphold, we can learn even more of him by asking, "How is God *not* like that? And does the opposite also hold true somehow?"

What God is . . .

Negative theology seeks to avoid boxing God in, but we do also need a positive theology. For God to be God, and not mere nonsense, we declare some truths by faith for which the opposite is *never* true:

- God is *good* and is never evil. He is the perfection of all we call goodness.
- God is *love* and every other aspect of God must align with his love.
- God is *light* and in him is no darkness whatsoever (1 John 1:9).
- God is perfect *beauty* and in him is no ugliness at all.
- God is perfect *truth* and let no one call him a liar.
- God is perfect *justice* and in him is no injustice at all.

Theology texts sometimes list God's goodness, love and justice among his 'attributes,' and dedicate chapters to describing God according to these attributes, almost scientifically. These descriptions can be quite dry and sterile, ascribing human ideas, concepts and analogies to God in a way that is pretty philosophical and, frankly, limiting. This is what negative theology had hoped to overcome in the first place. Negative theology sought to retain the majesty and mystery of God beyond our manuals and categories.

The Apostle Paul and his later theologians address this sterility by introducing another more dynamic phrase: ***divine energies****(energeia).*

Energeia is also translated in the New Testament as 'power' (Eph. 1:19), 'working' (Eph. 3:7; 4:16; Phil. 3:21; Col. 1:29) and 'operations' (Col. 2:12). We see God's energies at work when Paul

'Divine energies'

are God himself at work. They are not merely attributes of God, but rather, God himself in his actions, in his activity, in his self-revelation to us.

We'll never penetrate the infinite depths of God's *essence*, but God's *energies* do penetrate our lives and our world.

Another phrase we use for these energies is 'the grace of the Holy Spirit.'

says, "That energy is *God's energy*, an energy deep within you, *God himself* willing and working at what will give him the most pleasure" (Phil. 2:13 MSG).

Note that the *energies* are not merely considered attributes of God. The energies are God himself in action. Later theologians would specify this, speaking of them as 'uncreated energies.' In other words, when we say "God is love" or "God is good" or "God is light," we aren't merely describing his characteristics. We are saying God *is* love, goodness and light in his *energies*, just as we say God *is* Father, Son and Holy Spirit in his *persons*.

Why 'energies'? Because they describe who God is in his *actions*, in his *activity*, in his self-revelation. God *is* love experienced; God *is* goodness revealed. God *is* beauty, truth and justice—coming to us, manifesting himself in our lives. The uncreated energies are God himself, touching us, filling us and transforming us. We will never penetrate the infinite depths of God's *essence*, but God's uncreated energies penetrate our world and our lives. We use another phrase to describe this phenomenon: 'the grace of the Holy Spirit'!

So, while negative theology is a line of inquiry worth visiting—and we will—it cannot satisfy our hunger to *know* the living God. Doesn't the Bible show us a God who wants to be known and is always committed to making that happen? In negative theology, something is missing, even beyond the energies I've listed above. Or rather, *someone*! I'm referring to Jesus of course. To see the *only perfect image* that bears the fullness of 'the Good', of love, light, beauty, truth and justice—on earth as in heaven—we turn to the *'Incarnation'** (literally, the 'enfleshment') of God. We proclaim as truth the *good news* that God *has* revealed his character and nature in the person of Jesus of Nazareth. Through Christ, we can know God.

God is like Jesus

The Christian faith, at its core, is the gospel announcement that God—the eternal Spirit who

'Incarnation' refers to the great truth that in Christ, God became human. As John 1:14 says, 'the Word became flesh.' When we use the word Incarnation, some mistakenly reduce this to the initial event, the birth of Jesus. But the Incarnation refers to the whole life of Jesus and to Jesus himself. That is, Jesus *is* the Incarnation of God.

created, fills and sustains the universe—has shown us who he is and what he's like—*exactly* what he's like—in the flesh and blood human we sometimes call Emmanuel ('God with us'). Conversely, we believe Jesus has shown us the face and heart of God through the fullness of his life on earth: revealed through eyewitness accounts of his birth, ministry, death and resurrection. We regard this life as the decisive *revelation* and *act* of God in time and space. That's still a faith statement, but for Christians, it is our starting point. To look at Jesus—especially on the Cross, says 1 John—is to behold the clearest depiction of the God who is love (1 John 4:8). I've come to believe that Jesus alone is perfect theology.

When I say that God is *exactly* like Jesus, I don't mean we can reduce all that God is to a first century Jewish male. Nor would we claim anyone who encountered Jesus Christ could know all there is to know about God in his transcendent essence. But as we'll see, Jesus Christ is the perfected and perfect revelation of the nature of God because he *is* God. There is no revelation apart from him.

I don't shy from the word *'exactly'* because Scripture claims Christ is "the *exact* representation of God's being" (Heb. 1:3). Paul does assure us *all the fullness* of the God was pleased to dwell in Jesus' human body (Col. 1:19; 2:9). And we will repeatedly return to the truth that to see Jesus is to see God the eternal Word, who assumed flesh without ever once ceasing to be *fully* God.

Rejecting the un-Christlike God

I've also been pleasantly surprised how this proposition—the message that Jesus shows us what God is like—is often well received by those who don't profess Christian faith. If I say, "God is love and Jesus was love incarnate," no problem! Jesus is seldom the issue, even for a rabid, self-avowed 'non-Christian' such as satirist Bill Maher. His primary attacks are not against Jesus at all, but against Christians whose religion does violence in the name of the Prince of Peace. He castigates:

> If you're a Christian that supports killing your enemy and torture, you have to come up with a new name for yourself. ... 'Capping thy enemy' is not exactly what Jesus would do. For almost two thousand years, Christians have been lawyering the Bible to try to figure out how 'Love thy neighbor' can mean 'Hate thy neighbor.' ...
>
> Martin Luther King Jr. gets to call himself a Christian, because he actually practiced loving his enemies. And Gandhi was so f-ing Christian, he was Hindu. But if you're endorsing revenge, torture or war, ... you cannot say

you're a follower of the guy who explicitly said, 'Love your enemy' and 'Do good to those who hate you.' ...

And not to put too fine a point on it, but nonviolence was kind of Jesus' trademark—kind of his big thing. To *not* follow that part of it is like joining Greenpeace and hating whales. There's interpreting, and then there's just ignoring. It's just ignoring if you're for torture—as are more **Evangelical*** *Christians* than any other religion. You're supposed to look at that figure of Christ on the Cross and think, "how could a man suffer like that and forgive?" ...

> **'Evangelical'** when capitalized, refers to the movement associated with Protestant, Western Christianity, especially its conservative and revivalist forms.
>
> When in the lower case, 'evangelical' refers, in general, to the Christian faith and message of the 'evangel' (gospel) or good news that Jesus is Savior of the world.

I'm a non-Christian. *Just like most Christians.*

If you ignore every single thing Jesus commanded you to do, you're not a Christian—you're just auditing. You're not Christ's followers, you're just fans. And if you believe the Earth was given to you to kick ass on while gloating, you're not really a Christian—you're a Texan.[3]

Maher's unbelief is actually biting hatred directed against un-Christlike perversions of God, the projections of religious fundamentalists. Audiences find this commentary comedic because the irony is tragically accurate and laughably contradictory. Instead of reacting defensively or hanging our heads in silent shame, why not hear his indictment as a clarion call back to explicit Christlikeness.

At other times, atheism is self-created through some offense. We may despair of faith when a tragedy or disappointment makes nonsense of the God we inherited or imagined. Touched deeply by loss, our misperceptions of who God is, should have been or failed to be for us, can lead us from mere doubt to an active rejection of faith.

Charles Darwin exemplifies this experience. His discoveries about natural selection and the evolutionary process certainly undermined his faith in 'special creation,'[5] but they did not 'kill God' for him altogether. In fact, Darwin's theories were not generally regarded as problematic by key Christians of his day (the great battle comes later in America). Toward the end of his life, he wrote, "It seems to me absurd to doubt that a man may be an ardent theist and an evolutionist."[4]

'Cruciform'

means cross-shaped, or in the form of the crucifixion.

A *cruciform* God would be the God whose nature (love) is revealed through 'Christ and him crucified' (1 Cor. 2:2).

When his precious 10-year-old daughter, Annie, died in 1851, it broke his heart and crushed his faith. Darwin could hold the good purposes of God and the suffering inherent in natural process in healthy tension until he had to endure the terrible suffering of his little girl. It was too much. Whatever Darwin had believed about God, that belief could not survive his grief.

I wonder. In the case of the sardonic Bill Maher or the broken-hearted Charles Darwin, the real culprit may actually be an un-Christlike image of God. Which is to say, not God at all. If so, I'm inclined to agree with Walter Wink, who affirmed such atheism as a first step toward true worship, because it represents the rejection of an idol. That is, people like Maher and Darwin might be turning *from* – i.e., repenting. The next step, which I don't pretend they have taken, is a turning *toward* – i.e., faith. I say a Christlike God is worth turning to.

Trigger questions

When I personally turned my gaze to the God who is completely Christlike, I was confronted with how un-Christlike the 'church-God' or even the 'Bible-God' can be. Setting Jesus as the standard for perfect theology, many of our current Christian beliefs and practices would obviously face indictment. Even significant swaths of biblical literature don't line up well with the Christ of the Gospels. Claiming that God is revealed perfectly in Jesus triggers tough questions about the God I once conceived and preached. Jesus' life and character challenges my religious clichés and standby slogans—especially the rhetoric of supreme power and irresistible force. Christ never reveals God that way in his teachings and especially not in his Passion (that is, Jesus' arrest, trial, torture and death). Yes, he proves victorious, especially in his resurrection, but remember that Paul resolved to preach 'Christ and him crucified' (1 Cor. 2:2). You could resist him, you could mock him and beat him up. You could kill him. And we did. Our God is the **cruciform*** Christ, the 'weakness of God' (1 Cor. 1:25) who is stronger than men. Why? Because he operates by overcoming love, not by overwhelming force.

Seeing God this way inevitably triggers a barrage of tough faith-questions—an unavoidable domino effect of objections we're expected to ask with point-blank sincerity.

For example, if God is 'in control,' why the chaos in this world? If God is the loving Father Jesus proclaims, what about suffering and affliction? Why does God allow evil people to have their way? Why doesn't God prevent or protect us from natural disasters? And what's the deal with Jesus' death? Was God really punishing Jesus for our sins? And God's wrath? Why does God seem to over-react and get so violent in the Bible? Then there are the wars and merciless acts of genocide committed by God and in God's name! Didn't God incite these atrocities? The Bible says he did. How is that Christlike?

'Apologetics'

is not apologizing for faith. It is the study of how to answer objections to faith. The Apostle Peter wrote, "Always be prepared to give an answer to everyone who asks you to give the reason for the hope that you have. But do this with gentleness and respect" (1 Pet. 3:15). Sadly, if we don't trust the power of the gospel to ignite faith, we may lapse into apologetics to try to argue people into belief.

Didn't Jesus condemn that kind of behavior as immoral? Or is God beyond morality, unbound to his own requirements of justice and righteousness? "Do not kill, except when I say so." But lethal violence isn't the worst of it. What about hell? "I love you, but if you don't love me back, I will torture you with fire forever and ever!" Good and loving? What are we to think when the 'God of the Bible' seems so un-Christlike? Sometimes even Jesus seems to describe this kind of God. It's not as simple as tossing the Old Testament; God the vengeful king makes a cameo appearance in several of Jesus' parables. Awkward!

For some, these are not genuine questions. They are rhetorical charges meant to destroy faith and kill conversation. And too often, Christians have not faced these dilemmas honestly—we've often been evasive, defensive or aggressive. We've fired back at 'the enemy' (or at straw men), making ourselves look both mean and foolish. Lack of thoughtful engagement has left the church at large seriously shallow; it's spurred an exodus from our fellowships; and it's preempted many ever from darkening faith's door. We have also turned on our own, bullying those who wrestle sincerely with these hard questions. Are the questions themselves too dangerous? Does asking them warrant accusations of heresy? Why are we so afraid?

What if Christ is up to the challenge? What if, instead of throwing up our hands and muttering platitudes, we risked undergoing the devastating strength of these problems? What if, after enduring the purging power of our own atheistic doubts, we discovered we have a firm foundation? If Christ is the Truth, then a relentless quest for truth will lead us right into his arms, won't it?

And what if life itself offers us no choice anyway? The whole human pilgrimage through life, death and after-life is a refiner's furnace through which all of us pass. Everything that is combustible will be consumed; anything that can be shaken will be shaken. And what can't be shaken? Jesus, the Living Rock on whom the true house of faith will stand.

Removing boulders

On the ground, in the lives of real people, these questions are not mere recreational thought experiments. There is a critical life-and-death relevance about them. They matter deeply. They're intensely personal. And they're not too interested in a nuanced *apologetics** debate.

Last year, I gave a series of talks at a private Christian high school. I proposed that *if* God is real, then to call him God, he must be good, and the perfection of that goodness is seen in Jesus. I then shared 'The Beautiful Gospel,' which I will share later in chapter fourteen.

After the session a student approached me and asked for ten minutes of my time. We'll call her 'Jess.' She started,

"I am fifteen years old. I rejected Christianity when I was twelve.

But what you're saying makes sense to me. But I have questions. A *lot* of questions." Her eyes were serious, waiting for me to flinch.

"Good," I said. "Questions are good. Fire away."

The teenager's questions are the same ones I've been hearing for years. I've needed to work through them myself, and usually I treat them with a thorough, Bible-based response. But here was a teen with ten minutes and a heap of pain. Behind her questions were untold stories that were about to leak out. You might be alarmed by the frankness and substance of my answers, but the urgency of her situation warranted it. I hope you will stick with me as I explain how I could possibly say these things as the book unfolds. For now, here's a glimpse of our dialogue.

Jess: Why does Jesus seem so loving and God so mean?

Brad: God is not mean. He's exactly like Jesus. And Jesus is not mean.

Jess: Then why does God send people to hell to burn them forever and ever?

Brad: He doesn't. That would be silly. The God who is love, who is like Jesus, would never do that, would he? That would make no sense, would it?

Jess: No. But my Grandma was not a Christian and she died and now some of my family cries and cries because they say she's in hell? [Ah, the story peaks out.]

Brad: Well, I can maybe imagine someone who was truly *wicked perishing*. Like Hitler. But would you say your was Grandma wicked?

Jess: [Tears.] No.

Brad: But Jesus shows us exactly what God is like, do you think you could leave your Grandma in his caring hands?

Jess: [No hesitation.] Yes. [In prayer, she puts her Grandma in his hands. Peace.].

Jess: [A flash of anger.] But why does God command people to commit genocide in the Old Testament? Why would he kill all those people, including their children? And then the 32 virgins that the priests kept for themselves. What do you suppose they did with them? [Oh dear. She's been reading Numbers 31!].

Brad: Sex slaves?

Jess: Yeah.

Brad: If God were like Jesus, would he do that?

Jess: No.

Brad: Well of course not. Because God *is* exactly like Jesus.

Jess: Then why does it say he did?

Brad: You tell me.

Jess: Because they didn't know what God is really like? They just described him based on what they thought?

Brad: Sure. But can you imagine the Father in the Prodigal Son story, or the Father that Jesus prayed to, doing that?

Jess: No.

Brad: Well, then I guess he didn't. [Peace.].

Jess: [More tears.] I still have a lot of questions. God is the creator of everything and he's in control of everything and causes everything to happen for a purpose, so ...

Brad: No.

Jess: Huh?

Brad: Like rape? God causes rape? Rape is for a purpose?

Jess: No!

Brad: No! Rape is just evil. There's no lesson. That's not how God teaches lessons. And he doesn't *do* control. That's why terrible things happen. But we wouldn't want him to control us. Would you?

Jess: [Shakes her head no.]

Brad: So he never causes evil and he doesn't use control to prevent us from doing evil. But he *does* care. He loves and cares and wants to come heal those who've been hurt by evil.

Jess: I have three relatives who were molested, but I wasn't. I couldn't understand because people always say God is in control and everything happens for a reason. [Ah, there's the story again.]

Brad: So no, God didn't cause that in any way. But if God were like Jesus, would you be able to put your relatives in his care? Just like you did with your Grandma?

Jess: Yes. [No hesitation. She does it. Peace. More tears.]

Brad: Can you see them there? [She's nodding.] How are they? [More nodding.]

Brad: What are these tears about? Why are you crying?

Jess: Because I believe you.

Brad: So if God were like Jesus, could you put yourself in his hands, just like you did with your Grandma and your relatives?

Jess: Yes [No hesitation. And she does.]

As I read through that conversation again, I'm struck by how many huge boulders stood in Jess's way to faith. In the space of minutes, she had bombarded me with devastating issues, including hell, death and Grandma, the Old Testament and violence, creation and control, and then she threw in child rape. But through twenty years of pastoring, I can tell you that she is *not* exceptional. She fairly represents the sharp minds and broken hearts of up to ten million people who have left the church (in America alone) since the turn of the millennium.

I was also troubled by how simplistic and one-dimensional my responses sound. I haven't even made a case for them yet. But I risk the vulnerability of sharing this actual conversation in order to make a more urgent case: the desperate need for a thoughtful pastoral theology, an answer for our hope we have (1 Pet. 3:15).

Hopefully we can work toward a more beautiful answer than, "Yes, God is in control; yes, he commands genocide; and yes, your Grandma's in hell, along with all the rapists and probably you as well, one day."

The Father's love revelation

Again, the overarching question that ties *A More Christlike God* together is, "What is God really like?" I believe we're asking that age-old question afresh for several reasons, some negative and some positive. Maybe the *best* reason we're asking is because God initiated the re-asking. He is unveiling what he's like in a new way, which is really an ancient way, the Jesus way.

I'm referring to the way Christ has been refreshing our image of his loving Father, especially in the last thirty years. An ever-increasing proportion of believers have been remembering, preaching, singing and experiencing directly what we call "the Father's heart." So much so that a great number have nearly forgotten how threatening, judgmental and condemning the God of our childhood could sound. We really have moved on. Sometimes we forget the multitudes who fled through local church exits decades ago and have yet to receive the upgrade we now take for granted. Or did they flee precisely because, in their own spirits, God was already rehabilitating their picture of him, while the congregations they attended weren't ready to 'go there'?

Of course, not all of us cowered before the scary punisher-God—the 'Mighty Smiter'—but many readers will remember the hellfire messages and moralizing rants of itinerant revivalists and would-be prophets. Their tirades used to sound plausible. Now, having experienced the Father's heart, they sound more silly than scary, more suited to cartoon mockery. Some will recall the stifling standards of wool-slacks-holiness that set many of life's joys off limits. We were trained to obsess in indignation over all sorts of

'The church'

as a term has be used for (i) a vague universal idea, (ii) the visible kingdom of God on earth, (iii) any Christian institution or movement, (iv) local or trans-local fellowships or communities, (v) brick-and-mortar buildings and/or their worship activities.

I normally use 'church' to refer to the whole 'people of God' (1 Pet. 2:10) 'in Christ' (2 Cor. 5:17), re-deemed by grace through faith in his name' (John 1:12). I will specify with adjectives (ancient, west-ern, local, visible) when referring to particular fellowships or institutions.

'sins'—even ones that aren't found anywhere in our Bibles. According to Archbishop Lazar Puhalo, moral outrage at others' sin is often a confession of one's own deeply repressed cravings. Do we ourselves *need* hell to keep our envy of sin-ners at bay? One pastor in my city even confessed that without the threat of hell, he would not be a Christian. The grace and mercy of Christ was not enough for him, or, he thought, for his congregation. Throw in the odd witch-hunt and we have a revived Puritanism on steroids. But far from establishing righteousness, fear of the Punisher-God only provoked a disastrous counter-revolution of hedonism. "I'm going to hell anyway. May as well make the most of it."

Behind all of that toxic theol-ogy stood a broken or distorted image of God—quite ready to dole out violence. Repent and all is forgiven. But go and sin no more, lest something even worse should happen. The God perceived this way was harsh and volatile (with chapter and verse provided).

Then along came a new and wonderful epiphany. Or at least 'new' to many modern Evangelicals who had grown up on a diet of moralism and hellfire revivalism—just as it had been new for many of Jesus' first fans. Many were discovering the 'old, old story' afresh, like many previous generations who've experienced renewal.

Each of us had to experience this good news for ourselves. The revelation included:

- a fresh emphasis on God as the merciful and hospitable Father;
- who wins us by love rather than threats;
- who accepts and adores us while we're still a mess;
- who sees us as we are and heals us with hugs rather than blows.

We were learning at last that it's the "kindness of God that leads to repentance" (Rom. 2:4), and that it is only "the grace of God that teaches us to say no to ungodliness" (Titus 2:11-12).

What **the church*** at large needed more than anything—and what the world was more than ready for—is *a more Christlike God*

'The church' (cont'd)

is more than an institution. Teachers like Ignatius of Antioch and Justin Martyr saw the church as a *race—* the race of Christ in the place of the race of Adam.

Paul saw the church as Christ's *body*, in which we are included through baptism (1 Cor. 12:13).

The church is also a *faith family*, in which we are adopted or reborn as beloved children of God.

The church is also the Lord's *banqueting table*, where we are united by sharing his supper (Christ's body and blood) together.

and, by extension, *a more Christlike church* (because we mimic what we worship).

My impression is that this fresh awareness of the Father's love has become widespread, touching hearts across many nations. I first personally encountered the 'Father's Heart' through teachers at YWAM (Youth With A Mission) and in Vineyard conferences. I began to hear it in popular worship music, such as Brian Doerksen's *Father's House* album. I read it in books such as Brennan Manning's

Abba's Child and Philip Yancey's *What's So Amazing About Grace?*

Most importantly, the message of the Father's love was not only being preached, written and sung; many believers began to 'get it' at a heart-level that renewed their faith and transformed their lives.

My own circle of friends finally noticed that Jesus' favorite image of God was Father (seventy times in the Gospels!). Jesus showed us in the Gospels what fatherhood meant to him: extravagant love, affirmation, affection and belonging. It meant scandalous forgiveness and inclusion. Jesus showed us this supernaturally safe, welcoming Father-love, extended to very messy people *before* they repented and *before* they had faith. Or better, he was actually redefining *repentance* and *faith* as simply coming to him, baggage and all, to taste his goodness and mercy. He didn't seem to appreciate our self-loathing. The repentance he wanted was that we would welcome his kindness into our deepest needs and wounds.

Theologians such as James Alison and Anthony Bartlett taught me how the Jesus-event completely redefined *God* himself! We are rediscovering Jesus' revolutionary vision of *Abba* afresh in our generation. To call God *Abba* was to introduce a religion-shattering shift in how close and intimate we could be with God.

Add to Jesus' depiction of God as Father his startling Last Supper announcement, "If you have seen me, you *have* seen the Father" (John 14:9). Somehow we need to let his words jar us again. Maybe we're too used to the phrase, but it's what I've hinted at in the title. For our own sakes, we might take a break from trying to convince ourselves that Jesus was and is God and to spend this twenty-first century meditating on the truth that *God is like Jesus. Exactly* like Jesus. When the veil that obscured God was torn in two, what did it reveal? A Suffering Servant who hangs on the Cross (Zech. 12:10)! Thus, every human conception we previously associated with 'God' is uprooted, root and branch!

We begin by deconstructing false images—tearing down idols in the tradition of Jeremiah 1—before commencing with the work of construction. To this initial demolition we now turn.

Pausing to think

- What are some images of God common to our broader culture? How might those who don't profess faith imagine God? How do you think they differ from God as he truly is? How might they have developed such an image of God?

- Compare the image of God among various church-cultures and Christian movements. Contrast the images of God in different religions. How might these variant visions of God reflect the worshipers themselves?

- What suspicions do you have about the God of your tradition? Of your personal understanding? If God were bigger and better than those boxes, what is it that God might want to reveal to you?

- If we are prone to distorted or limited images of God, how might we break *out* into a clearer vision? How might God break *in* to show us the truth?

- What was it that Jesus wanted us to see about God? How was his vision of God different than anything previous? How might his vision of God still be different than your own?

Pausing to pray

God, who are you? I want to know you but my vision is so distorted, my mind is so small, my heart is so constricted. How could you live in such tiny boxes? Ah, but you don't! I do! Rescue me from the prison of my puny understanding! Turn on the lights so I can catch a glimpse of the same Eternal Love that Jesus revealed. Give me the gift of Christlike vision that burns through the fog that blinds me to pure Goodness. Lord, let it be!

Un-Christlike Images of God 2

"Who made who?"

– ACDC –

"We become what we worship."

– G. K. Beale –

Projections and Reflections

Over the next two chapters, we will consider how our ideas of God might be glorified projections of ourselves and conversely, how we inevitably become like the God we worship. After setting up the question with a surprising guest voice, I will suggest a few examples of the common, contemporary false images of God: the doting grandpa, the punitive judge, the deadbeat dad and the curious Santa Claus blend.

We will then analyze two conceptions of God that compete throughout Christian history and, indeed, appear within the Bible itself. Finally, I will propose that our false images of God can be overcome by a shift from biblical literalism to a return to Christ himself as our final authority—a move which challenges the un-Christlike religious ideas of God so often reinforced by 'cherry-picking' Scripture.

Who made who?

I recall the chorus of an ACDC song in 1986 that asked,

Who made who? Who made you?

Who made who? Ain't nobody told you?

Who made who? Who turned the screw?

The song was originally written for the Stephen King movie, *Maximum Overdrive*, in which the machines of the world turn on their human makers. But when the song came out, I was prompted to pose the question concerning the God I worship. Did God create me in his image? Or had I created God in my image? Who actually made whom?

Actually, given my solid Baptist indoctrination, I can't take credit for inventing anything, especially not God. To be a good boy—something I desperately wanted—was to accept and affirm as true whatever was revealed to me through my beloved parents and the particular church culture in which we were completely immersed. Was the faith I had received real? Or was ours the latest iteration of many projects under construction over generations and centuries? Our religion had obviously evolved over time. Had our God also evolved?

If I had been born in the outback of Afghanistan or India, would I not have simply and sincerely conformed to the local religion and believed in a distinctly dissimilar homegrown God? If I mistakenly believed my God had a different name and extra appendages, would he love me any less? If I had prayed to this alien God, would it have been a false God? Who was I to say that my God was the more authentic 'model'? Why would I suppose their God was evil and mine good? Or that my God would hear my prayers but theirs were deaf? Why should I believe my God is so pleased with my worship as to give me heaven? Is he so offended by counterpart children and their counterpart gods that he would reject their sacrifice as he had rejected Cain's? In an accident of birth and borders, would I now escape while God consigned them to the Lake of Fire?

Were these questions a sign of heresy or sanity? "Who is God?" I wondered? Indeed, *what* is God?

What is God?

Now for our surprise guest. In a talk to Hindus entitled "What is God?"[1] Indian yogi and mystic, Sadhguru, teased his audience about how the God we imagine can be an amplified mirror of ourselves.

When you were born and you opened your eyes; you saw creation. Before you came here, so much had happened. Obviously you did not create it. So you thought, there must be a Creator. This is how you come to the Creator, isn't it? The moment you thought there must be a Creator, because you are in human form you thought, "It must be a big man. A small man like me cannot do all this. It must be a big man. Just two hands? How can he do so much creation? Must be eight hands!" Isn't it so? If you were a buffalo, you would really be thinking, "God is a huge buffalo." Isn't it so? You go and ask a buffalo and you will see. The buffalo will insist, "God is a huge buffalo. Maybe four horns."

He goes on to joke about the Ugandan dictator, Idi Amin, who declared that God is black. And Sadhguru agrees, "If white people can have a white God, why can't black people have a black God? But of course both are confused because God is really brown, isn't he! After all, God had visited India. Isn't it so?"

I beg your pardon; didn't *she*? The old holy man pressed: "Do you really believe God is a man? Or could God also be a woman?" In India, he recalls, they 'solve' this dilemma by invoking *every* kind of god: man gods, woman gods, cow gods and monkey gods—every conceivable god to suit a myriad of tastes and temperaments. Gods that crawl, that creep and fly. Even factory-made gods you can buy and keep in your pocket.

The guru laughs, "As long as man is the most powerful force on the planet, God is man. But as women gain more power, why not a woman? And suppose dogs gain even more power, they will ask,

'Why is God not a dog? Actually, the spelling is closer. Isn't it so?'"

The joke prepares us for a pointed critique. He is warning us: your *idea* of God may be no more than an exaggerated version of yourself. Moreover, he thinks, the problem worsens in that we don't even have an accurate understanding of ourselves. If we can't define what it is to be human—this small piece of creation—how do we dare limit the source of creation to our definitions? With his charming and witty approach, Sadhguru makes the challenging charge: "Whatever knowledge you have about God is just pure nonsense—cultural nonsense. Depending upon what kind of culture you are in—it is that kind of God, isn't it?"

His conclusions are not that different from those of the early Christian father, St. Gregory the Theologian, who said, "It is difficult to conceive God but to define Him in words is an impossibility. … it is impossible to express Him, and yet more impossible to conceive Him."[2]

Both Yogi Sadhguru and St. Gregory, in the end, believe that we cannot claim to truly know or grasp God; we can only *experience* God. Now in the guru's particular form of faith, you experience God by 'dissolving into it.' Yet this too is surely a cultural expression: the perspective of an individual man who experiences life in India as one drop in an ocean of over a billion citizens. Isn't it so?

*Projections** and reflections

In other words, the great peril is that we worship *ourselves* via an image of God *we create* out of *our own* temperament. Then, easily enough, we find scriptures to establish our image as 'biblical'!

As a Christian, am I not also in danger of conceiving Jesus, not as he really is, but more as an upgraded version of myself? So we have Prozac Jesus versus cage-fighter Jesus; hippy Jesus versus Rambo Jesus; American Idol Jesus versus United Nations Jesus. Or think in terms of our twentieth century heroes: Gandhi Jesus, Martin Luther King Jr. Jesus, John Lennon Jesus and Ronald Reagan Jesus. Or pick your favorite Hollywood actors who have played Jesus. Was it Max von Sydow (1965)? Ted Neeley (1973)? Jim Caviezel (2004)? Or Diogo Morgado (2013)? Ewan McGregor (2015)? So many to choose from!

On the much grander scale of national culture, isn't it amazing how closely God resembles our respective nations? From my experience in America, I can assure you that God is exactly like America. All of God's attributes are reflected beautifully in the values of her founding fathers and in the righteousness of her central collection of causes. Do you believe that? Or might the truth be precisely the opposite? What if the God 'in whom we trust' is exactly what the nation sees in the mirror and deifies according to her own exceptional ambitions?

'Projection' is a psychological term describing how humans defend themselves against unpleasant impulses by denying their existence in themselves and attributing them to others.

I'm using the term to describe traits in us that we attribute to (that is, project onto) God, ranging from pleasant to hostile.

Thus, God becomes a reflection of our own temperament.

A strange thing happens. If you drive north, passing through Canadian immigration, what will you find? God has adapted to the nationalist passions of Canadian worshipers! The God who lives south of the 49th parallel seems obsessed with freedom and capitalism. But somehow when he visits his chalet in Canada, the same God (supposedly) is more enthusiastic about tolerance and

'The New Atheists' are a particular stream of public voices who directly attack religious faith (especially Christianity) as a dangerous and violent delusion that needs to be actively repressed and destroyed.

The New Atheists include scientists and writers, such as Richard Dawkins *(The God Delusion)*, Daniel Dennett *(Breaking the Spell)*, Sam Harris *(The End of Faith)*, and Chris Hitchens *(God is Not Good)*.

the common good. Look for God in China and you'll see his dedication to harmony and honor. Latin Americans and Italians are really into family (a la *The Godfather* trilogy), so what does their Catholic God look like? The Holy Family is huge, right? Jesus, Mary and Joseph. And so it goes: the highest moral values of any given people group get stamped into their image of God, are reinforced by their worship and downloaded back into their people (times ten for *fundamentalists**).

It can't be helped. Religion is a human phenomenon. People are built for worship. Every society and culture composes its own way(s) to approach the divine. We develop ideas about God. Different ideas—sometimes bad ideas, even deadly ideas. But, as I say, it can't be helped. Or maybe it can be!

Cleansing the palate

So far, I've said nothing here that the **New Atheists*** aren't preaching with great fervor. Their salvos against faith can be bitter and hit close enough to home to trigger shame and defensiveness. To the degree that they are truth-tellers (not to be overestimated), they are helpful to me in small doses. Reading them is like drinking saltwater to induce vomiting when one needs to purge the poison of toxic religion. Unfortunately, saltwater itself is also poisonous in any significant volume. The effects of drinking it include dehydration, delirium and impaired judgment—symptoms commonly observable among New Atheist groupies. Honestly, if Christianity needs a course correction, we'll do much better than looking to our haters for help.

We need an alternative metaphor and practice, especially if God is not merely a delusion and much more than a projection. If there is a God of love revealed in Christ, I don't need or want to be purged of the faith, hope, love and life I've experienced in Jesus. The condemnation, cynicism and judgments of the New Atheists prove every bit as ugly as what we see in their strange bedfellows: the scribes and Pharisees of *fundamentalism.* *

'Fundamentalism' is an ever-shifting term that has now become a pejorative synonym for extremism. Here, it refers to a branch of any religion, ideology or movement (including atheism!) that becomes dogmatic, militant and repressive, set in its resolve to purge their movement or society of the perceived heresies of their opponents.

What is the alternative?

We can start with a sober awareness of how we obscure God with our own ideas and ideologies. We can recognize our vulnerability to worn out superstitions and hidden agendas. But instead of purging ourselves with the saltwater of scorn, we could *cleanse our palates* with the living water of Truth. Cleansing the palate (taste buds) is a common ritual for wine tasters and fine diners. It refers to clearing your mouth of previous tastes before trying the next course. You don't have to swallow saltwater or poke a finger down your throat. All it requires is a little fresh water and a few bites of bread or some sorbet.

Many of us carry a bad taste in our mouths—some old hurt that has misinformed our image of God. It's high time we cleansed our palates of that bitterness. I believe God's healing grace (the bread) and Jesus' gospel truth (the water) can wash out the sour and prepare us for the sweet, to where his Word (Jesus) becomes like 'honey on our lips' (Ps. 119:103). We'll *taste* and see that God really is good (Ps. 34:8).

In practice, what will this look like? We will start by identifying and tracing some of our putrid pictures of God to their roots. Then we will displace these images by saturating ourselves in a *prayerful experience* of the Christ-story. We want to approach the Gospels afresh—without assuming we remember them clearly—intent on a living-grace encounter that leads to intimate friendship with Jesus.

Common Un-Christlike Images

Unhealthy ideas about God are often rooted in the bitterness of our own hearts. People instinctively push their highest expectations and deepest disappointments onto God, especially when their hearts are somehow afflicted or infected with sorrow. These projections form a broken image of God. Let's review four common examples of these un-Christlike images. These include:

- *God the doting grandfather*
- *God the deadbeat dad*
- *God the punitive judge*
- *God the Santa Claus blend*

God the doting grandfather

Taking these in order, *God the doting grandfather* begins with the fantasy of a God who is syrupy 'nice' and rather naïve. Grace, in this model, imagines that God spoils his grandkids with whatever they want, while turning a blind eye to their escalating misbehavior. Similar metaphors include God the *fairy godmother* who grants every wish, and God the *genie in the lantern* who serves at our command. More grotesquely, how about God *the sugar daddy*—the wealthy old man who spends lavishly on his young gold-digging mistress while she barters her phony affections to siphon off his inheritance.

A God who does whatever I please at the prayerful snap of my fingers—wouldn't that be nice! We can surely find biblical promises to fortify this picture. I'm a huge fan of Psalm 37:4 where we are told, "Take delight in the Lord and he will give you the *desires of your heart.*" And didn't Jesus also say, "Ask and it will be given to you; seek and you will find; knock and the door will be opened to you" (Matt. 7:7). In fact, he assures us, "If you believe, you will receive *whatever* you ask for" (Matt. 21:22). Glorious faith-promises from the 'Good Book'!

But also perilous. There are two deep ditches to avoid here. On one side, we might infer a 'whatever-you-want' fairytale God from these texts. And on the other, we might so over-react to them that we discard them as meaningless. I've certainly done my time in both ditches!

In the first case, I remember being very optimistic about God's willingness to 'show up' and do whatever we needed, especially as we ministered to broken people. His will seemed obvious to me and seeing his will done should be a simple matter of asking. As long as my will and his will looked the same, no problem. It's not that I was making obviously selfish demands of God. But doesn't Psalm 91 assure God's children, "No harm will overtake you; no disaster will come near your tent" (v. 10)? Then God should honor his word, right? And if James 5 claims that the elders' prayer of faith would heal the sick, it should work, right? If even a mustard seed of faith can move mountains, then trusting in the living God to overcome

'Spiritual director'

refers to a mentor relationship that assists with spiritual development.

Ironically, the best directors are *non-directive* listeners. They ask insightful questions that lead 'directees' to self-discovery, contemplative awareness and clarity for their life journey.

My spiritual director, Steve Imbach, co-founded *Soulstream*, a dispersed contemplative community.[3]

obstacles ought to be no problem. As the bumper sticker says, "The Bible says it, I believe it and that settles it." It's a great formula as long as it works.

Until it doesn't. Until tragedy strikes. Until a person or family or local church you care about unravels, implodes or dies. Until a friend is abducted and abused. Until another falls off the wagon and overdoses. Until another's life is permanently altered by a car accident or incurable disease. As strokes and cancers, mental illness and suicide, earthquakes or tsunamis have their day and do their worst. Until you yourself do your worst, harm others and would rather die than face it. Until the God who hears doesn't answer and the God who 'saves' doesn't rescue. Until you realize that God, in fact, allows absolutely anything—every kind of evil and depth of suffering.

It strikes me that the same phenomenon occurs when we liberally use the phrase, "the Lord told me," to justify our own desires, only to have our hopes dashed on the cruelties of life.

At that point—and I've been there many times—God the doting grandfather, fairy godmother, genie in the bottle is so disillusioning that we either lose our faith or we lose our illusions.

Thankfully, Steve Imbach, who is my ***spiritual director,**** walked me through this painful discovery. I underwent a 'hell year' in 2008. Everything in my life seemed to be coming apart, and God was obviously allowing it! I expressed my anxiety and anger to Steve, horrified that God might stand back and allow it to all blow up.

Steve asked, "What if he does?"

I replied, "If God won't hold things together, then *I* need to!" My Messiah complex was showing!

Steve asked, "And when you talk to God about it?"

I shouted back, "He's not OBEYING me!"

Busted! In a later chapter, we'll look more deeply at the problem of suffering, but for now, here's the point: my image of God as *my obedient servant* was exposed. My most noble prayers of intercession were nothing more than efforts to manipulate God and manage others. I expected God to answer—to *obey* me—and when he didn't, I was outraged. For the first time in my memory, I no longer trusted God. So I placed my trust in myself. I would hold my world together. But I couldn't do it. I can only thank God that my desperate delusion was not sustainable! Nor was my conception of God. At that point, my odd blend of arrogance and self-pity needed to hear the author of Hebrews:

> Don't feel sorry for yourselves. Or have you forgotten how good parents treat children, and that God regards you as his children?
>
> My dear child, don't shrug off God's discipline, but don't be crushed by it either. It's the child he loves that he disciplines; the child he embraces, he also corrects. God is educating you; that's why you must never drop out. He's treating you as dear children.
>
> This trouble you're in isn't punishment; it's training, the normal experience of children. Only irresponsible parents leave children to fend for themselves. Would you prefer an

irresponsible God? We respect our own parents for training and not spoiling us, so why not embrace God's training so we can truly live?" (Heb. 12:5-9 MSG)

'Contemplative prayer'
usually refers to silent listening, expectant waiting, openness and surrender. Such prayer comes from a place of peace, but doesn't sabotage faith-filled expectancy.

When I discovered God's willingness to allow affliction—and the surprising relief of accepting this reality—I was tempted to swerve wildly into the other ditch: passivity and fatalism. Letting go of prayer as leverage with which to manage God and others, I inclined to the other extreme, which says, "Prayer doesn't change things. It only changes you." (Another bumper sticker proverb—one for each ditch!) Such prayer becomes exclusively about inner transformation, not outward circumstances. We accept life on its own terms, reality as it is, and at most, we pray for peace in the storm. There's something to this line of thought. Remember the 'Serenity Prayer' often quoted by the 12-step recovery movement? The complete and unabridged original version, composed by Reinhold Niebuhr (1892-1971), says:

> God, give us grace to accept with serenity
>   the things that cannot be changed,
> Courage to change the things which should be changed,
>   and the wisdom to distinguish the one from the other.
> Living one day at a time, enjoying one moment at a time,
>   accepting hardship as a pathway to peace,
> Taking, as Jesus did, this sinful world as it is,
>   not as I would have it,
> Trusting that You will make all things right,

if I surrender to Your will,
So that I may be reasonably happy in this life,
and supremely happy with You forever in the next.
Amen.[4]

I have found a lot of peace from this prayer. I truly love it. But it's not my only prayer. Here's why: In my newfound fear of being disappointed again, I was drawn to either not praying at all ... or purposely crafting *'contemplative prayers'** that desperately avoided the possibility of disappointment. Prayers that asked nothing of God and expected nothing from God—prayers that required no faith at all.

This didn't sit well with me because I know the Gospels too well. I couldn't escape the value Jesus puts on asking, seeking and knocking in faith. Doting grandfather aside, I desired to remain faithful to Jesus, who both congratulated faith and rebuked his disciples' lack of it. The Christ of the Gospels made it pretty clear that faith matters, but what does that mean? I was completely done with striving to muster self-induced psychological states of certitude. According to the Apostle Paul, even faith is a gift (Eph. 2:8). But if so, how do I get it? How does it work?

You can see my dilemma. What to do? How to pray?

When in doubt, I usually run to a trustworthy elder. I put the question to Eugene Peterson, author of *The Message Bible*. His answer in two words: "Be disappointed." That is, without placing demands on God or enslaving him to my agenda—*and* without the frenzied cries of the prophets of Baal (1 Kings 18)—Peterson called me to risk disappointment. Pray for heaven to touch earth *and* grieve because heaven is not earth.

For me, staying between the ditches means learning how to empty myself of willfulness and to surrender my life (if only for a moment) to the supernatural love of God. I can then open myself to partnership with God as he directs, remembering I'm the servant, not him. Some days, I pray only the *Jesus prayer* ("Lord Jesus Christ, have mercy on me.") or the prayer Jesus gave us (the 'Our Father,' which includes plenty of sincere requests).

On my more courageous days, I tell him exactly what I'd like to see happen, but I leave the outcome to his love and care. He has enabled me to risk trusting again, whether the results are glorious or disappointing, because in either case, God is a loving Father who is always close. We can contrast this to its opposite: God 'the deadbeat dad.'

'Prayer ministry'

can range from licensed counselors to volunteer laypeople who have learned to pray with people through spiritual and emotional wounds. It's sometimes called 'inner healing'[6]

The last chapter of my book, *Can You Hear Me?* is a manual for my own approach to prayer ministry, called 'listening prayer.'

God the deadbeat dad

I have less experience with God *the deadbeat dad* (or alternatively *absentee landlord*), because unlike many of my friends, neither my dad nor my mom ever abandoned me. As a boy, I saw my dad as chronically tired from working very hard. My own children would say I'm a dad who travels a lot. But neither generation knows the pain of a broken family or permanent loss of support from a parent. For those who do, that sense of abandonment easily casts a shadow on their impressions of God. It makes them feel like orphans.

They imagine *the God who abandoned me*. God, the Dad who was *powerless* to intervene when I was bullied. God, the Dad who *walked out* the door one day and never came back. God, the Dad I needed to *listen* and *reply*, but never visited or answered my calls. God, the Dad I needed to *show* me how to grow up. God, the Dad I needed to be *proud* of me when I succeeded and *supportive* when I failed. God as *absence*—absence so painful that we need a breather. I remember these silly lyrics from spoof song by Ming Tea (and sometimes sing these lines to my boys in jest):

> Daddy wasn't there to change my underwear!
> It seems he doesn't care. Daddy wasn't there!
> If you got a Daddy issue, here's a Daddy tissue.[1]

The sad and serious truth is that many of God's people, whether they had a dad or not, suffer from what we call an 'orphan spirit.' They've never known the love of God as Father or Mother. God seems perpetually distant, absent and silent—disconnected. In fact, our society is broadly afflicted with this sense of isolation. They are crying out for spiritual mothers and fathers who will adopt them and mentor them.

Today, ministries abound that serve to meet these needs and heal these wounds, both in the church and the world. Think of the Big Brothers/Big Sisters organization, and the many mentoring and spiritual direction networks. Then there are the many sports coaches and clubs leaders who volunteer to invest in our youth. Think of the thousands of parents who adopt children, but also the host of adoptees on a quest to search out their birth-parents. Behind all of this, I believe, is a deeper spiritual thirst to know God as Mother or Father. Thankfully, God seems committed to reciprocating, mediating his love through the examples above, but also directly in this 'Father's Heart' season of Christianity.

A growing number of *'prayer ministries'** are learning to help wounded people reconnect with God. One of their approaches is to ask God, "Would you show us the moment when this disconnect happened? Would you bring to mind a time when this person came to feel like an orphan?" As they pause in silent prayer, a specific memory or series of memories may bubble up. It could be a critical moment of abandonment or one example of many. The person receiving prayer is invited to express honestly what happened and how it felt. They may express hurt and anger, fear or grief, whatever. And then we (prayer ministers) simply ask God to come into that moment with His healing love. We ask God to draw close so the one receiving prayer can see, hear and feel the love he has for them. In essence, we pray Paul's prayer to the Ephesians:

> [14] For this reason I kneel before the Father, [15] from whom every family in heaven and on earth derives its name.
>
> [17] ... And I pray that you, being rooted and established in love, [18] may have power, together with all the Lord's holy people, to grasp how wide and long and high and deep is the love of Christ, [19] and to know this love that surpasses knowledge—that you may be filled to the measure of all the fullness of God. (Eph. 3:14-19)

I'm overjoyed to say that for almost twenty-five years, I've seen God faithfully answer this prayer, whether in an instant or through a process, for all who are willing to open themselves to God's love. They come to know God as a continually present, intimately close Parent—neither silent nor distant, regardless of their performance.

God the punitive judge

Speaking of performance, being 'good enough' leads to our third broken image: God the *punitive judge*. Secondary versions of this could include the *meticulous micro-manager* or the *harsh taskmaster*. This brand of 'god' is still very popular among fundamentalists—religious and atheist extremists alike. The former like how it galvanizes their self-righteousness and judgment; the latter use it to energize their cynicism. In the light of Jesus Christ, such a god might have been a passé artifact—a curiosity for archaeologists.

But he's so *useful* as a bludgeon for combatants on the right *or* left! Here's an example of one of Christianity's 'cultured despisers' who would shame believers by describing the God of the Christian right as a *prurient voyeur*:

> His invisible hand is everywhere, say His citizen-theologians, caressing and fixing every outcome: Little League games, job searches, test scores, the spread of sexually transmitted diseases, the success or failure of terrorist attacks (also known as 'signs'), victory or defeat in battle, at the ballot box, in bed. Those unable to feel His soothing touch at moments such as these snort at the notion of a god with the patience or the prurience to monitor every tick and twitch of desire, a supreme being able to make a lion and lamb cuddle but unable to abide two men kissing. A divine love that speaks through hurricanes. Who would worship such a god?[7]

Again, beware of too much saltwater—this stuff can make one soul-sick—but let's use the opportunity to examine the God we know and profess: do you live under the tyranny of the *punisher Judge*? Here are some possible indicators:

In your family or faith background,

- Even apart from religion, were successes praised and failures punished? Was there an obvious distinction between good and bad behavior accompanied by rewards or penalties? Were there mixed messages that added anxiety?

- Did you frequently hear about God's condemnation of sin? Were these sins spelled out in detail along with their potential consequences?

- Did you often hear hell-fire and brimstone preaching with a high-strung call to repentance with many tears?

- Were you exhorted to examine and review every sin before the Lord's Supper under threat of eating and drinking damnation on yourself?

- Was there a keen sense of exclusion and embrace—us and them, insiders and outsiders? Did your sins endanger your sense of belonging? Did you recognize loved ones or yourself as black sheep in this system?

- Was there an urgency around 'End Times' judgment either in this world or the next? Were you afraid of being 'left behind' or on the precipice of the Lake of Fire? How often were Jesus' words used to scold for having 'lost your first love' and warned that he will 'spew you out of his mouth'? (Rev. 3:16).

In your own heart today,

- Are you tormented by old guilt about wrongs done? Are you stuck in remorse and regret no matter how sincerely or often you've tried to say 'sorry'?

- Do internal voices accuse and condemn you for being a 'bad' girl or boy? Do you punish yourself with hurtful words (such as 'stupid') or exercise self-imposed consequences when you stumble?

- Do you ever inflict self-harm?

- Are you obsessed with measuring up or feel like you're 'not good enough'? Do you ever feel there's something wrong with you, but can't put your finger on it?

- Do you struggle with shame?

- When you imagine 'Judgment Day,' what do you expect? Does it cause fear?

- When circumstances don't go your way, do you think perhaps God is punishing you? When things go well, do you assume God is rewarding you? What does grace mean to you in that case?

I'm able to rattle these questions off quite quickly because most of them describe my own angst as a born-and-bred Evangelical revivalist. 'Revival' sounds like a positive word. Who wouldn't want God to revive us? But *'revival-ism'** as I recall it implied a noxious recipe of nearly all the above. Why?

When we idolize the great 'revivals' of history and compare them to our current spiritual state, we *never* measure up. Some assume if revival isn't sweeping the land, then someone is to blame and the revival-*ist* is the heroic prophet called to point the finger and lead the people out of bondage. There's sin in the land to be opposed or sin in the camp to be exposed. Who shall we scapegoat this time around? Thus, the accuser is given free rein to point the finger at 'the lukewarm church' and the hedonism of 'the world.' If we can rile ourselves into a weeping lather, perhaps the 'breakthrough' will come. Conversions will abound, church buildings will be filled and the city will be transformed. All that stands in our way is the sin that holds back the blessing. But hatred of sin and self-hatred and hatred of the sinner are a very thin line, aren't they?

'Revivalism'

2 Chron. 7:14 says, "If my people, who are called by my name, will humble themselves and pray and seek my face and turn from their wicked ways, then I will hear from heaven, and I will forgive their sin and will heal their land."

Revival-*ism* refers to the Evangelical pursuit of the prophetic promise via 'revival meetings' and 'crusades' until revival culture becomes its own religious system and industry.

Having once been immersed in this sort of *revivalist culture,* I can tell you about its God. We'll say more later but I can assure you: he's very angry. Only his mercy has restrained him from crushing sinners already, like the putrid bugs they are. But one day the time for repentance will run out and God's wrath will be poured out in rivers of their blood as deep as the bridles of the horses. I know this because I braced myself through many evangelistic sermons that proclaimed it. I know this because I read it in Jonathan Edwards' "Sinners in the Hands of an Angry God," the ultimate Revivalist sermon. I know this because I myself preached it.

In response, allow me two brief points. First, does this sound like Jesus of Nazareth to you? I know some reference such wrath to the Jesus of John's Revelation. But remember Jesus of Nazareth, who dined with sinners, welcomed prostitutes and tax collectors, advocated for the adulteress and restored the disqualified. I *never* see him spouting hatred against the sinner or using the Law to accuse and condemn. Rather, when he preached, "Repent," it was embedded in this message: "The Kingdom of God is at hand! Repent and believe the Good News!" The *only* time I see him point the rebuking finger is at the oppressive religiosity of the first century revivalists!

Second, Jesus' response to sinners is never condemnation, but an invitation into the unfailing love and enduring mercy of his Father. God has indeed rendered a decisive judgment through the Cross, and his verdict is "Mercy!" Sometimes Evangelicals imagine their Catholic brothers and sisters as more religious than themselves because of the robes and rituals, bells and smells, etc. But in this century, Pope Francis bears a far more gracious and 'evangelical' message than any of the revivalist preachers I was raised on. At his first Good Friday Mass as pope, he said,

> One word should suffice this evening that is the Cross itself. The Cross is the word through which God has responded to evil in the world ... a word which is *love,*

mercy, forgiveness. It also reveals a judgment. Namely, that God, in judging us, loves us. Let us remember this: God judges us by loving us. If I embrace his love then I am saved. If I refuse it, then I am condemned, *not by him*, but by my own self, because *God never condemns, he only loves and saves.*[8]

This is surely an echo of Jesus' words in John 3:16-17. "For God so loved that world that he gave his only begotten Son, that whoever believes in him should not perish, but have eternal life. God did *not* send his Son into the world to condemn the world." In other words, Jesus does not come to announce condemnation from the Father, nor even to save us from the condemnation of the Father, but rather to reveal the love of the Father for those already perishing and suffering condemnation. Instead of a punishing Judge, the Father of Jesus waits on, watches for and then runs to those who've come to the end of themselves.

The Santa Claus blend

To round out our selection of false images, understand that ideas of God are often as complex as those who hold them. We should not be surprised to find a blend of all three previous examples in what I call the *Santa Claus blend*. Christmas has a powerful impact on children, who may laminate their 'theology of Santa' onto their idea of God when the two are held closely together on Christmas Eve.

On the one hand, Santa is very legalistic and judgmental. "He's keeping a list (of sins?); he's checking it twice. He's going to find out who's naughty or nice" (like the Lamb's book of life?[9]). Children are exhorted to behave or else. Even insomnia on Christmas Eve is threatened, because, "He sees you when you're sleeping; He knows when you're awake" [even if you fake it!]. Nor can you hide your hypocrisy because, "He *knows* if you've been bad or good; So be good for goodness sake!" Were you good enough?

The point is entirely anti-grace. Those who behave are good and can anticipate rewards. Those who misbehave are bad and should fear exclusion from the joy to come. Sound familiar? Small wonder if children infuse their understanding of Jesus with this Revivalist-Pharisee-Santa, especially when nativity truth mingles so closely with the Santa legend.

The flipside is that Santa is also treated like a doting grandparent from whom we can ask *anything* we want. We can mail a list of requests to the North Pole or endure sitting on his knee for a portrait photo, whispering our every wish into his ear. Sort of like, "Ask me anything in my name, and I will do it" (John 14:13-14), right?

And Santa never disappoints? Until the tree features missing or mistaken presents! "Hey! Where's my pony and why the stupid socks?" (But say, "Thank you"!) Also, there's the nonsense magic that's afoot! I reasoned to myself as a child, "Our fireplace is too narrow for his belly. And how does he get to every home in the world in one night?"

Imagine the hybrid theology of prayer that emerges: we ask God for every desire, hoping our faith measures up; we are disappointed by unanswered prayer; and we confuse faith in God's loving care with contriving belief in God's magic. See how we nurture disillusionment!

Finally, Santa lives far away and visits only once a year—and only in your sleep. How different from Jesus who said, "I am *with you always*," who we trust to "*never leave* us or forsake us." At the same time, from a young age, I also learned to believe God is in 'heaven' (further than the North Pole) and coming again some day (hopefully *after* next Christmas!) like a "thief in the night"!

The Jesus of the Gospels

While the purpose of this chapter was to name and expose some false images of God, I can't help but remind readers of the true Image, Jesus Christ. Specifically, I believe the best way to purge ourselves of these damaging distortions is actually *not* by binging on cynicism. Nor are we sustained by an occasional visit to a prayer minister. Rather, we have our hearts washed by continually immersing ourselves in the beauty of Jesus as he's portrayed in the Gospels. Those stories are the most potent prescription for the spiritual poisons we've ingested.

For example, does the Gospel Jesus ever seem like a doting grandfather? A punishing judge? A deadbeat dad? Or Santa Claus? No. What was he really like? Even a brief sampling of his words and works is good for the soul. For now, I'll remind you of just one beautiful image of God, evident in the Christ of the Gospels: he's the *Restorer of lives.*

Jesus is the One who sat by the well and restored the Samaritan woman to her place in her community. He restored Zacchaeus' integrity and offered him friendship. He saved and restored the woman caught in adultery to morality and life. He restored the paralytics, the blind and the deaf to wholeness. He restored outcasts such as lepers and the bleeding woman. He restored the sanity of the demonized. Even harshest rebukes were offers of restoration to the unrepentant. When we see Jesus in action, we are seeing the true heart of God, the Restorer of lives.

Summary

In this chapter, we've seen a swirl of personal impressions of God, distortions typically formed amidst our faith-families of origin from an early age. Beyond these images, abiding conceptions of God recur throughout history and theology. Some of them may even compete within the Bible itself. To these we will now turn.

Pausing to think

- Which of the projections of God most resonated with you? When was that image first rooted in your heart?

- Our broken images of God are often inferred from real life experiences. Have you ever felt God doting on you? Abandoning you? Punishing you?

- We hear that God sees our every act and every thought. Do you imagine God forgetting every wrong (1 Cor. 13:5) or remembering them all for future reference (Rev. 20:12)?

- Is God someone you flee in fear or hide from in shame? Or is your instinct to run to God? Does God's nearness inspire dread or joy? When have you been most thankful for and to God? Most disappointed or disillusioned with God? Most angry with or hurt by God?

- What is your most dominant image of God? What does that say about your own belief system? Your own temperament? Your own faith community?

Pausing to pray

God, free me from every slanderous misrepresentation of you that I've believed. Heal my heart in the places that make me afraid of you. Please liberate me from any sick notions that prompt me to run away. If you aren't a doting grandpa, a deadbeat dad or a punitive judge, then who are you? I would welcome whatever rehabilitation I need in my view of you. Lord, let it be!

Freedom or Love?   **3**

Competing Values in Western Culture

"I will what I want."
– Under Armor ad –

"Yet not my will, but yours be done."
– Jesus (Luke 22:42) –

Competing images

This chapter will be our first step to understanding the two *principal competing images* of God throughout the history of religion: the God of pure will (or freedom) and the God of pure love (or goodness). This divide effects virtually every faith tradition and cuts through the heart of most of them. These two images clash within the 'biblical religions' of Judaism and Christianity and even collide on the pages of our Bible!

Again, remember: we are imitators of the God we worship, for good or ill. These primary images of God contend for our allegiance. And they define the highest moral calling of each of their followers. So thinking about moral values is a good first step toward comprehending these competing versions of God.

A completely free God who is pure will produces worshipers who reflect him by championing freedom at all costs. This God does whatever he pleases, even beyond good or evil. I would argue that a willful God produces willful people who ultimately do whatever they please. They will see themselves either as God's agents or, in their willfulness, reject God to become his rivals.

On the other hand, a completely good God, whose nature is

pure love, produces people who imitate him by exemplifying love. That God, who willingly laid down his life for others, inspires loving followers who truly are free—free to move beyond the slavery of self-seeking into self-giving, sacrificial love.

Your highest moral value

Let's do a thought-experiment: if you were God, what kind of God would you be? The image of God we hold in our hearts becomes clear when we run into our own personal dilemmas: freedom versus love, rights or responsibilities, our interests or somebody else's. How do we make choices when we can't have it both ways—when it's a matter of 'him or me' or 'us and them'? Our varying perceptions of right and wrong, and the moral choices we make in the moment, are a snapshot or echo of this ongoing rivalry between two visions of God. It cuts even deeper than—*and across*—labels such as 'left' or 'right' or 'conservative' and 'liberal' in the culture wars of religion and politics today.

So let me ask, what is your highest moral value? When the pressure is on, what 'law' gets the last word and determines your actions? Consistently, the top two answers I hear are 'love' and 'freedom.'

And who doesn't love both? We like the two to co-exist in perfect harmony. And they can. But as we'll see, in both earth and heaven, one is always primary. Either freedom reigns or love reigns, both in God and in people.

Let's start with people.

When freedom reigns: a critique

What happens when we feel our freedom—our *rights* or our *security*—being threatened? In our era, the chief moral imperative has become *defending our freedom*—it's considered the height of all we deem honorable and valorous.

We live in a culture that so totalizes freedom that anyone who presents an obstacle or becomes a hindrance to what *I* want is attacking *my* freedom. I will perceive intrusions on my way of life as the enemy, whether it's a family member, a foreign militant or a government regulator. Whether they're trespassing on my property or regulating the size of my soft drink or rifle clip, impositions on my freedom are considered offensive and immoral—*attacks*—because my personal autonomy (self-rule) comes first. More important than life itself? Apparently. Remember Patrick Henry, the great revolutionary, who said, "Give me liberty or give me death." Or, in the words of one-time NRA president, Charlton Heston: "I'll give you my gun when you pry it from my *cold, dead hands*."[1] Their point was that for some, life without freedom is not even worth living. They will die to defend it or take out anyone who dares breach it.

On the other hand, Christ commands us to love our enemies and to overcome evil with good. He calls us to make love our first allegiance—and his love *frees* us to do so. Freedom in Christ, ironically, is freedom from the tyranny of our own paranoia-producing self-will and fear-driven self-preservation, which we've tragically mislabeled 'freedom.'

But what if someone menaces our security, whether in our homes or at our borders? How we respond to our enemies becomes a real quandary when loving one's enemy and defending one's freedom come to a showdown. Our instinctive response in the moment of truth will depend on whether love or freedom is our *highest* calling.

Let's unpack these competing values a step further. Freedom, rightly understood, is a gift that Christ wishes for everyone, and indeed died to give us. Remember, I'm not arguing against freedom. Genuine freedom is a gift of Christ's sacrificial love, *not* the vacuous promises of grandiose political movements or sabre-rattling politicians. But freedom defined as *my rights* or *my security*—just *how* important is it? Is it *all*-important? Life and death important?

Let's be practical. *How* would you defend your freedom if someone invaded your home tonight? Really? Are you prepared? Or is this just a pretend ego-fantasy? Surprised in the middle of the night, would your cunning defense plan work? Would it make you and your family safer? Or would it actually escalate the danger?

Or what if someone attacked your country? We're no longer being hypothetical. Would you kill them? How would you go about this? What should be done that won't make the mutual hatred and escalating violence even worse over the next decades? What about those who only *might* become a threat? Would you invade their homes or countries first? Would you go get them *before* they could get to you? If you only *suspected* they *might* be planning to attack your freedom, would you snatch them, jail them and torture them to find out, before they had committed an actual crime?

A silly question? Not at all, and especially not for Christians. In fact, in a 2009 poll conducted by the *Pew Forum on Religion and Public Life*, 54% of people who attended church services at least once per week and *62% of white Evangelicals* agreed that using torture against *suspected* terrorists is often or sometimes justified."[2]

How is so much hostility and death possible for 'freedom-loving' Christian people? Well, that majority mindset is not only possible but considered *morally necessary* so long as freedom-as-self-will stands as our premier value. It is the inevitable fruit of our commitment to defending *our* rights and freedoms, *our* peace and security, from every hindering authority, obstacle or inconvenience. Moreover, that kind of freedom demands someone else's rights and freedoms to be sacrificed, their peace and security violated. Unfortunate.

Ironically, since 9/11, our aggressive program for defending freedom has also significantly impinged on our own freedoms and endangered our own children. Am I wrong, or have not our governments, media outlets and pulpits created a culture of crippling fear—reinforced by legislation—that has self-sabotaged our own freedom in the name of protecting it from others?

Then consider how many casualties we've incurred in preemptive sorties supposedly meant to make us safer. It wasn't safer for those we sacrificed on the altar of our freedom. As the body counts have risen over the last decade-plus, I remember Jeremiah's prophecies condemning those who worshiped Molech by binding their firstborn to the fires of child-sacrifice. But if freedom says it's 'necessary.'

Consider the possibility that the very act of placing freedom before and above love has actually perverted the definition of 'freedom.' Freedom has popularly come to mean *being* what I want, *getting* what I want and *doing* what I want. I am captain of my ship—I set my course according to my desires.

'I make the path'
Alice in Wonderland [3]

Alice:
From the moment I fell down that rabbit hole I've been told what I must do and who I must be. I've been shrunk, stretched, scratched, and stuffed into a teapot. I've been accused of being Alice and of not being Alice but this is *my* dream. *I'll decide* where it goes from here.

Bayard:
If you diverge from the path . . .

Alice:
I *make* the path!

Is this the 'freedom for which Christ set us free' (Gal. 5:1)? Is this the 'freedom' the Spirit of the Lord brings (2 Cor. 3:7)? Has our idolatry of self-will really freed us from fear? From the power of Satan, sin and death? From oppression, obsession and addiction? From the economic, political and religious beasts that devour?

What we now typically call 'freedom' sounds more like the idolatry of pride to me.

While Christians once saw true freedom as a blessed *byproduct* of living according to *virtues* revealed by God, we now frequently see freedom as living the values we *create* without hindrance. Jesus taught that *his* truth sets us truly free to follow the path of love that *he* created. But now, western culture defines freedom as forging one's own path, willing one's own destiny.

Take a typical line from any presidential address (Republican or Democrat): "*Nobody* gets to write your destiny but *you*. Your future is in *your* hands. Your life is what *you* make of it. And nothing—absolutely *nothing*—is beyond your reach."[4] Such lofty language recalls the story of the tower of Babel in Genesis 11, where a people who sought to "make ourselves a name" soon found that pride comes before a fall.

The modern rhetoric of freedom (as personal autonomy) makes for an inspiring screenplay, a rousing State of the Union address or an inspiring sports ad. From the Pilgrims at Plymouth Rock to today, we have embraced the promise of freedom from religious and political oppression. Excellent. So now, ours is a shining future and limitless destiny. *We* make our world, *we* declare our independence and *we* choose our fate. We are free! And woe to those we enslave or eradicate on the way to making that dream happen. It's our God-given right!

Right or wrong, isn't this exactly how we live? The stubborn fact is that freedom has come to mean, "I do what I want to do to get what I want to have—according to *my* conscience, *my* desires, *my* convictions, *my* passions—myself, *my* way."

This type of *freedom* is really about *will—my will be done*— what I'll call 'the primacy of the will,' self-will or willfulness. We talk about freedom, but when the *will* rules, it actually craves mastery and power. Far from 'live and let live,' self-will imposes itself on the other—whether it's the most vulnerable in our society or a terror suspect in some out-sourced dungeon. So our 'free will' grows brutish, employing coercion, domination and lethal force.

Ultimately, the very thing we called 'freedom' becomes a form of slavery—what novelist David Foster Wallace called the 'slavery impulse.' He criticized our culture for exposing our children to this message from their earliest years:

> That *you* are the most important and what *you* want is the most important. And that your job in life is to gratify your own desires. ... This does not work as well when it comes to educating children or helping us help each other know how to live ... and to be *happy*—if that word means anything. Clearly it means something different from 'whatever I want to do'—'I want to take this cup right now and throw it! I have every right to! I should!' We see it with children: that's not happiness. That feeling of having to obey every impulse and gratify every desire seems to me to be a strange kind of slavery.[5]

Thus, when freedom is primary, the will becomes self-centered, then dominates others, and finally becomes captive to its own demands. But there is another way.

When love reigns: a cross

On the other hand, what happens when love reigns? Could God's love for us somehow make loving God (worship), loving one another (fellowship), loving our neighbor (compassion) and loving our enemy (forgiveness) our highest moral vision?

Notice that I'm not talking about just *any* kind of love, just as it doesn't do to exalt just *any* kind of freedom. We needn't pause for more than a moment to state the obvious. *God's* love is obviously *not* what we mean by loving chocolate or 'falling in love' or 'making love.' *God's* love is clearly something other than the 'free love' of the sexual revolution. It's not merely the romantic drama depicted in Hollywood or Bollywood, Bieber or Gaga. God's love is specific. God-love is also more than just one type of love in the variety pack. God *is* love and so defines love. All other claims to love either relate to God's love or fail to be love at all. Savoring chocolate, adoring a loved one and even sexual intimacy can dimly reflect something of God's love *or*—as with obsession, addiction and exploitation—they maybe become entirely anti-love.

When we see a dysfunctional relationship, we might warn the abused party, saying, "That's not love," or "He doesn't love you!" By what criteria? Well, we might say, "Love is this," or, "Love is not that." By whose standard? Ultimately, we know what love is and what it isn't by God's standards of a compassionate heart, self-giving care and selfless commitment. God showed us this perfectly in Christ. But even before that, he graciously embedded it in creation—in us.

What if grace were to generate a love more compelling than even our own freedom? It sounds terribly self-defeating—and it is (sort of) and yet there's something counter-intuitive that plants self-giving and self-sacrifice as the seeds of human flourishing. Remember Jesus' words:

> [23] Whoever wants to be my disciple must deny them-selves and take up their cross daily and follow me. [24] For whoever wants to save their life will lose it, but whoever loses their life for me will save it. [25] What good is it for someone to gain the whole world, and yet lose or forfeit their very self? (Luke 9:23-25)

> [24] Very truly I tell you, unless a kernel of wheat falls to the ground and dies, it remains only a single seed. But if it dies, it produces many seeds. [25] Anyone who loves their life will lose it, while anyone who hates their life in this world

will keep it for eternal life. [26] Whoever serves me must follow me; and where I am, my servant also will be. My Father
will honor the one who serves me. (John 12:24-26)

Take up your cross? Lose your to life to save it? Die to live? Hate
your life? Serve? Follow? Jesus' words rebel against every instinct of
self-will and worldly freedom I can imagine! Imagine saying this at
a commencement speech for college graduates! And yet Jesus says
it. To me. To you.

Easier said than done, for sure, but also not totally unfamiliar.
Isn't this the basic principle in a marriage covenant? For marriage
to work, partners must repeatedly put love ahead of their own interests. Every time we say no to our own whims and wants for the sake
of husband or wife, self-will (my freedom to do as I please) bows
to self-giving love. Self-centeredness dies another little death and
yet, amazingly, unselfish love causes both spouses to flourish. Love,
if primary, leads to the genuine freedom of abundant life together.
But when willfulness has its way, partners start pining for what? For
'freedom,' especially if they experience their partner as self-centered
and loveless. Clearly, healthy marriage occurs where mutual, self-
giving love—not self-willing freedom—takes the lead.

Another example of the primacy of love is parenting. Talk
about infringing on freedom! Women willingly go through great
agony for the sake of childbirth. Parents learn that love makes great
sacrifices. We sacrifice sleep, time, hobbies and even careers for the
sake of our children. Love changes mountains of diapers, tidies up
thousands of messes, supervises years of homework and sits through
endless practices and performances. Love trades in the convertible
for the mini-van and makes countless taxi runs! Freedom can 'make
babies,' but only love raises them! On the other hand, love is meant
to define the relationship and sexual intimacy of 'making babies,'
just as it leads to the great sacrifices involved in *birthing* and then
raising children.

In fact, only two things can cause parents to forsake a child: the necessity of love for the child's sake or the demands of freedom for the parents' own sake.

Beyond the rigors of marriage and parenting, God can fill and transform our hearts so that love becomes our 'prime directive,' or as the philosopher Immanuel Kant said, our 'categorical moral imperative.' Jesus called love of God and neighbor, 'the greatest commandment' (Matt. 22:36). In fact, if by grace, "I am crucified with Christ: nevertheless I live; yet not I, but Christ who lives in me" (Gal. 2:20), then what won't 'Christ-in-me' do for love? Christ's love surrenders willingly to the Father's will as its highest good. *Christ's love is the true freedom—freedom to love, empowered by our risen Love!* Love-sponsored freedom sacrificially serves one's siblings-in-Christ, extends mercy to the needy, and lays down its life in the cause of justice. We've seen such love in the lives of famous saints such as Mother Teresa and Martin Luther King Jr., but also in countless anonymous heroes who show us the high road of costly, 'Christly' servant-love.

Christlike love is willing, not willful. Consensual, not coercive. Faithful, not forceful. It serves and defers for the sake of a higher good than one's own way. In using terms like self-giving, sacrificial and forgiving, I am making Christ's passion journey from Gethsemane to Golgotha my central and abiding referent for extreme love. He prays the words of surrender as he kneels in the garden:

"My Father, if it is possible, may this cup be taken from me. Yet ..." (Matt. 26:39).

"My Father, if it not possible for this cup to be taken away unless I drink it, *may your will be done*" (Matt. 26:42).

See Christ lay down his rights, his personal freedom and his will for the sake of the Father's saving cup of 'co-suffering love.' When he is betrayed and Peter would 'defend freedom,' Jesus says,

"Put away your sword. Shall I not drink the cup the Father has given me?" (John 18:11) And so he does, from his trial and torture to his death on the Cross.

"*This*," says John, "is how we know what love is: Jesus Christ laid down his life for us. And we ought to lay down our lives for our brothers and sisters" (1 John 3:16), for our neighbors (Mark 12:31) and our enemies (Matt. 5:44). For disciples of the Lamb, laying down our lives means laying down the sword of coercion and lethal force, and picking up the Cross of self-giving, radically forgiving love.

This 'ought' sounds like law and obligation—and yes, Jesus calls it a commandment—but this is not a new religious ladder to climb. Rather, it is what you become when Love comes to live inside of you. What Christ asks is that we willingly receive God's transforming grace and surrender to the impulses of Christ's love in our hearts. Once we let go of the willful 'No!' in our hearts, this naturally supernatural process of grace simply unfolds.

Pausing to think

- Review in your mind the difference between the worldly freedom of willfulness and the godly freedom of willingness. How would you explain the difference? Can you think of examples?

- What are the perceived payoffs of being your own master and doing whatever you will? What are the costs? To you? To others? How have you experienced the bondage of willfulness?

- Think about what God says about love and what Jesus showed us about love. Compare this to cultural pop-references to love. How does human love best reflect God's love? When is it virtually the opposite?

- Have you experienced love and freedom competing in the face of an important decision?
- Which won out? What tended to be the tipping point?
- How does putting love first lead to a greater freedom than demanding my own rights and freedoms? Can you give an example from your life?
- Recall my descriptors for 'Christlike love.' Willing versus willful, consensual versus coercive, faithful versus forceful. Where might boundaries fit in? What would a healthy, loving "No" look like?

Pausing to pray

God, something in me wants freedom but finds it slipping whenever I chase it. But you claim that the love of Christ is my path to true freedom in Christ. How can this be? You say that in losing my life I will find it! Truly? My life is so often about getting my way. What if I let go and prayed, 'Not my will but yours'? That scares me, but here goes. Lord, let it be!

God of Will or God of Love? 4
The Willful God in Biblical Religion

"Does God command a thing because it is good,
or is it good because God commands it?"
– Plato (Euthyphro) –

God's essence: freedom or will?

What do our ethics of freedom or love—willfulness or willing-ness—have to do with competing images of God? Only everything! Our highest moral values are ultimately an echo of the God we believe in (or once believed in).[1] We can trace our ethics to our understanding of God's essential nature. Namely, if your highest value is freedom (as self-will), the God you know (and may have received or rejected) is one whose nature is *pure freedom* or *pure will*. If your highest value is love, the God you know (and are most likely to love), is probably the God who is *pure love* or *pure good*. This crucial distinction impacts our worship, our theology, our faith-practice—indeed, our every decision—so it deserves a clear explanation.

Those who see God's essence as his *freedom* or *will* say, "God is God, so he is free to do or say or require whatever he wills, and that makes it good." This God determines, governs and commands absolutely everything. Because he is omnipotent (that is, all-powerful), nothing happens unless he ordains it. He is almighty. Sovereign. He is 'in control.'

The strongest version of this theology, still very popular, says that God foresees everything and whatever he foresees, he also 'foreordains.' In other words, he appoints and determines every event ahead of time, to the finest detail. Even before he created the world, God decreed everything, including the fall of humanity. He chose and predestined a specific class of people (the 'elect') to be his beloved children and decided that others would be left to defy him and be consigned to an eternity in hell—even before they were born! Why would he do that? "To the praise of his glory!"[2]

In other words, *because he can.* This God is *free* to do anything he *wills*, and if he does, because he is God, that makes it good. God's will, in this picture, determines what is good.

'Triumphalism'

refers to a narrow focus or boastful pride in the superiority, dominance or victory of one's faith or one's God, to the exclusion of the realities of weakness and denial of suffering.

When our faith is triumphalistic, those who suffer (think of Job) may infer they have failed God or be accused of being too weak in faith.

If God, in his anger, *wills* to enslave or annihilate a nation, he can and will do it. It is God's *right* to command his armies to massacre whole nations—including their women, children and animals. To obey this command is righteousness; and to disobey is rebellion. For example, in 1 Samuel 15, God supposedly instructed Samuel to command King Saul to destroy all the Amalekites—even their women, children and animals for things their forefathers did centuries earlier. But when Saul spares some of them, Samuel is enraged and condemns this act of mercy as rebellion, then dramatically and prophetically strips Saul of his kingdom.

Because God willed it, even genocide is seen as holy. In fact, it is regarded as worship, with the victims offered as one's gift to God!

Furthermore, if God chooses to summon an evil empire to siege and pillage his own people, to tear open the bellies of pregnant women and kill every unborn child (Hosea 13), the fact that God elected to do so makes that slaughter righteous! Whenever God deputizes human servants to exercise these judgments, including acts of extreme violence, remember: "It is better to obey than to sacrifice." Violent atrocities committed in obedience to this God are not considered immoral or sinful. In fact, to disobey God's command in those instances is compared to the sin of witchcraft (1 Sam. 15:23), which carried the death penalty.

And so we see, just as with people, a God who is pure freedom is also utterly willful. Add to this willfulness the fact that God is all-powerful, and you get a *triumphalistic** deity who can be dangerously violent. This God is an irresistible force to be feared and obeyed, worshiped and loved, or else!

The willful God in Christian history

The image of God as pure will and utter freedom can be quite appealing when shaped according to our self-interests. But when the brutality and violence of the willful God becomes overt, the image conjured is unsavory to our modern minds. Indeed, I personally find such a God abhorrent—evil, in fact. However, the truth about God is not discerned by our personal tastes of what is sweet or sour. *If* God is pure will—even a divine tyrant—then we'd better submit, like it or not. The fact is, historically, such a God recurs in various forms throughout Christian history and even within the pages of the Bible. The willful God has been taken very seriously by many major Christian theologians and teachers. Just a quick sample for our history buffs:

- *Early Church—Augustine (354-430 AD):* In the early Latin church, Augustine was a bishop whose influence grew in the west and had an enormous role in shaping both Catholic and Protestant theology. In an introduction to Augustine's famous *Confessions*, we read that, for Augustine, God's 'sovereign grace' is his *freedom*,

> "*To act beyond any external necessity whatsoever*"—to act in love beyond human control or understanding; to act in creation, judgment, and redemption; to *freely* give the Son of God and the Spirit of God for salvation, empowerment, and guidance; and "to shape the destinies of all creation and the ends of the two human societies, the 'city of earth' and the 'city of God.'"[3]

Augustine begins with God's freedom to love and forgive and save, in which he is accountable only to himself. Magnificent! But Augustine is quick to add that it works both ways. God is also free to judge and condemn and damn. According to Canadian scholar, Ron S. Dart,

> Augustine took a position at times quite at odds with the Alexandrian Christianity of Clement and Origen. It is in Augustine that notions such as election, double-predestination, God's sovereignty, just war and God's *willing* and *choosing* reach a place and pitch that has much in common with the God of Biblical Judaism. ... [We see] in Augustine the return to a *willing*, choosing sovereign God, not bounded by goodness or justice. Such a God could and would use his freedom to elect whom he willed for salvation and whom He willed for damnation. This is not a god [we can] truly trust.[4]

• *Medieval Theology—Voluntarism (1300-1500 AD):* During the chapter of Christian theology we call 'late scholasticism' (leading up to the Protestant Reformation), another school of thought emphasized God's freedom. It was called **voluntarism.** * The major names associated with it are Henry of Ghent, Duns Scotus and William of Ockham. Following Augustine, voluntarism places God's will prior to his goodness. The motive is again a defense of God's freedom. They expand the primacy of God's will, not only over creation, but also over God's own nature. According to Orthodox theologian David Bentley Hart, the voluntarists "placed an unprecedented emphasis on God's sovereign will as being the first and highest and primary attribute in God."[5] They sought to defend God's almighty power by making his will absolute, *even beyond good and evil.* "God does not command that which is good, that which is good is good because God commands it. That is, his will is not obedient to his nature as God; his will does not follow from his divine goodness."[6] So again, happily, God can forgive liberally without being bound to

> **'Voluntarism'** refers to the primacy of freedom of the will in God or people— it is prior even to love as the primary attribute of God.
>
> Thus, 'whatever God wills is good' versus 'God only wills what is good.' For people, it means that freedom, not love, is the highest moral obligation.

some law higher than grace—*but* God can also condemn individuals and destroy nations justly, *only because he wills it.* Moreover, in this view, to be omnipotent, God not only *allows* evil—he eternally, permissively *decrees* it.

• *Reformation Theology—John Calvin:* In the early 1500's, John Calvin was a European reformer whose theology was later made popular in America through the revival preaching of Jonathan Edwards. Calvinism continues to undergird much of Evangelical theology to this day. However, Calvin took the 'sovereign will of God' another step further. He claimed, "*All events* take place by God's sovereign appointment."[7] In other words, there is no difference between God's permission and God's purposes. What he *allows* is what he *commands.* Even evil? Consider these two claims:

Thieves, murderers, and other evildoers, are instruments of divine providence, being employed by the Lord himself to execute the judgments which He has resolved to inflict.[8]

The devil, and the whole train of the ungodly, are, in all directions, held in by the hand of God as with a bridle, so that they can neither conceive any mischief, nor plan what they have conceived, nor how they may have planned, move a single finger to perpetrate, unless in so far as he permits, *nay, unless in so far as He commands*; that they are not only bound by His fetters but are *even forced to do him service.*[9]

Thus, according to Calvin, God is not only beyond good and evil, but everyone who does evil is merely acting as his instrument and at his command. When an evil person or even the devil commits evil, it is because the Lord not only permitted it—he *commanded them* and *forced them* to do it. Every act of terror, every rape and murder, every genocide or infanticide, every cancer and heart attack, every famine and plague are all in the service of God's ultimate purpose: that you would fear him and glorify his name.

• *Radical Puritanism—Oliver Cromwell:* Calvin's theology carried over into the U.K. scene as English Puritanism. For those who confuse the Puritans with quaint images of the Mayflower

---

'Neo-Reformed' or 'New Calvinist'

refers to the current iteration of classic Calvinism (the theology of John Calvin). It typically retains the five major Reformed 'doctrines of grace' under the acronym TULIP:
total depravity; unconditional election; limited atonement; irresistible grace; and, the perseverance of the saints.

Pilgrims (1620) and Thanksgiving turkeys, it's important to distinguish them from the blood-soaked English Puritanism of Oliver Cromwell. Cromwell believed God actively controls history, continuing to engage directly in conquests and regime changes, exactly like those we see in the chronicles of Israel's history. He proclaimed that God had providentially appointed him and his armies as chosen instruments. Cromwell sought to purify Great Britain as a self-proclaimed Joshua, quoting the OT to justify mass murder and ethnic cleansing, and to dissolve the monarchy and then the parliament. His pitiless revolution of terror lasted from 1642-60.[10] During a nine-month campaign in Ireland, the war, famine and plague that followed killed over 500,000 men, women and children. Remember, this blitzkrieg was undertaken in the name of Jesus Christ, the 'Lord of Armies,' under whose sovereign orders Cromwell claimed to march.

We can be thankful that the ferocious extremes of Cromwell's theology no longer persist today. Or do they? I dare say they do: the old Christian 'crusades' and Islamic *jihads* continue to mirror each other wherever God's name is invoked in today's military conflicts. Prayers are offered and pleas for victory invoked, with both sides calling on the God of Abraham to advance their cause in the name of freedom. Does God pick sides? Since he is all-powerful and 'in control,' some see God as the ultimate Mastermind, Zeus-like, standing above the fray while simultaneously directing all the warring sides as pawns on a chessboard. Why? According to many popular End Times preachers, God is inexorably and pitilessly maneuvering the nations toward Armageddon, the great holocaust of humanity that ushers in Christ's glorious return.

- *Neo-Reformed theology today:* Thankfully, not many competent theologians get so carried away. Nevertheless, the image of God as sheer will has seen a resurgence among some popular **'neo-Reformed'*** or 'new Calvinist' teachers of our day. In March

2009, *TIME magazine* ranked neo-Calvinism as one of the "10 Ideas Changing the World Right Now."[11] Some of its most popular voices have included John Piper, Mark Driscoll, Kevin DeYoung and Tim Keller. Many are active in networks such as "Acts 29" and "The Gospel Coalition." It's extremely important not to paint the whole movement with one brush, as they can range from flaky (the infamous Westboro Baptists, who picket gay and military funerals) to wise and fruitful (e.g., Tim Keller).

For our purposes, I will cite John Piper, whose preaching ministry has spanned decades and whose voice is broadly received. He is also the most articulate modern teacher in the voluntarist stream of Augustine and Calvin. Again, remember the emphasis is on defending God's sovereign will as absolute. God is self-reliant and self-determined. He can do as he pleases and exerts control over every event, which includes governing evil for good purposes. In the aftermath of 9-11, here was his response:

> I'm coming to those families and I'm saying when they ask me, "Do you think God ordained the death of my daddy?" I say, "*Yes.* The Lord gives and the Lord takes away. Blessed be the name of the Lord. ... But the very power by which *God governs all evils* enables Him to govern your life. ... Where would we turn if we didn't have a God to help us deal with the very evils that He has ordained come into our lives?
>
> [Jesus could have] easily blown those planes off course by a little puff of wind, and He didn't do it. Therefore God was right there, *ordaining* that this happen, because He could have stopped it, just like that."[12]

Now here's an except from Rev. Piper's blog, where he recounts a conversation with his daughter in the wake of the Minneapolis bridge collapse in 2007 (13 people were killed, 145 injured):

We prayed during our family devotions. Talitha (11 years old) and Noel and I prayed earnestly for the families affected by the calamity and for the others in our city. Talitha prayed, "Please don't let anyone blame God for this but give thanks that they were saved." When I sat on her bed and tucked her in and blessed her and sang over her a few minutes ago, I said, "You know Talitha, that was a good prayer because when people 'blame' God for something, they are angry with Him, and they are saying He has done something wrong. That's what blame means: accuse somebody of wrongdoing. *But* you and I know that God did not do anything wrong. God always does what is wise. And you know that God could have held up that bridge with one hand." Talitha said, "Yes, with His pinky." "Yes," I said "with his pinky. Which means that God had a purpose for not holding up that bridge, knowing all that would happen, and He is infinitely wise in all that he wills." Talitha said, "Maybe he let it fall because he *wanted* all the people of Minneapolis to *fear* Him." "Yes, Talitha," I said, "I am sure that is one of the reasons God let the bridge fall." I sang to her the song I always sing:

> Come rest your head and nestle gently
> And do not fear the dark of night.
> Almighty God keeps watch intently
> And guards your life with all his might.
> Doubt not his love, nor power to keep,
> He never fails, nor does He sleep.

I said, "You know Talitha, that is true whether you die in a bridge collapse, or in a car accident, or from cancer, or terrorism, or old age. God always keeps you, even when you die. So you don't need to be afraid, do you?" "No," she shook her head. I leaned down and kissed her.

"Good night. I love you."[13]

John Piper's basic logic follows this track: when you feel like life is out of control and you are afraid, remember that God is all-powerful and that he is in control. If he's in control, you don't need to be afraid. It's *all* in God's hands. The concern is pastoral, with a heart to minister comfort. That worked for Talitha. I'm less sure it will work for the thousands upon thousands of Burmese women who have been raped and beaten, whose husbands have been tortured and murdered, and whose children have been abducted for conscription into a child army. In Rev. Piper's model, God both *ordains* and *governs* every evil, according to his design and purpose, so that we will fear him. This includes the Nigerian schoolgirl abductions by Boko Haram and the beheadings and atrocities by ISIS (and these religious extremists would completely concur). If God is in control—if he not only allowed, but also *willed* for tragedy and evil, natural and moral, to happen—he must certainly be all-powerful. But can he be said to be good?

I don't like it, but what I *like* doesn't get to be the criterion for truth. Take note: this image of God is not merely Augustine, Calvin or Piper's fanciful interpretation of the difficult scriptures. This way of seeing God really does appear plainly within the Bible.

The willful God in Jewish scripture

In the Hebrew Scriptures, or Old Testament, the fact is that Yahweh is reported to have committed or commanded these types of 'evils' frequently, embedding them right within his Law. The 'Christian West' (whatever that means) normally condemns genocides or slavery as obviously evil—injustices to be opposed.

Also, when an earthquake or tsunami destroys a city and buries its inhabitants, we instinctively pray and mobilize to bring relief. Why? Because we know (from the Bible?) that oppression and affliction are bad and we say, "Evil triumphs when *good* men do nothing."[14]

But what if God *wants* slaughter or *commands* slavery or *sends* calamity? Considerable portions of the Bible attribute plagues and famines and sieges and massacres to God, either by his direct intervention or as he delegates destroying angels or marauding armies. God's casualties are measured in the tens and hundreds of thousands. Entire cities and people groups are supposed to have been massacred by divine command. Men and women are put to the sword, their children enslaved and the virgins divvied up as spoils. And the Bible does not say God *allowed* it. In many cases, we read that he required it, at least if *we* require that God's call to slaughter be read literally. Indeed, the **cynical*** despisers of Scripture count on it.[15]

> ### 'Cynicism and literalism'
>
> The most devastating attacks on Christianity come not through clever arguments, but by a cynical reading of Scripture as if it was all meant to be read literally.
>
> Cynicism is clever, trendy and even a bit prophetic, but in the end functions only to steal hope.

And yet we believe God is good. Remember, we first heard that God is "gracious and compassionate, slow to anger, abounding in loving-kindness" in the Jewish canon (Exod. 34:6; Ps. 103:8). So what makes these more disturbing 'mighty acts of God'—normally considered evil—somehow *good*? One answer: merely the fact that God *willed* them. According to this image of God, the highest moral standard in heaven is God's sovereign will. A few passages appear to say exactly that. The psalmist sings, "Our God is in heaven; he does *whatever pleases him*" (Ps. 115:3). Isaiah chimes in,

> "I form the light and create darkness; I bring peace and *create evil* [or calamity]; I, the LORD, do all these things."
> (Isa. 45:7 KJV).

Remember Job? God bragged about Job's righteousness to Satan. Then according to Job chapter 1, Satan goaded God into a wager whereby he was given the green light to ruin Job's life. After suffering the loss of all his children, property and health, Job laments in an agonized defense before fools, complaining to God about his misery. And what is God's answer? In Job 40, we read:

¹ The LORD SAID TO JOB:
² *"Will the one who contends with the Almighty correct him?*
   Let him who accuses God answer him!"
³ Then Job answered the LORD:
⁴ "I am unworthy—how can I reply to you?
   I put my hand over my mouth.
⁵ I spoke once, but I have no answer—
   twice, but I will say no more."
⁶ Then the LORD SPOKE TO JOB OUT OF THE STORM:
⁷ "Brace yourself like a man;
   I will question you,
   and you shall answer me.
⁸ *"Would you discredit my justice?*
   Would you condemn me to justify yourself?
⁹ *Do you have an arm like God's*
   and *can your voice thunder like his?"*

What do you hear in God's response? Be honest. I hear an almighty deity shouting down a broken man: "Who are you to question me? How dare anyone judge me? I'm God almighty!" (Job 38:1-3; 40:1-7; 42:1-6).

Job knows. "I know you can do all things; no purpose of yours can be thwarted" (Job 42:2). In other words, Job resigns—"You're right. You're almighty. You're God. You can do whatever you want and no one can stop you. You win." I sometimes wonder if Job also whispered under his breath, "Yes, but are you good?"

Of course, there's more going on here—something more brilliant and beautiful than divine bullying, but for the theologian who sees sovereign will as God's essential nature, there doesn't need to be. God does whatever he wills and if Job or Jonah or I don't like it, so what? God is God and we're not so, we're told, don't question him.

In truth, the major takeaways from Job are nothing like that. We're to learn (in contrast to Job's foolish friends) that calamity is *not* a sign that we've been bad or that God has abandoned us or is intent on punishing us. We're to notice that God *does speak*—all along, all the time and in many ways (Job 33:12-30)—and *why*? To warn us, to restore us and to rescue us. God's is not a callous will but a loving heart—not setting us up for harm but ultimately, working to redeem us. How? Through a forthcoming Mediator!

> ²³ If there is a messenger for him,
>> A *mediator*, one among a thousand,
>> To show man His uprightness,
> ²⁴ Then *He is gracious* to him, and says,
>> '*Deliver him* from going down to the Pit;
>> I have found *a ransom*';
> ²⁵ His flesh shall be young like a child's,
>> He shall return to the days of his youth.
> ²⁶ He shall pray to God, and He will delight in him,
>> He shall *see His face with joy*,
>> For He *restores* to man His righteousness.
>> (Job 33:23-26)

The willful God in the New Testament

These competing pictures of God-as-will versus God-as-love aren't restricted to the Old Testament. Some would like to forego the problem by distinguishing between 'the God of the Old Testament' (the vengeful and violent one) and 'the God of the New Testament' (the gracious and merciful one). Then it's simply a matter of jettisoning Yahweh in favor of Jesus. But it's not that simple. The New Testament is written on the foundation and as the fulfillment of the Old. Jesus is revealed as Yahweh incarnate. The Old Testament can depict God as vengeful, but also reveals him as gracious—it may describe him as violent, but also shows him to be merciful. He's not to be reduced to a retributive warrior—Yahweh is first and foremost all about restoration. It depends what lenses you're wearing as you read the Hebrew records.

So it is in the pages of the New Testament. My son, Justice—who clearly distinguishes between God's life-giving justice and our death-dealing judgment—had words with a hate-spewing street-preacher this week. When Justice challenged him, asking, "What about the truth that God is love? Why aren't you sharing that with these people?" the evangelist replied, "God is love, *but,*" and produced a Bible marked with a bright highlighter. He showed my son verse after verse (always devoid of context) where he had underlined 'hate,' 'anger,' 'wrath' and 'judgment'—including many examples from the New Testament.

The preacher had highlighted portraits of God in Jesus' parables, Paul's epistles and John's revelations that seemed every bit as punitive as Israel's darkest versions of Yahweh. Sure enough, God *is* sometimes described as an exacting Master (Matt. 19:28-35), avenging Landowner (Mark 12:1-12) or retributive Judge (2 Thess. 1:6-10). This fiery preacher wielded such New Testament texts to paint an image of God as willful, coercive and destructive—on purpose! He wanted Justice to see that wrath and retribution are woven throughout the tapestry of the New Testament—including the words of Christ.

In fact, he happily envisioned Jesus himself as the blood-drenched, conquering Warrior of Rev. 19:11-19. Too many preachers positively revel in that image. For example, as Mark Driscoll (former pastor of Mars Hill Church in Seattle) once said,

In Revelation, Jesus is a prize-fighter with a tattoo down his leg, a sword in his hand and the commitment to *make someone bleed.* That is the guy I can worship. I cannot worship the hippie, diaper, halo Christ because *I cannot worship a guy I can beat up.*[16]

I find that picture extremely troubling because it clashes with the image of humility, grace and mercy of the Father, revealed by Christ's words, works and most especially his Passion. I see no resemblance between that ruthless conqueror and the Jesus we *did* in fact beat up: the compassionate healer whose commitment to love led him to bleed for us.

Brandishing the New Testament as the hate-literature of God also ignores the obvious intended trajectory of revelation from Old Covenant to New. God didn't evolve; our conception of him did, in greatest part because Jesus came to show and tell us exactly who God is in ways *no* prophet had the capacity to anticipate—not Moses, David or even Isaiah.

For example, we read in John 1:17 that Moses gave us the Law (a system of rewards and punishments), but Christ brought us grace and truth. We read in 2 Cor. 3:9ff that Moses' covenant brought condemnation but Jesus' covenant brings righteousness, true freedom and transformation.

What's happening here? Rather than replacing Yahweh of the Old Testament with the Christ of the New, these authors emphasize that Moses' revelation of God as the just Judge (the law-bringer) is being eclipsed by Jesus' greater revelation of God the loving Father (the gospel-giver). They preach the same God, but through a different lens. With the restorative lens of Jesus and his glad tidings, Yahweh comes into focus as that gracious Father whose judgments *are* mercy. Whatever maleficent image we see is the result of distorted vision, whether ours or the stories' characters or their human narrators. Through a retributive lens, even Jesus appears vengeful and violent.

Remember, it's not only the vengeance or violence from which I'm recoiling: the real problem is the portrait of a God whose *un-Christlike naked will* eclipses love and trumps grace—a coercive *force* incongruent with Christ's *cruciform* revelation of his Father's love.

Some disciples of John Calvin parade Paul's reflections in Romans 9 as an example of God's will-to-choose. They see Paul bombarding readers with a series of Old Testament passages to assert God's freedom, and so he does. But these interpreters exploit the text to pose the utter willfulness of God *to hate, exclude and condemn*—the flip side of God's grace. With that lens, yes, you could argue that:

[13] Just as it is written: "Jacob I loved, but Esau *I hated.*"

[14] What then shall we say? Is God unjust? Not at all!

[15] For he says to Moses,

"I will have mercy on whom I have mercy, and I will have compassion on whom I have compassion."

[16] It does not, therefore, depend on human desire or effort, but on God's mercy. [17] For Scripture says to Pharaoh:

"I raised you up for this very purpose, that I might display my power in you and that my name might be proclaimed in all the earth."

[18] Therefore *God* has mercy on whom *he wants* to have mercy, and he hardens whom *he wants* to harden. [19] One of you will say to me: "Then why does God still blame us? For who is able to resist *his will?*" [20] But who are you, a human being, to talk back to God? "Shall what is formed say to the one who formed it, 'Why did you make me like this?'" [21] Does not the potter *have the right* to make out of the same lump of clay some pottery for special purposes and some for common use?

If read through the lens of absolute will, this passage seems to describe a God *worse* than retributive and vengeful, because those attributes are merely angry reactions to wicked people. But these paragraphs don't say that. They go further. They actually suggest that God made some people wicked—*created them to be damned goats*—in the first place, because he willed it. And if he then punishes them also for it, don't cry foul! Who are you to judge God? This interpretation of Romans 9 hails God's sovereign will in pre-choosing (electing) some to salvation and actually creating others for the sole purpose of damnation—why? To glorify himself as we cower in gratitude.

As Justice's street-preacher said, "Hey, some people are goats, and God hates the goats." He wasn't sure who the goats were (but he was sure he wasn't a goat), so he preached God's hate to everyone, 'butchering' the very text he alluded to (Matt. 25:31-46).

Do we *really* believe *that* is Paul's intent in Romans 9? The reason he wrote the epistle? The point and flow of his argument? Ludicrous! That approach makes nonsense of Paul's life mission *and* his purpose in writing Romans. Worse, it represents God as unjust, unholy and unloving. Because this text is so critical to one's view of God's love and will, and because it's misread when isolated, let's pause to see its piece in the bigger puzzle of Romans.

- Paul begins Romans with the content of his ministry: 'the Gospel of God' (1:1-4).
- He describes his call to bring the good news of God's faithfulness to all nations (or Gentiles) (1:5).
- He proceeds to argue at length for the universality of the gospel's availability and significance. He announces the inclusion of Greeks and barbarians, Gentiles and Jews (starting in 1:14-16), even those in Rome.
- Thus, the apostle's theme is the universal availability of divine salvation to *all*: past, present and future. Understanding the arc of Paul's argument opens up what he's doing in Rom. 9-11 by addressing Israel.

- Throughout his letter, Paul quotes his opponents and their favorite exclusion texts, then turns those same texts against them (a method called 'diatribe'). In Romans 9, Paul takes passages his adversaries have used to paint God as a willful hater, but he applies them to magnify God's *freedom-in-love* to graciously extend salvation to the Gentiles.

- Then Paul answers another question: Does God's faithfulness include Israel, even when they've rejected Christ? Yes, God is *free-in-love* to save them also!

- God's redemptive plan—his *freedom rooted in love*—is irrevocable and his mercy will reach the Jews, just as it had also been reaching the Gentiles.

Given the context, we at least know this: Paul's enemies *never* accused him of preaching a willful and exclusionary God. Their angst was always about his message being *too* gracious, *too* inclusive and *too* willing to save anyone. Their God—*not* Paul's—was the 'goat-hater' of raw will.

Word association

Let's conclude this chapter by gathering some common biblical and theological words associated with a God whose essence is pure will:

- King, Master, Warrior, Conqueror
- sovereignty, dominion, control, intervention
- almighty, omnipotent, invincible, supreme
- power, force, authority, rule, command
- punishment, retribution, vengeance, wrath

We cannot simply do away with these descriptions of God. They appear in our Bibles as important truths. They represent major themes and revelations of God from Genesis to Revelation, including the Gospels. So we can't and won't start snipping them from the pages of Scripture.

On the other hand, we will need to learn how to read these themes with fresh eyes and gospel lenses. When religion represents God's *will* as absolute—the primary attribute of his nature—an idolatrous and un-Christlike portrait of God emerges. Competing and contradictory images inevitably pop up everywhere. Our theology and even our Bible begins to unravel. To redress this problem, the following chapter will refound our footings on the following assumptions:

- God's essence in not pure *will*.

- His essence is selfless *love*.

- God's primary attribute is not *freedom*.

- God is first of all *good*.

- God's nature is totally *Christlike*, and, we'll see, *cruciform*.

Pausing to think

- Does God command a thing because it is good, or is it good because God commands it? What do you think?

- If we say God is all-powerful, does that mean he could do *anything,* including what for us would be evil? Is it still evil if God does it? Or commands it?

- What do we do with scriptures that seem to make God complicit in such evils? How do we reconcile these texts with the Father of love revealed through Jesus?

- How might you answer those who assign God's will to every event, including natural calamities and even the wicked acts of free people?

- Where do we see examples of God putting his love ahead of his freedom or power in the Old Testament? In the New Testament?
- When God is depicted as putting love and compassion ahead of law, judgment and wrath, how does this affect your posture toward him? Your emotions about him?

Pausing to pray

God, you are free, you are almighty in power, you are just and righteous in your judgments. Most of all, we hear that you are love. Your compassion extends to everyone and your mercy gets the final word. I don't care whether or not you could create a stone too heavy for you to lift. What I need is to know whether you care, if you are kind and how much you love me. Not just on paper, but here, today in my real life. Lord, let it be!

Word Made Flesh   **5**
The Christlike God[1]

*"He was incarnate by the Holy Spirit
of the virgin Mary, and was made man."*
– The Nicene Creed –

"Colossal power . . . tiny little living space."
– Disney's Aladdin –

In this chapter, I propose Jesus as the lens through which to clarify our vision of God. But really, 'lens' doesn't say it strongly enough. Jesus is not just a filter through which God is seen—Jesus *is* that God. God is, was and always will be exactly like Jesus. The apostles explicitly testified that *all the fullness* of God was enfleshed *in* Christ—that Jesus of Nazareth was the perfect human image of the invisible Spirit of Divine Love.

As we'll see, because God is fully revealed in Jesus—exactly like him—then God is a self-giving lover, and not a conquering emperor, like Constantine for example. We will need to address both the problem of a seemingly two-faced God (love versus force) and an apparently two-faced Christ (Lamb versus Lion; the suffering Servant versus the bloody Warrior on the white horse). We will acknowledge Christ's complete and utter victory but identify the *way* of his victory as self-giving love.

Incarnation: becoming flesh

Let's begin with an old Christian term we usually associate with Christmas: '*Incarnation*' (see glossary). Historically, Christmas season was a sacred feast celebrating the Incarnation, literally the *enfleshment* of God Almighty. But even Christians who haven't forgotten the word altogether often mistakenly reduce the meaning of Incarnation to the nativity scene in Bethlehem. That's understandable, because Incarnation has to do with 'becoming flesh'—and certainly Jesus' birth marked the event when God appeared in a human body. But it's actually much bigger than that. First, the Incarnation refers to the entire life of Christ, when God tangibly walked the earth for over three decades. And second, Jesus of Nazareth *was* the Incarnation of God. When Jesus went public, King Herod was worried he was a reincarnation of John the Baptist, but he didn't know the half of it. Jesus was *not* a *re*-incarnation; he was *the Incarnation* of the God of Israel, and indeed, the universe.

The early church, drawing from her rich tradition of the Gospels and epistles, hymns and liturgies, creeds and councils came to this consensus: "We believe in one God, the Father almighty ... and in one Lord, Jesus Christ. Light from Light, very God from very God ... of one essence with the Father."[1]

This reflects the language Paul used to teach the Corinthians:

> For us there is but *one God*, the Father, from whom all things came and for whom we live; and there is but *one Lord*, Jesus Christ, through whom all things came and through whom we live (1 Cor. 8:6).

In other words, Jesus and the Father are distinct 'persons,' and yet they share the fact that together, they (along with the Holy Spirit) are 'one God' or 'one Lord.' God and Lord are synonymous here.

So this God—this Lord—"became flesh and tabernacled [that is, 'pitched his tent'] among us for a while" (John 1:14, my translation). Astonishing! Hopefully, we can regain the astonishment that overcame the shepherds as first witnesses. But it's not easy to relive this amazing news when we've been so conditioned to it.

Recently, I was able to revisit the wonder of the Incarnation by hearing it through the fresh ears of a native spiritualist / social worker. She had popped into a university where I was teaching "The Gospel in Chairs" (or "The Beautiful Gospel"[3]), a version of the Jesus story I will recount in chapter 14. Afterward, she approached me, absolutely gushing. She said, "I'm not a Christian, and I wouldn't use the same language as you, but this is exactly the message people need to hear!" She talked about how 'Universe' fills everything with love and never abandons or rejects us. And then her eyes grew as she experienced her 'Aha!' moment there and then. Animated, she exclaimed, "What if ... what if 'Universe' wanted to communicate that love too us? What if the best way to do it was to come as one of us!" Peter Fitch, my friend and host at the university, replied, "Yes, that's pretty much what we're saying." Jesus came from his Father into the world to reveal God in a way we could see, hear and touch. Imagine: the God of the universe who "dwells in unapproachable light," but if you had a smartphone, you could have posed for a 'selfie' with him![4] Astonishing!

So, in the flesh and blood person of Jesus, we have the only life ever lived that *perfectly* reveals the true nature of God, as far as it can be revealed in a human being. New Testament writers remind us that Jesus of Nazareth was more than a wandering peasant-prophet from Galilee. They insist he was and is the *exact image* of God's essence, the *precise imprint* of God's being (Col. 1:15; Heb. 1:13). They testify that in Christ, "all the fullness of the Godhead lived in a human body" (Col. 2:9). John's first epistle contends for the central Christian truth: that Jesus Christ came 'in the flesh' (1 John 4:2). 'Flesh' as in a tangible body. 'Flesh' as in authentic humanity. 'Flesh' as in the full range of physical limitations, human emotions and depths of suffering common to us all.

In simple terms, we say that Jesus showed us *exactly* what God is like, not just a facet of divinity; Jesus was the one true and living avatar of the transcendent God. When the Apostle Philip asked him,

"Show us the Father and that will be enough for us," Jesus himself declared, "Don't you know me, Philip, even after I have been among you such a long time? Anyone who has seen me has seen the Father" (John 14:9).

"I and the Father are one," he says (John 10:30).

That is, Jesus on earth unveiled God in heaven. His apostles confirmed that in Christ, they had experienced the impossible: they had seen God, heard God and touched God (1 John 1:1-2). They knew face-to-face fellowship with the Almighty because Jesus was in truth the very face of God (2 Cor. 4:6).

These are profound claims, not only about who Jesus was and is, but even more importantly, these claims mean that Jesus is the decisive revelation of who God is and the radical re-definition of what God is like. If so, then understand: God is entirely Christ-like! Archbishop of Canterbury Michael Ramsey once said, "God is *Christlike*, and in Him there is no *unChristlikeness* at all." Or as the American preacher, Brian Zahnd, declares, "God is like Jesus – God is exactly like Jesus – God has always been exactly like Jesus." Thus, God did not merely *become* Christlike. God always, eternally has been. So what does, 'exactly like Jesus' mean? That depends on who you ask! Let's start from the beginning.

'God is like Jesus'

"God is Christlike and in him is no un-Christlikeness at all."
– Ab. Michael Ramsey

"God is like Jesus— exactly like Jesus— God has always been exactly like Jesus."
– Brian Zahnd

Birth of a king

When Christ was born, angelic messengers were dispatched from the throne of God to announce the arrival of a king—*the* King. "Glory to God in the highest," they sing, "and on earth, peace to those on whom his favor rests" (Luke 2:14).

When we think about kings and kingdoms, we think of glory, of ruling and reigning; we speak of sovereignty, authority, power and might. So when we imagine God as King, we proclaim his reign in word and song, just as the multitudes do in the heavenly visions of Revelation 4-5. We project our loftiest ideas of worldly monarchs onto God and try our best to amplify them to divine heights. Twentieth century theologian Karl Barth referred to this phenomenon as defining God as man in capital letters! Christ is worshiped, crowned and enthroned as King of Glory, majestic in his universal dominion—imagery drawn from the world of human monarchs.

All of these terms draw on the royalty theme. When we use the king metaphor, we might imagine that God is a king like our kings, except more! They are powerful; he is all-powerful! They rule nations; he rules the universe! In fact, since he is the king-of-kings, that makes him an emperor! Emperor of the universe! We imagine the mightiest emperors of history: Tutankhamen, Nebuchadnezzar and Alexander the Great. We picture the Roman Empire, the Chinese dynasties and the British Commonwealth. And really, history's most exceptional empire still exists: the United States of America! Yet they must all finally bow, as one day every knee shall bow, in submission to the Emperor of All and his Son, the Lord Jesus Christ.

Such a God is very appealing. I can trust a God who is 'sovereign.' I want a God who is 'in control.' I like my God to be bigger, wiser and stronger than any other ... mainly because he is *my* God. And woe to the bully who picks on me! I put my hope in this warrior-king, 'the mighty smiter' who avenges me and wins the day, whether now or on the Day of Judgment. Glorious!

Such glory makes for great hymnology. Moreover, these descriptions are biblically true, right? Or course! The king metaphor reminds us that God gets the last word. It calls us to allegiance, obedience and worship. Thus it becomes very natural for us to conceive of God's *sovereignty* in terms of *imperial dominance*.

The emperor image

Eusebius certainly thought so.[6] He was the bishop of Caesarea in the fourth century and has been called the 'father of history.' Among his written works are his "Oration in Praise of Constantine," proclaiming the thirtieth anniversary of the first Christian emperor's reign. In his grand speech, Eusebius reasons that through the power of the Cross, every demonic hindrance to the global reign of God—the Emperor in heaven—has been removed. Therefore God's kingdom will now advance unchecked until it covers the whole earth. Having defeated their false gods, the Prince of Peace will rule over all nations in one united empire, just as the prophets foretold. Moreover, Christ's imperial kingdom was spreading rapidly through the conquests of his earthly co-regent, the emperor Constantine and his armies. In battle after battle, Constantine subjugated all foreign enemies under the sign of the Cross, just as Israel had (sort of) behind the Ark of the Covenant. And so God's kingdom and glory was to cover the earth via the imperial might of the Holy Roman Empire, baptized by the approval of the institutional church. Eventually every knee would bow to Christ through the victory of Constantine, and bring about an era of eternal peace. In Eusebius' words,

> And thus the Almighty Sovereign himself accords an increase both of years and of children to our most pious emperor, and renders his sway over the nations of the world still fresh and flourishing. ... He appoints him this present festival, in that he has made him victorious over every enemy that disturbed his peace: He it is who displays him as an example of true godliness to the human race. ...
>
> Invested as [Constantine] is with a semblance of heavenly sovereignty, he directs his gaze above, and frames his earthly government according to the pattern of that Divine original, feeling strength in its conformity to the monarchy

of God. And this conformity is granted by the universal Sovereign to man alone of the creatures of this earth: for He only is the author of sovereign power, who decrees that all should be subject to the rule of one.[7]

Note here how Eusebius defines God's 'sovereignty.' It relates to victory through violence and peace via conquest; monarchy through force and coercive power; rule through decrees and reign as subjugation. Rebellion—polytheism, pluralism and democracy—would be trodden underfoot for the sake of God's kingdom.

Now to be fair to both Constantine and Eusebius, understand that Christianity had experienced periods of horrendous persecution. The prisons sometimes had no room for criminals because they were full of bishops and priests, tortured for their faith and disfigured by the mutilations of their captors. Imagine, now, the emperor, whether or not you believe his conversion is genuine, signs and enforces the *Edict of Milan* (313 AD), which allows for religious freedom of all faiths, but also the active promotion of Christianity. Moreover, he sponsors and presides over the great Council of Nicea (the first ecumenical council, 325 AD), the first successful attempt to bring consensus across all of Christianity. From this initiative, we receive the first draft of the Nicene Creed, which finally defines the nature of the Son of God and his relationship to the Father. We use that creed to this day as our standard for *orthodoxy*.*

Furthermore, for a long time, wherever Emperor Constantine marched, chaos became peace and

'Orthodoxy'

refers to theology that conforms to the plumb line of "faith once delivered" (Jude 3) by Christ through the apostles and defined by the early church fathers in the creeds and councils of the ancient church.

Christianity was able to take root.

What does all this imply? For Eusebius, God's kingdom had come "on earth as it is in heaven" *through the lifework of Constantine.* The *earthly emperor was now the image and agent of the heavenly King,* with the institutional church written in as his happy chaplain, confidant and cheerleader!

In hindsight, such claims seem impudent and audacious—yet they persist throughout the ages in various forms, draped in terms such as "divine right of kings," "manifest destiny" and, more recently, "American exceptionalism."

Remember *how* Jesus came

But wait a moment.

Remember the Incarnation? The almighty Creator God who both pre-existed and birthed our whole universe had *already* come. Christ *already* established his kingdom. Remember also *how* he arrived. It was no military parade! Remember, the royal proclamation of the angels indicate a trudging journey, a smelly donkey, a tiny village. Recall the "No Vacancy" sign and of course, the crowded manger-cave. God, bursting into this dimension, crowning from between a virgin's legs! God, a helpless newborn, wailing for momma's milk. God, filling his first swaddling diaper with meconium! God, whisked away at night by a refugee family, barely ducking Herod's sword, hunkering in Egypt.

God came to earth, *this* way, on purpose! And *how* God came is itself an essential revelation of his true nature.

Remember Jesus! Remember that he—not Constantine—represents the *only perfect image* of God. Recall *who* Jesus was on earth: *how* he arrived, *how* he lived, *how* he died and *how* Jesus overcame—his *way* of overcoming represents the *only exact* revelation we have of God's sovereign reign!

If God sent his Son to reveal himself, if Jesus showed us how true sovereignty works, what real power does, and what victory looks like—*on earth as it is in heaven*—then let me propose that the King of Heaven rules and reigns, not like Constantine, but like Jesus of Nazareth. If Jesus is a king, he is not like any king we have conceived. When we remember the babe in Bethlehem, or the servant washing his disciples' feet or the crucified King of the Jews, we must say that his kingdom is an upside-down kingdom! If Jesus is to be called king, then he is a humble king, an ironic king—virtually an anti-king! Christ himself said so:

> [25] But Jesus called them to *Himself* and said, "You know that the rulers of the Gentiles lord it over them, and those who are great exercise authority over them. [26] Yet it shall not be so among you; but whoever desires to become great among you, let him be your servant. [27] And whoever desires to be first among you, let him be your slave—[28] just as the Son of Man did not come to be served, but to serve, and to give His life a ransom for many." (Matt. 20:25-28 NKJV)

Theologian Derek Flood comments,

> Jesus models the way of God, not as one who 'lords it over others' but as the servant Lord, and calls for us to embody that way too. Following Jesus means rejecting the way of domination, the way of worldly kings.[8]

Lowly king

The subversion of worldly kingship is evident from birth to death and at every stage of Christ's life. Yes, Jesus Christ reveals the power, sovereignty and victory of the God's kingdom. But in so doing, he undermines our default notions of power, sovereignty and victory. In fact, Jesus forever redefines our vision of God-as-king!

Christ indeed is our king, but the Cross reveals that he is a *lowly* king. This word 'lowly' has two senses in Hebrew, Greek and English. On the one hand, lowly can refer to humiliation—as in crushed, broken or brought low with grief. On the other hand, lowly *primarily* means humility or meekness. Both senses apply to Christ, but in very different ways. Christ suffered the *humiliation* of mockery, beatings, crucifixion and death. This humiliation was a *temporary experience* Christ overcame through his resurrection and ascension to glory. But Christ was also lowly in the sense of his *humility*. Christ's humility reflects his own character, and also reveals the eternal nature of God. It is the latter lowliness—this humility—to which Jesus refers when he says, "Take My yoke upon you and learn from Me, for I am gentle and *lowly* [*humble*, NIV] in heart, and you will find rest for your souls" (Matt. 11:19 NKJV).

So too Christ draws close to the lowly (versus the proud)—the humiliated and the humble. The Good News is that he is looking to rescue and lift up the lowly (the humiliated) and, at the same time, wants to reproduce his lowliness (humility) in us. God, speaking through Isaiah the prophet, says, "I live in a high and holy place, but also with the one who is contrite and *lowly* in spirit, to revive the spirit of the *lowly* and to revive the heart of the contrite" (Isa. 57:15).

Christ's lowliness of humility is a revelation of the Father's humility. Humility is an eternal attribute of God that we see in the Incarnation and especially in the Passion. But also, Christ experienced and participated in the lowliness of our humiliation, so that we, with

'Crucifixion versus Cross'

We can think of the *crucifixion* as what we did to Jesus—the sin of torturing and murdering God's Son. We can think of the *Cross* as what Jesus did for us—offering his life in self-giving love and radical forgiveness.

him, might be lifted out of humiliation. The first 'lifting up' is *to* the Cross (humility). The second 'lifting up,' is *from* the crucifixion (humiliation).

As we launch into this idea of the Cross as a revelation of God—a *theology of the Cross,* so to speak—readers may find it helpful if I distinguish between the *crucifixion* and *the Cross*.

The Crucifixion and the Cross

When we read the New Testament accounts of Christ's death, we are struck by both the ugliness of the crime and the beauty of the One who endured it. We note the irony of how an instrument of torture becomes a work of art.

I will usually use the word *crucifixion* to refer to the sinful act of evil men who tortured and murdered the Son of God. When I mention *the Cross*, I will have in mind the self-giving, servant-love of Christ, in which his blood symbolizes his mercy and forgiveness poured out onto the world. In other words, the crucifixion is what we did to him—we took his life. The Cross is what Christ did for us—he gave his life.

The New Testament does not strictly use the words this way, but I will do so in order to retain both perspectives. So when we think about the *crucifixion,* we may recall Jesus' parable of the tenants (Mark 12:1-12). The owner of the vineyard (representing God) expects the tenants to respect and receive his beloved son (v. 6), but they murder him (v. 7) and the owner is furious (v. 9). Jesus uses this parable to prophesy how the temple authorities will conspire in his death. So too, in retrospect, Stephen the martyr indicts the religious leadership, saying, "Was there ever a prophet your ancestors did not persecute? They even killed those who predicted the coming of the Righteous One. And now *you have betrayed and murdered him*" (Acts 7:52). Thus, Jesus and the witnesses in Acts saw the *crucifixion* as an ugly homicide.

But when we speak of *the Cross*, we behold the great love Jesus has for us in giving his life (1 John 3:16). The Cross is how "God showed his love among us" (1 John 4:9-10). When Paul says he will only "boast in the Cross of our Lord" (Gal. 6:14), he means *all* that Jesus did for us in his death. I capitalize 'the Cross' because that image is so central to describing who God is and what Christ does that the word is virtually synonymous with Jesus' name! We might say the Cross is a short way to say 'the person and work of the crucified Christ.'

This distinction also clarifies what God the Father is doing *and not doing* on Good Friday: he is *not* a co-conspirator in the *crucifixion* of his own Son, nor does he get any pleasure out of betrayal, punishment or killing. Rather, the significance of the *Cross* is that "God was *in Christ*, reconciling the world to himself ..."

How? By graciously, mercifully *"not* counting our sins against us" (2 Cor. 5:19). And by powerfully, victoriously conquering Satan, sin and death on our behalf.

The Revelation par excellence

In John's first epistle, he makes two absolutely vital claims: "God is love" (1 John 4:16) and "This is how we know what love is: Jesus Christ laid down his life for us" (1 John 3:16). In other words, as we 'zoom in' on Jesus' revelation of the nature of God, he draws us to "a hill far away, on an old rugged Cross." The portrayal *par excellence* of God's very being is the Cross of Christ. Just about every great painter in history has tried to produce a work of art that captures the beauty and power of the crucifixion scene. I am saying the Cross is Jesus Christ's own masterpiece, capturing the beauty and power and face of God the Father.

So now, in the next section—*the cruciform God*—we will examine the way in which the kingdom and the power and the glory of God come into their sharpest focus at Calvary.

Pausing to think

- Consider the following passages:
  - Phil. 2:1-11
  - John 12:27-33; 16:33-17:5
  - Rev. 5:1-10; 12:1-12
- What are these texts saying about God's self-revelation in and through Jesus? What is revealed about God's eternal nature?
- How do these texts associate glory and the Cross? When is Christ glorified according to John's Gospel?
- What does 'Lamb' imagery communicate? How does Christ reign as Lamb? Why Lamb as opposed to Lion?

Pausing to pray

God, you are free, you are almighty in power, you are just and righteous in your judgments, but most of all, we hear that you are love. That your compassion extends to everyone and your mercy gets the final word. You care, you are kind and you love me. Not merely on paper, but here, today in my real life. Lord, let it be!

Part II
The Cruciform God

- In which we see Christ—and particularly *Christ crucified*—as the climax of God's self-revelation.

- What does Jesus show us about the nature of God?

- What does the Cross demonstrate about the nature of God?

- How does the Cross represent God's consent to the world and to human freedom?

- What does the Cross reveal about the way God participates in the world?

- How is the Cross a response to the problem of suffering?

Of Lions, Lambs and Donkeys 6
Kenosis—Cruciform Power

"He came the first time as the Lamb of God;
he comes again as the Lion of the Tribe of Judah."
– Ray Pritchard (Sound the Trumpet) –

"He divinizes with the frailty of his immanent touch,
and in the wounding of his fragile being
he reveals the fullness of the divine glory."
– Aaron Riches (Ecce Homo)

Most world religions have chosen to use a wide variety of animals to portray their gods. Some are majestic, others comical or even grotesque. While visiting temples in Asia I saw ornate golden elephant gods, giving the impression of nobility and power. The ancient Egyptians liked to carve superhuman animal-human hybrids. Even the newly freed Jews experimented with a great golden calf. Each faith wanted to communicate something of its gods' wealth and power. Christendom loves to symbolize the over-coming power of Christ as a great eagle or kingly lion. If it hadn't been for the humble life and gruesome death of Christ, I doubt we would have pictured God's Messianic King as a slain lamb or a peasant so familiar with donkeys. Apparently wealth and might weren't foremost in God's priorities for self-revelation. But God did communicate exactly what he wanted to reveal about himself, and he did so in Jesus, using images we doubtless would have avoided.

To echo one of our primary themes, the images of God we choose, as people and as Christians, are typically not very

Christlike. Again and again Christ must set the record straight: God is completely Christlike—lamb-like and *cruciform*, divine humility incarnate (literally). Gold, rippling muscles, immeasurable wealth and overwhelming power—are these 'God'? Aren't they more in the realm of pride? Is God like Jesus or is he like Zeus? Or Lucifer?

Kenosis: cruciform power

In the great hymn of Philippians 2, we read:

… Christ Jesus, [6] who, although He existed in the form of God, did not regard equality with God a thing to be grasped, [7] but emptied Himself, taking the form of a bond-servant, and being made in the likeness of men. [8] Being found in appearance as a man, He humbled Himself by becoming obedient to the point of death, even death on a cross. [9] For this reason also, God highly exalted Him, and bestowed on Him the name which is above every name, [10] so that at the name of Jesus, EVERY KNEE WILL BOW of those who are in heaven and on earth and under the earth, [11] and that every tongue will confess that Jesus Christ is Lord, to the glory of God the Father (Phil. 2:6-11 NASB).

The key term in this passage is 'emptied.' *Kenosis** is Paul's Greek word, but it's so important we've adopted it into English. *Kenosis*—self-emptying—will become all-important shortly, so fair warning: I'll be using it and its adjective form—*kenotic*—a lot.

Some believe that *kenosis* means that God *gives up* his divine attributes or *hides* or *hinders* his own nature in order to become incarnate. He either puts on something (like wearing a disguise) or takes off something (like disrobing). Certainly the fullness of the divine nature is *concealed* in some ways in the Incarnation. But it is uniquely *revealed* in Christ as well. "We beheld his glory," says

John (John 1:14). So then, our descriptions of the Incarnation must not construe Jesus as less than human or less than divine. Historic Christianity affirmed that in the Incarnation, Christ was and is *fully* human and *fully* divine at all times. In fact, he *must* be fully human in order to experience our death, *and* fully divine in order to overcome that death. In the Incarnation, God the Son assumes (takes on) humanity, makes it his own, and in so doing, not only restores but perfects humanity.[2]

I must emphasize: any kind of '*kenotic* theology' that makes Christ less than God is certainly *not* what I'm talking about. The early church was clear: Christ never ceased to be fully God and fully man. Paul says in Colossians that *all the fullness of the Godhead* dwelled in Jesus' human body (Col. 2:9). So I am espousing an altogether different *kenotic* vision than those who mistakenly empty Christ of his 'Godness.' Far from giving up, hiding or hindering God's nature, we shall see that Christ's *kenotic* and *cruciform* life is the revelation par excellence of God's glory. *Kenosis* is not a surrender of the divine attributes; *kenosis* defined as self-giving or self-donation is the premier expression of God's nature—of God's love and grace—seen most clearly on the Cross. In other words, while the early church typically used *kenosis* only to describe the

---

Kenosis, kenotic

Greek for *emptying*, used by Paul in Philippians 2 to describe Christ's self-emptying power, self-giving love and radical servanthood, revealed in the Word becoming flesh and particularly seen in the Passion of Christ.

Kenosis expresses God's glory, rather than diminishing it. *Kenosis* reflects God's self-giving, cruciform *kenotic* love.

Incarnation, the Incarnation itself is all about revealing who God is in both his self-giving humility and his self-revealing glory.

Kenosis as I conceive it is the same idea we get from the Beatitudes, "Blessed are the *poor in spirit*" (Matt. 5:3). In other words, not 'full of ourselves,' *emptied* of egotism, *void* of willfulness, *bankrupt* of selfishness. Humble, generous, effusive in his love. That's *kenosis*. That's Jesus. That's God! And so Paul encourages those who claim to follow Jesus to imitate Christ by being *kenotic* in our relationships. He points to Jesus as the supreme example.

Typically, Philippians 2 is used to describe the Incarnation in this way:

- God was the almighty King of heaven who reigned as all-powerful Lord of the universe;

- God incarnate (God the Son, Jesus) temporarily become a humble, meek and even weak servant during his earthly sojourn, even to the point of death; but now,

- Christ has ascended to his sovereign throne at the Father's right hand, where he has resumed universal dominion and control forever and ever.

The passage *almost* relays that narrative. Many think it does, because the *kenosis* is framed in Jesus descent to earth and ascent back into heaven. But I believe we must push *kenosis* even further.

What if? What if Jesus' humility, meekness and servant heart were never a *departure* from God's glory and power, but actually *define* it and *demonstrate* it? Take your time—read that sentence again. What if *kenosis*—self-emptying power, self-giving love and radical servant-hood—expresses the very nature of God! What if God does rule and reign, *not* through imperial power but through *kenotic love!* What if the first beatitude—"Blessed are the poor (void, empty) in spirit; theirs is the kingdom of heaven" (Matt. 5:3)—is a vision of the glory of God lived through Christ! Why? Wherever God, wherever Christ, wherever *we* risk emptying ourselves of self-will and self-rule to make space for the other, that is where the supernatural kingdom-love of God rules and reigns. Thus, *kenosis*, which is to say *love* (!), is the heart of who God is. Not lording over, but always coming under; not triumphing through conquest, but through the Cross. God's being and God's power *are* his *kenotic* love.

So when I say *kenosis*, I am talking about love. Cruciform love, as revealed through Christ's Passion, is none other than authentic, willing consent to 'otherness.' Love is, by nature, willing and consensual, self-giving and self-sacrificial. The Apostle John clarifies this in his first epistle. John says "God *is* love" (1 John 4:8). Then he says, "This is how we know what love is: Jesus Christ *laid down his life* for us. And we ought to *lay down our lives* for our brothers and sisters" (1 John 3:16). This is John's version of *kenosis,* though he prefers the term 'laying down' (ἔθηκεν; *ethēken*).

So while God in his fullness is far beyond our comprehension, who God is can be known through the revelation of the Cross, by which we mean cruciform love, by 'laying down his life.' Love is not merely one of God's attributes. Love is who God is in his very nature. God *is* Love in a way that exceeds character qualities. God *is* living love. Let's gather these thoughts:

- God is Love.
- We know who God is and what love is as we behold the Cross of Christ.
- The God who is living love defines that love as *cruciform,* which means he is continually giving himself, emptying himself and laying down his life for us.
- Jesus came to show us who God is and what God's glory is. He reveals and even (re)defines God. The Trinity revealed in Jesus is *cruciform.*

If Christ's *kenosis* reveals self-emptying, self-sacrifice and servanthood as who God really is, we'd better have a closer look. We're peering into a very deep well! As it turns out, *kenosis* emerges from the unfathomable mysteries of the Godhead.

We see the *kenosis* unfold in Christ's Passion, and before that, enacted in the creation of all things. And even prior to creation and redemption, if *kenotic* love is actually *who God is,* we will find it in the very heart of the Father. How so? It's what theologians call the Father's 'eternal generation' of the Son, which means God the Son is *begotten* by the Father, but never created. There was never a time when God the Son did not exist, and yet he's a Son who has a Father! That Father has forever been pouring his life into the Son in self-giving—*kenotic*—love. The twentieth century Catholic theologian, Hans Urs Von Balthasar, acknowledges the wonder of this revelation, far beyond any human comprehension, yet revealed on the Cross. He writes,

'Trinitarian love'

If God is love in the very life of the Trinity, one way to see love function within the Trinity is:

God is Love =
Lover (Father),
Love (Holy Spirit),
and Beloved (Son).

> We shall never know how to express the abyss-like depths of the Father's self-giving, that Father who, in an eternal 'super-*Kenosis*,' makes himself 'destitute' of all that he is and can be so as to bring forth … the Son.
>
> God, then, has no need to 'change' when he makes a reality of the wonders of his charity, wonders which include the Incarnation and, more particularly, the Passion of Christ.[3]

Thus, the self-giving love seen in Christ's Passion becomes the clearest expression of the glory of God the Father (and Son and Holy Spirit). Of course, the glory of God is not only self-giving love but self-giving is intrinsic and even central to it. We won't let wrong triumphalist (see glossary) leanings rob us of the glory of God that is overwhelming in its manifestation of light and power and holiness that upholds the universe. But the *kenosis* is that the Word voluntarily and out of love forgoes this expression of glory for (and this is the mind-blowing part) an existence in which this glory is revealed to the world through and in his human frailty. So that's mind-bending, especially when we remember the kind of glory he came from and is rightfully his.[4]

Nevertheless, Christ's Passion is not only an *image* of the Trinity; it is the 'inner life of the Godhead.' As philosopher George Grant once wrote, "The Trinity is no analogy. It is simply the clearest word to express what is seen directly in the Passion of Christ."[5] To look at the Cross is to see God. Grant even claims that beholding the Cross is the *only* avenue by which we arrive at a true doctrine of **trinitarian love.** *

Behold the Lion – I saw a Lamb

We'll want more evidence for this proposal, but this is a good start. Most Christians will accept a lamb-like picture of God, but many also rush to balance it out with the more triumphant, ferocious lion portrait they see in Revelation. As if Christ consists of one part mercy (the Gospels) and one part mayhem (Revelation). We'd better take a look at that mysterious book in the back of our Bibles and discover its surprising decryption key.

I often hear the adage, "Jesus came the first time as a lamb, but next time he's coming as a lion." I cringe at the glee in the tone. It's like the old 1970's bumper sticker that said, "Jesus is coming back, and he is pissed off!" Do the 'prophets' of the Second Coming realize what they are saying? They seem to mean that Jesus came as

---

'Anthropomorphism'

is a description of something not human (like a tree) or more than human (God) using personal human characteristics.

Bible authors speak of God's 'anger' to describe experiences of the consequences of sin. But with God, reactive emotions, such as 'anger,' are anthropomorphic, to be read figuratively, not literally.

Anthropomorphisms read literally reduce God into a human projection—an idol—whereas Christ truly unveiled God.

---

a suffering servant the first time, but next time, he will appear as the victorious king. Okay, sure, "He will come again in glory to judge the living and the dead," we read in the Nicene Creed. "Riding the clouds, he'll be seen by every eye, those who mocked and killed him will see him, People from all nations and all times will tear their clothes in lament. Oh, Yes." (Rev. 1:7 MSG).

Again, how many times have we heard it preached: "Last time he came in love (for me), next time he comes in wrath (for my enemies). Last time he came to save the lost; next time to punish the wicked."

Why? Because love wins ... but not really, not completely? Having given love its best shot, Christ must return with plan-B: fierce, blood-drenched and merciless. No more 'mister nice guy'!

I've heard the returning Christ depicted as *Braveheart's* William Wallace—face smudged blue with war paint, muscles rippling, claymore flashing, on a righteous rampage. Perhaps you have never heard Christ's glorious victory reduced to a blood-soaked military campaign, in which Jesus personally kills millions of people, his white robes soaked in their blood—literally. I have. Many of them (transcripts available on request)!

"Enough!" he seems to roar across the world in rebellion. The Warrior pours out violence and calamitous destruction. Rivers of blood flow to the horses' bridles as the vengeful Rider wields his cruel swift sword. What I'm hearing is, "God once tried being the cross-bearing servant, but praise the Lord, next time around he will be the sword-bearing, flesh-tearing warrior." Sing it with me:

> Mine eyes have seen the glory of the coming of the Lord;
> He is trampling out the vintage
> where the grapes of wrath are stored;
> He hath loosed the fateful lightning of His terrible swift sword: His truth is marching on.[6]

Hallelujah! Booyah!

I beg your pardon? Let's pause for a double-take.

Christ's work on the Cross and his power in the Resurrection were insufficient? Now he's reverting to actual wrath and violence on the majority of the human race?

Orthodox theologian Father Alexandre Turnicev, recoils at the crassness of taking such end times visions literally:

> This archaic conception perverts the evangelical texts in a literal, coarse and materialistic way, without penetrating the spiritual meaning of the mysterious images and symbols. This conception has increasingly been exposed as an intolerable violation of Christian conscience, thought and faith. *We cannot allow that the sacrifice of Golgotha has proved powerless to redeem the world and conquer hell.* Otherwise we should say: *creation is a failure, and Redemption is also a failure.* It is high time for all Christians to testify in common and ... revolt in horror before these materialistic, **anthropomorphic*** representations of hell and the final judgment, ...

It is high time to end all of these monstrosities from past ages, often blasphemous, doctrinal or not, which make our loving God what He is not: a 'foreign' God, who is merely an "allegory of earthly kings and nothing else."[7]

Hallelujah! And if I may, *Booyah!*

Not that this is a modern objection. Take John Cassian, one of the pre-eminent church fathers (c. 360-435), who said,

And so as without horrible profanity these things cannot be understood literally of Him who is declared by the authority of Holy Scripture to be invisible, ineffable, incomprehensible, inestimable, simple, and uncompounded, so neither can the passion of anger and wrath be attributed to that unchangeable nature without fearful blasphemy.[8]

But where did we get this lion-lamb dichotomy? It comes from Revelation 5. And what does the text actually say? John sees a heavenly scroll representing world history. No one can open it, so he begins to weep. An elder in heaven interrupts, "Stop weeping; *behold, the Lion* that is from the tribe of Judah, the Root of David, *has overcome* so as to open the book and its seven seals" (Rev. 5:5).

Pause. John is told of a Lion who can resolve history (an excellent definition of 'sovereignty'!). Why a lion? Because lions are kings; lions are powerful; lions are victorious. Yes. That describes Jesus. Furthermore, we read that this Lion 'has overcome.' Already. Done. Finished. *Fait accompli.*

How? When?

John turns and looks, and what does he see? Surprise! "A Lamb standing, as if slain" (Rev. 5:6). 'Standing' because he is alive—'as if slain' because he was crucified. Jesus is a Lion because he is the king who has *already* overcome; he is a Lamb because that victory came, not someday through violence and conquest, but already, through *kenosis*—through sacrificial love. And this Lion-Lamb is worthy to rule, why?

Those worshiping at God's throne tell us:

> Worthy are You to take the book and to break its seals; for You were slain, and purchased for God with Your blood men from every tribe and tongue and people and nation (Rev. 5:9 NASB).

Jesus' global, universal and eternal kingship was established at the Cross and confirmed by his resurrection. His dominion over every people group will not be won through a someday-sword, but has already purchased by his blood. His kingdom grows now—a patiently expanding regime of love, forgiveness and reconciliation.

So the image of the Lamb becomes the key to interpreting Revelation.[9] By way of confirmation, let's briefly note Revelation 12. It's a notoriously difficult chapter to interpret, but this idea of overcoming by the blood of the Lamb—the crucifixion—could not be more plain.

> [10] Then I heard a loud voice in heaven say:
> "*Now* have come the salvation and the power
> and the kingdom of our God,
> and the authority of his Messiah.
> For the accuser of our brothers and sisters,
> who accuses them before our God day and night,
> has been hurled down.
> [11] They triumphed over him by the blood of the Lamb
> and by the word of their testimony;
> they did not love their lives so much
> as to shrink from death."
> (Rev. 12:10-11)

When has the kingdom of God and authority of his Messiah arrived? When was Satan hurled down? When did the martyrs triumph? The voice in heaven says, "Now." And when is this 'now'? We discover the 'now' by asking the 'how?' *How* did the martyr-saints overcome the evil one? Their victory is already effective now, because it was forever rooted in the blood of the Lamb, which is to say, at the Cross. And, as we'll see, Jesus says so himself in the Gospel of John.

The Cross: Christ's glorious throne

> Forgiveness shows God's will most fully done.
> There on the Cross the myth of hell is cleft,
> And the black garden blazes with the sun.
> Hold close the crown of thorns, the scourge, the rod,
> *For in His sweat, full front, the face of God.*[10]
> (George P. Grant, "Good Friday")

John 12 recounts the triumphal entry of Zion's king, astride a humble donkey, not cantering on a proud warhorse. The crowds, waving palm branches, begin chanting for their king: "Hosanna! Blessed is he who comes in the name of the Lord! Blessed is the king of Israel!" (John 12:13). The crowd is quoting Psalm 118, a messianic prophecy concerning the triumphal entry. When we read this sentence, we're to recall the whole context (the italics are mine for emphasis):

> [15] Shouts of joy and victory
>   resound in the tents of the righteous:
> "The LORD'S RIGHT HAND HAS DONE MIGHTY THINGS!
> [16] The LORD'S RIGHT HAND IS LIFTED HIGH;
>   the LORD'S RIGHT HAND HAS DONE MIGHTY THINGS!"
> [19] Open for me the gates of the righteous;
>   I will enter and give thanks to the LORD.
> [20] This is the gate of the LORD
>   through which the righteous may enter.

²¹ I will give you thanks, for you answered me;
 you have become my salvation.
²² The stone the builders rejected
 has become the cornerstone;
²³ the LORD HAS DONE THIS,
 and it is marvelous in our eyes.
²⁴ The LORD HAS DONE IT THIS VERY DAY;
 let us rejoice today and be glad.
²⁵ LORD, SAVE US!
 LORD, GRANT US SUCCESS!
²⁶ Blessed is he who comes in the name of the LORD.
 From the house of the LORD WE BLESS YOU.
²⁷ The LORD IS GOD,
 and he has made his light shine on us.
 With boughs in hand, join in the festal procession
 up to the horns of the altar.
²⁸ You are my God, and I will praise you;
 you are my God, and I will exalt you.
 (Ps. 118:15-16, 19-28)

This passage is about the royal procession of 'the right hand of God' (a title for Messiah) as he enters the city gates and proceeds to the temple, where we expect him to be enthroned as Israel's king. But alas! The builders of the temple—the religious establishment (of course)—reject him! Yet God takes the stone they have rejected and makes him the Chief Cornerstone, appointed and crowned by heavenly mandate to be King and Savior. Thus, his violent rejection by the religious elite becomes the path of ascent into his place and his role as 'the right hand of God.'

In this picture, riding on a donkey denotes humility, but John also notes the backstory to this image. In retrospect, the apostles will remember the verse: "Do not be afraid, Daughter Zion; see, your king is coming, seated on a donkey's colt" (John 12:13, citing

Zech. 9:9). Again, there's a context. What we read in Zechariah is no Rose Parade! This is about Messiah coming in glory and power to crush the enemy and liberate his nation.

> 8 But I will encamp at my temple
>   to guard it against marauding forces.
> Never again will an oppressor overrun my people,
>   for now I am keeping watch.
> 9 Rejoice greatly, Daughter Zion!
>   Shout, Daughter Jerusalem!
>   See, your king comes to you,
>   righteous and victorious,
>   lowly and riding on a donkey,
>   on a colt, the foal of a donkey.
> 10 I will take away the chariots from Ephraim
>   and the warhorses from Jerusalem,
>   and the battle bow will be broken.
>   He will proclaim peace to the nations.
>   His rule will extend from sea to sea
>   and from the River to the ends of the earth.
> 11 As for you,
>   because of the blood of my covenant with you,
>   I will free your prisoners from the waterless pit.
> 12 Return to your fortress, you prisoners of hope;
>   even now I announce that I will restore
>   twice as much to you.
> 13 I will bend Judah as I bend my bow
>   and fill it with Ephraim.
>   I will rouse your sons, Zion,
>   against your sons, Greece,
>   and make you like a warrior's sword.
> 14 Then the Lord will appear over them;
>   his arrow will flash like lightning.

The Sovereign Lord will sound the trumpet;
he will march in the storms of the south,
¹⁵ and the Lord Almighty will shield them.
They will destroy
and overcome with slingstones.
They will drink and roar as with wine;
they will be full like a bowl
used for sprinkling the corners of the altar.
¹⁶ The Lord their God will save his people on that day
as a shepherd saves his flock.
(Zech. 9:8-16)

The context is obviously Messianic. The prophet looks ahead to a mighty liberation. He uses the imagery of sword, bow and shield—of destruction and victory. The result will be freedom and peace, because every enemy will be vanquished. If we take these images literally, as the crowds heralding Jesus probably did, it is actually a profoundly accurate prophecy ... of Constantine, that Christian emperor who so impacted the direction of Christendom! Zechariah foresees world peace and religious freedom. But how? Through religion-blessed, God-on-our side conquest via militaristic violence.

So the fact that, in this text, the King comes "lowly, riding on a donkey" sticks out like a sore thumb. Maybe Zechariah originally thought Messiah would slip into the city in disguise, sneak into the temple, and begin the coup that would lead to ultimate victory. If so, the crowds of Palm Sunday sure blew Jesus' cover! The whole city was talking about it. The Pharisees were in a panic: "Look how the whole world has gone after him!" (John 16:19).

Yes, Pharisees, you've got it. Not just Jerusalem or Israel—the whole world! So much for stealing in under cover!

But Zechariah's donkey verse is fulfilled not only in Jesus' choice of transportation. The humility and lowliness of Christ are

'Literalism'

insists on reading and interpreting the whole Bible literally, as the only way to acknowledge its truth.

No one actually does this—but some claim to do so faithfully.

The reality is that Scripture uses many non-literal genres, including metaphor, hyperbole, poetry, parable, apocalyptic and more.

The authors require us to interpret such styles symbolically in order to discern their intended meaning.

who he is. It's not merely his mode of travel; it's Jesus' method and means of salvation, ultimately as a slain lamb, the humiliation of a Roman crucifixion.

As in Psalm 118, we see our hero pass through the gates of the city and set up camp in the Temple, just as Jesus did. But if we don't allow *literalism** to corner us, we'll see that even in Zechariah, Messiah's mission is far greater, far more ambitious than beating a few armies to save a small nation and become the local regent.

His plans are for an all-encompassing peace, one that extends to all peoples and nations, where the boundaries of his reign extend from sea to sea, to the ends of the earth. He intends to make all people his people. He means to save the whole world from every oppressor and free every prisoner from 'the waterless pit'—that is, death itself! And he tells us how: the blood of his covenant.

What the prophet may not have known: that the Lamb slain and the blood shed is that of the Messiah himself. The Cross itself would be his ultimate victory.

Jesus saw it and, eventually, so does John. It makes sense to the apostles, but only after the fact. They begin to understand

Jesus' words in light of his 'victorious death.' They finally see that his glorification and crucifixion, his victory and his death, his *cruciform* power, are one and the same.

Immediately after the triumphal entry account, John records these pivotal words of Christ:

> [23] Jesus replied, "The hour has come for the Son of Man to be glorified. [24] Very truly I tell you, unless a kernel of wheat falls to the ground and dies, it remains only a single seed. But if it dies, it produces many seeds. [25] Anyone who loves their life will lose it, while anyone who hates their life in this world will keep it for eternal life. [26] Whoever serves me must follow me; and where I am, my servant also will be. My Father will honor the one who serves me.
>
> [27] "Now my soul is troubled, and what shall I say? 'Father, save me from *this hour*'? No, it was for this very reason I came to *this hour*.
>
> [28] Father, *glorify* your name!"
>
> Then a voice came from heaven, "I have *glorified* it, and will *glorify* it again."[29] The crowd that was there and heard it said it had thundered; others said an angel had spoken to him.
>
> [30] Jesus said, "This voice was for your benefit, not mine. [31] Now is the time for *judgment on this world; now the prince of this world will be driven out.* [32] *And I, when I am lifted up from the earth, will draw all people to myself.*" [33] *He said this to show the kind of death he was going to die.*
> (John 12:23-33)

Likewise, in Jesus' high priestly prayer of John 17, we read:

> [1] After Jesus said this, he looked toward heaven and prayed: "Father, the *hour* has come. *Glorify* your Son, that your Son may *glorify* you. [2] For you granted him *authority*

over all people that he might give eternal life to all those you have given him. ³ Now this is eternal life: that they know you, the only true God, and Jesus Christ, whom you have sent. ⁴ I have *brought you glory on earth* by finishing the work you gave me to do. ⁵ And now, Father, *glorify me* in your presence with the *glory* I had with you *before the world began*. (John 17:1-5)

Jesus' focus here is on the 'hour,' a major theme in John that focuses on the events leading to and including his crucifixion. Having been outed by the triumphal entry, and escalating the drama in the Temple, there is no turning back. His hour has come. But see how Jesus understands it? The hour of his death also marks the hour of his glorification. Should the Father save him from this hour? No! It's why he came. And now that the hour has come, the Father and Son will be mutually glorified.

Unlike the synoptic Gospels and Pauline epistles, which usually associate glory with the resurrection, in John's Gospel, the 'hour' of Christ's execution *is* the hour of his exaltation. Jesus is the serpent 'exalted / lifted up' on the wooden stick (John 3:14). When he is 'exalted / lifted up' from the earth, he will draw all people(s) to himself (John 12:32). Thus, the language of glory and the exaltation / lifting-up of Christ are synonymous in John. For John, the Cross is the diadem of God's unprecedented self-revelation.

But there's more. John actually treats the crucifixion as:

1. The judgment of the world.

When? Now. This hour. On the Cross. In judging Christ, the religious and political powers of the world system stand judged. In fact, even as Pilate interrogates Jesus, we read, "Therefore when Pilate heard these words, he brought Jesus out, and sat down on the judgment seat at a place called The Pavement, but in Hebrew, *Gabbatha*." (John 19:13). Who sat in the 'judgment seat?'[11] In English—and in many paintings—it looks like Pilate is seated there.

But in Greek, John intentionally makes it ambiguous—it could also be Jesus sitting in Pilate's seat as the governor runs in and out, between Jesus and the crowd (like a servant) seven times! John writes this way purposely, habitually and ironically to ask the reader, "Who is really on trial here? And who is the true Judge?" Jesus has told us: the world stands judged. And in fact, the Cross becomes the *judgment seat* upon which Christ sits, indicting and condemning the *system* of the world, even while forgiving and saving the *people* of the world.

2. The judgment of the Satan.

When? Now. This hour. On the Cross. Remember reading in Revelation 12 that the "accuser of the brethren has been hurled down"? How? By the blood of the Lamb. And here it is again: "the prince of this world [the devil] is *driven out*" (John 12:31). Paul agrees. Whether we see his 'rulers and authorities' as religious, political or demonic, the apostle assures us that on the Cross, "When He had *disarmed* the rulers and authorities, He made a public display of them, having *triumphed* over them through Him" (Col. 2:15).

The 'lifting up' that draws all people. Again, John uses a double entendre. 'Lifted up' is the language of exaltation, of enthronement, of glorification. But John sees Jesus' hidden meaning and points it out. He's referring to the way he'll die—he'll be 'lifted up' onto the Cross. It will be his throne. He is declared King by Pilate himself. "Behold, your king," he says, presenting Jesus in royal robes with a crown of thorns (John 18:14), and again on the plaque announcing, "Jesus the Nazarene, King of the Jews" (John 18:19) in Hebrew, Latin and Greek (that is, *all people* in that world).

3. Authority over all people.

Through the victory of the Cross, Jesus receives kingdom authority over all people and can grant eternal life to all those the Father has given him (that is, given authority over).

The fact is, in John, Jesus virtually treats the Cross as the Final

Judgment! The world is judged, Satan is defeated and Jesus is glorified. He is given all authority and reigns in a kingdom that advances in the same way it came: through the *kenotic* power of love.

How do we know what God is like? By recalling that God is 100% Christlike and by remembering how Christ humbly laid down his life. That is, the crucified and glorified Christ—the apex of God's *kenotic* power and '*cruciform*' love—is our clearest image of God's very nature from beginning to end! The Cross is the all-encompassing revelation of the Christlike God.

In the next chapter, we will see that the crucified Christ shows us how God created the world and how he reigns in it—a theology of the Cross as consent and participation.

Pausing to think

- How does Christ's *kenosis* reveal God's nature as self-emptying, self-sacrificing and self-giving?

- How is God (Father, Son and Spirit) *cruciform*? How is God's cruciformity true prior to the Incarnation?

- Why would John associate the Cross with Christ's glorification rather than the resurrection or ascension?

- How does the Cross symbolize Christ's enthronement as King? What images and details does John use in his Passion narratives to highlight this theme?

- If Jesus, rather than Constantine, shows us the true nature of God's heavenly government, how have we erred in imagining God as almighty Emperor?

- How does the Lamb-like reign of God look in the world today?

Pausing to pray

God-in-Christ, victorious Lion, merciful Lamb, I'm grateful that you overcame, but not a global bloodbath or through merciless force, but through self-giving love.

Victory through a loving Lamb, impaled on a crosspiece? A King crowned with thorns, pinned to a death-machine? Totally powerless, and yet a force more powerful! It's true. You've won by winning my heart! Lord, let it be!

The Cross as Divine Consent 7

Readers may not be aware that 'forced marriages' (not just 'arranged') are still very common in our world—and not only in foreign cultures in far away lands. Versions of forced marriage have been imported to North America. In my province (British Columbia), couples marrying outside their religion or race have been murdered for eloping with their true loves. I've also seen reports of reprisals against freethinking brides in the form of face-mutilating acid attacks. Meanwhile, the phenomenon of child-brides continues to be a broadly accepted practice overseas. I recently saw a wedding photo of an older man sitting with his bewildered eleven-year-old bride. Repugnant! Forced marriage is so offensive to my Western mind that I bristle to think of it.

It causes me to wonder about the image of God as a Bridegroom. Does he compel and coerce relationship with us, or does he patiently invite and romance? Easy answer: God has given us free will and we can freely accept or reject his proposal. He doesn't force anyone to enter the eternal marriage covenant with him. But what if you decline? Not that God will *make* you say "I do." But if you don't, what about the ultimatum?

Doesn't the Bible itself threaten us with retributions far worse than acid in the face? "Please accept my proposal, my beloved … or I'll throw you in a lake of fire." Where's the freedom in that kind of ultimatum? Where's the *consent*? That's what we'll discuss in this chapter.

'Pleroma'

means *fullness,* as in, "In Christ lives all the fullness (*pleroma*) of God in a human body" (Col. 2:9 NLT).

Following authors such as P.T. Forsyth, I take the next step: *kenosis* IS the *pleroma* of God, which brings about the *fullness* of Christ's redemption in us, "that we may be filled to the measure of the fullness of God" (Eph. 3:19).

We have seen that God's self-revelation is perfected in the Passion of the Christ. Our God is Christlike and therefore his kingdom, power and glory are unveiled as *cruciform* (Cross-shaped) and *kenotic* (self-giving) love. We've worked these terms thoroughly enough now that I hope you understand them and are comfortable using them. The truth is that *cruciformity* and *kenosis* are not temporary conditions of God's history, restricted to a first century Jewish long-weekend or even to the whole of the Incarnation of Christ. They describe God's divine identity—not just what he is like, but who he is.

In the *kenosis* of Incarnation, God emerges from the unapproachable light (1 Tim. 6:16) and condescends to our form (Phil. 2:7), veiling himself in flesh precisely in order to *unveil* the glory of divine love, but in a way we could hear, see and touch (1 John 1:1). Even the secrecy of the Incarnation is not truly God in disguise; Christ reflects accurately God's genuine nearby-hiddenness within the fabric of creation. That is, God is Christlike in his secret presence within creation, including the obscure Preacher who emerged from Nazareth. *Kenosis* actually reflects God's triune, unchanging and eternal nature—who God was, and is and is to come—"now and ever and unto ages of ages" (in the words of the ancient doxologies). The Cross reveals God's person (who he is) but also his kingdom (how he reigns). Yes, the Cross is a strange way to reign! But that's exactly what we're to see: the kingdom reign of God is *cruciform* and *kenotic* from Alpha to Omega, from before creation to the restoration of all things in Christ—and at all points in between.

In the next few chapters, we will begin to explore the grand mystery of *how* a *kenotic, cruciform* and Christlike God can reign—can be present, active and 'sovereign'—in the world, when he is neither *coercive* nor *controlling*, but nevertheless infinitely *close* and *caring*. We'll notice together how such a God rules, saves and serves by grounding and filling all that is with the power of love—a divine love with a particular content defined as *consent* and *participation*.

Further, we'll see that we surrender to God's reign, cooperate with the Spirit's grace, and receive Christ's salvation in the same way: by *consent* and *participation*. The fullness (in Greek, the **pleroma***) of God's saving comes as God *participates* fully in the human condition—from birth to death—and *consents* to enduring temptations, trials and even the extreme humiliation of crucifixion. The fullness of our salvation comes as we *participate* in Christ's death and as we fully *consent*—cooperate and surrender—to his grace.

Speaking poetically, I will suggest that, incredibly, the timeline of the entire human saga—and in fact all of cosmic history—is spanned by Jesus' outstretched arms, nailed to that horizontal cross-piece! Imagine: the universe and all that is in it forever embraced within the distance between the spikes in each of Christ's wrists! Those arms stretch even wider than the epoch from Adam's fall to our redemption. They encompass the alpha and omega of God's eternal intentions.

The Cross as consent

The Cross is a picture of the Christlike God, a portrait of love, and a symbol of *consent*. Exactly what do I mean by 'consent'?

The Cross is the perfection of consent because Christ rules through love rather than coercion—through persuasion rather than force—through revelation rather than domination. Thus, God's consent is far greater than merely 'allowing,' as if he just sits back and watches the tragedies of life, uninvolved and passive. No! God's consent is a great 'in-between' initiative. He opens his arms wide in welcome. He acts decisively in love. God's own kiss. Specifically, the Cross-as-consent comes to symbolize the Father's love for the world and the Son's obedience to the Father. The Cross—the cruci-fied Christ—is our bridge, our mediator, our *consent-between*. Let's expand on these ideas for a moment.

1. Consent is the divine act of love between Father and Son. Some have said that as the Father kisses the Son, the Holy Spirit is the kiss. The Son shows his love for God the Father by continually consenting—obeying, surrendering, yielding—to his Father's will (and God's will *is* love!). Jesus only ever said what the Father told him to say; only did what he saw his Father doing.

> [19] "Very truly I tell you," said Jesus, "the Son can do nothing by himself; he can do only what he sees his Father doing, because whatever the Father does the Son also does. [20] For the Father loves the Son and shows him all he does" (John 5:19-20).

But the Father-Son consent is also mutual. Verses later, Jesus says, "Moreover, the Father judges no one, but has entrusted all judgment to the Son, that all may honor the Son just as they honor the Father, who sent him" (John 5:22).

This same kind of deference defines the Spirit. As Jesus said,

But when he, the Spirit of truth comes, he will guide you into all the truth. He will not speak on his own; he will speak only what he hears. (John 16:13).

Jesus embodied this Trinitarian consent in his life and ministry, not only obeying the Father explicitly, but also modeling obedience to the Father when the Father chose to speak to the Son through others! He was not ignorant of the Father's will but, rather, so attentive to the Father's voice that he could hear and obey it in the moment, even through indirect means.

Consider the wedding at Cana (John 2). The wine has run out and Mary taps Jesus for a solution. To that point, Jesus had been obediently waiting on his Father for the go-ahead to launch his ministry. So he says, "My hour has not yet come" (v. 4). Mary, Jesus' mother, apparently gets the nod from Jesus' Father. "Do whatever he tells you," she says to the servants. You know the rest: Jesus performs his first glory-revealing sign (v. 11), turning the water into wine. If Jesus' hour had not yet come, why did he do the miracle? Was he mistaken? Was he disobedient to the Father's timing and will? Not at all. As always, he was obeying his Father, but this time, his Father's will is revealed to him by hearing the Father's voice in the moment as his mother signals his time has come.

Similarly, when the Syrophoenician woman (Mark 7; Matt. 15) appeals to Jesus for the deliverance of her demonized daughter, Jesus resists, citing the mission his Father had given him: "I was sent only to the lost sheep of Israel" (Matt. 15:24). Is he lying? No. He is serving entirely under the direction of his Father. But when she cleverly insists, he is amazed at her faith and is moved to respond by healing the daughter in that moment. Again, is he disobeying? Bending the rules? No, he has the humility to perceive this God-given faith as a sign from the Father—the mission is shifting now. And in Mark's version, Jesus journeys to Decapolis, an apparently Gentile region.

But most of all, we see Christ's ultimate consent to his Father's will when he agrees (through tears of anguish) to drink the cup of suffering and death—the cup of God's co-suffering love for the world. Gethsemane becomes the ultimate expression of Son to Father consent. He prays, "My Father, if it is possible, may this cup be taken from me. Yet not as I will, but as you will" (Matt. 26:39). Moreover, we see the divine self-giving will of the Word (God the Son) and the human life-giving willingness of Jesus (the Son of man) revealed as one and the same. That is, in perfect surrender, Jesus' "Not my will, but yours" comes out as a single-minded willingness to give his life in love for the sake of the world.

2. Consent is also the divine act of mediation between God and the world. The Father kisses the world, and the Son is his kiss. The Father gives over—consents and relinquishes—his only begotten and dearly beloved Son into a hostile world and into the hands of hateful men. This profound act of surrender on the Father's part would seem insanely un-Godlike if we didn't know the rest of the story. Indeed, that wicked men could take the life of Yahweh's Messiah is so offensive to most Muslims that they cannot accept it. It just can't be. They believe that Jesus is indeed God's Messiah, that he is alive now and will return in glory to conquer the anti-Christ and reign in the world (it's true!). But would the Father be so meek as to give consent to an actual, ignoble death of his anointed King? Most Muslims are unable to go there.

On the other hand, John reminds us that Jesus' consent is active and at his own initiative:

> [17] The reason my Father loves me is that I lay down my life—only to take it up again. [18] No one takes it from me, but I lay it down of my own accord. I have authority to lay it down and authority to take it up again" (John 10:17-18).

The authority to lay down his life, as opposed to having it taken, can prove to be a valuable point of contact in inter-faith dialogue with our Muslim friends, who abhor the idea that God's Messiah could simply be killed by wicked men.

It also leads us beyond the Father's consent. The Son—the Mediator or Middleman between the Father and world—shows the Father's love for the world by his own life-giving love, even consenting to our hateful rebellion and murderous rejection in the crucifixion. In fact, in the Gospel of John and the Book of Acts, the authors frame the story so that the Father foresees and the Son orchestrates the events in which our own ugly schemes are co-opted by God's willing consent for our salvation! In retrospect, we come to see Christ's consent framed as giving up his life in an extraordinarily Trinitarian move of God. His surrender to the Father's will in Gethsemane opens up the way of everlasting love and radical forgiveness, turning our heinous crime into the means of our redemption.

3. Consent is our response to the Cross of Christ and the grace of God. As the Father kisses the world through the life and death of his Son, we receive his kiss by consent. The Son does not force himself into our lives or make us receive his love. But he does invite us to willingly respond to the offer of relationship with God. He initiates and we respond ... always by consent.

But remember, if consent comes with an ultimatum tied to a deadline—if lack of surrender is threatened with eternal conscious torment—then the offer is devoid of real love. We're left with no more than a pseudo-choice and not genuinely allowed to withhold consent.

Wayne Northey, a pioneer practitioner in restorative justice, described the dilemma for me this way (I'm paraphrasing):

Imagine there is a fabulously wealthy king who looks out the window of his castle one day and, in the distance, sees a beautiful Cinderella-type peasant living in the slums. His heart is ravished and he thinks, "This is the perfect bride for my son, the prince."

Unlike other kings—wicked worldly kings—he cannot just abduct her and make her a slave-concubine of his son. He must genuinely invite her to take the hand of his son voluntarily. So, along with his entourage and his son, they make their way out of the palace into the squalor beyond the moat, searching hut to hut and through the markets until they find her. The offer is made:

"Young lady," says the king, "this is my beloved son, the prince of this kingdom and heir to all that is mine. I humbly beseech you to come out of your life of poverty and oppression and to join my son in holy matrimony, enjoying all of the benefits that come with a princess' life." The offer seems to be too good to be true. All she needs to do is consent to the proposal.

But there's a hitch. The king continues, "There is a deadline. If you don't say yes by such-and-such a date, we will arrest you, put you in our dungeon, where torturers will fillet you alive for endless ages, supernaturally keeping you alive such that your torment is never-ending. Moreover, after the deadline, your decision is irrevocable. No repentance is possible. The dishonor of your rejection is too great to warrant any second chance. The consequences of refusal are without mercy and utterly irreversible."

As the king, the prince and their cohort leave, the prince turns and says, "Oh yes, please hurry. And always know that I will love you forever and for always … but only until the deadline."

Is this our gospel? If it were, would it truly be a gospel that preserves the love of God, the freewill of humanity and the mutual consent inherent in and necessary to God's invitation? I don't buy it any more. Without going into great detail here, might I suggest that because God, by nature, is the eternally consenting Bridegroom, there are two things he cannot and will not do:

- He will not ever *make you* marry his Son, because an irresistible grace would violate your consent. Your part will always and forever be by consent.

- His consent will *never end*, because a violent ultimatum would violate your consent. Divine love will
always and forever be by consent. Emphasis on *forever*. "His mercy endures *forever*" (Psalm 136). "I have
loved you with an *everlasting* love; I have drawn you
with *unfailing* kindness" (Jer. 31:3).

I don't believe the divine courtship involves wearing you down
with his love until you give up. It's simply that he'll always love
you, with a love that even outlasts and overcomes death (Song of
Solomon 8). The Bible at least hints (Rev. 21-22) that the prodigal
Father will wait for you, invite you and keep the doors open for you
until you're ready to come home. He'll wait for you forever.

Consent from the beginning

Consent then, like the Cross, encompasses love, surrender,
submission, invitation, hospitality and receptivity to love. Christ
consents—yields, submits—to the Father, to *kenosis,* to humility, to
servanthood and to death (Phil. 2). Beautifully, mercifully, powerfully—even ironically—through the Cross, Christ is exalted to the
highest place and makes all things new. Consent, then, is a synonym
for the Cross and for God's love. It is an *active* and *responsive* love
for God and for others that never degrades into mere passivity and
acquiescence.

Consent is therefore a major active ingredient in the Cross-love
of Christ. But remember, this vision of the Cross-as-consent is bigger than six hours one Friday. If it describes the Christlike God as
he always is and always reigns, then it structures the universe and
spans the breadth of history, from before the beginning until after
the end. How so?

Fair warning: I believe what I'm about to say about *consent*
is true—necessarily true—but only in combination with the
participation piece that follows. Without the critical element of

God's presence and participation, the following point does not stand alone as true. God's consent on its own can feel like God's absence, as abandonment and forsakenness, as distance and silence—all of which are real human experiences that need to be validated (e.g., Ps. 6; 13; 22). This experience of absence and isolation—of being forgotten or even cursed by God—lies at the heart of the so-called 'problem of evil.' The many (usually failed) rational attempts to reconcile how a good God can allow the horrific suffering we see in our world are called *'theodicies.'** The Book of Job is a very early attempt at a thoughtful theodicy. We'll give that topic a whole chapter, but for now I will say that only a *cruciform* theodicy can avoid calling evil good or condemning the victims of natural tragedies or human evils.

Natural law and human freedom are *not* the only players, *not* the final word, *not* our ultimate reality. We can't and won't stop there. There is a third pervasive and active presence at work: grace. God's *presence-as-grace* is real and essential to a Christlike vision of the world. With that stipulation, we proceed. How does God's *kenotic* reign look across the ages?

'Theodicies'

are rational attempts to reconcile the problem of why suffering or evil pervades our world.

If God is all-good and all-powerful, where does evil come from and why does God allow it?

One theory, first conceived by Kabbalism (the mystical wing of Judaism), is that in the very foundations of creation, God 'withdraws' or even 'dies.' Not literally, of course. The idea is that God dies to being all there is and controlling all that is. Simone Weil proposed a Christian version of this theory. Namely, in the beginning, out of his fullness, the Creator emptied himself—*kenosis!*—to make space for creation so that we could authentically live and move and have being. Poetically speaking, he is "the Lamb who slain from the foundation of the world" (Rev. 13:8).

Another caveat: 'foundation' implies more than 'the beginning,' when the world was founded. God's being (his willing love) is the foundation on which his creation continually rests. He's not just *a being* like all other beings who starts the creation clock. He is *being itself*, on and in whose self-giving love we utterly depend for our very being. Without the living, loving God as our foundation, we don't exist—nothing exists.

And yet, even as God is the foundation before and beneath our every moment and every breath,

> ## 'Secondary causes'
>
> God *consents* to the free (and often catastrophic) play of secondary causes. That is, he allows *natural law* and *human freedom* to act.
>
> God is ultimately responsible for all that is—for natural law and for human freedom—but we say he doesn't *directly* cause or control humans actions or natural events.

we behold that God as none other than a slain Lamb! The One on whom we utterly depend for existence runs the universe by the hospitality of yielding (and by participation).

God is ultimately the source and cause of all that is. Good. Sometimes we refer to God as the *primary* or *first* cause. And as first cause, God is Good and all he does is goodness. But there are also **secondary causes.*** Secondary causes include *natural law* and *human freedom.*[1] We refer to them as secondary causes because while God caused them, they also cause things that God does not directly cause. That is, God *consents* to the free (and often catastrophic) play of these secondary causes—he allows *natural law* and *human freedom* to do their thing. God is ultimately responsible for all that is—for natural law and for human freedom—but we would say he doesn't *directly* cause or control humans or nature in whatever they do. I'll be more specific.

Natural law refers, obviously, to the laws of nature. On the one hand, these laws perfectly *consent* to the Creator who established them. Gravity, for example, is good and does exactly what it is supposed to do. It always obeys its own God-given rules. Rigidly. Unbendingly. Gravity is necessary for our survival, but is also able to crush and destroy anything in its path, without malice or mercy. Gravity perfectly consents to God's law, and gravity can kill, but when it does, we don't say God did it. And yet God consents to gravity's work, even at its cruelest.

In making space for secondary causes, God doesn't directly interfere with every natural disaster. Tectonic plates shift, weather patterns come and go, all consenting to the design God gave them. But when the plates rub and cause an earthquake or when winds blow and cause a hurricane, God consents, even when it wipes a city off the map! But unlike our ancestors, we mustn't assume the carnage ensued by a direct 'act of God,' nor cast blame on those we think God must be punishing.

So too with the human freedom. God risked giving us the capacity to freely consent to his will or to willfully reject it. This freedom is another major secondary cause. Ironically, in using our freedom to reject God, we actually become enslaved in a thousand different ways. Autonomy ('freedom' from God), the disaster of Eden, is really a delusion that chains us. We become slaves to impulses and compulsions and temptations and addictions, to fears and rages and so on. And in our slavery to willfulness and selfishness, we do wicked things and cause much pain. God's good gift has become, through our defiance, a death-dealing or life-harming secondary cause. And God consents. He does not prevent or inter-rupt every wicked human act.

Jesus explains this principle clearly in Luke's Gospel.

> [1] Now there were some present at that time who told Jesus about the Galileans whose blood Pilate had mixed with their sacrifices. [2] Jesus answered, "Do you think that these Galileans were worse sinners than all the other Galileans because they suffered this way? [3] I tell you, no! But unless you repent, you too will all perish. [4] Or those eigh-teen who died when the tower in Siloam fell on them—do you think they were more guilty than all the others living in Jerusalem? [5] I tell you, no! But unless you repent, you too will all perish." (Luke 13:1-5)

Do you see how Jesus addresses both secondary causes: the *natural law* of the falling tower and the *human freedom* of Pilate's massacre? He's critiquing their assumption that you can tell who is righteous or wicked by the circumstances that happen to them. The Jews of Jesus' day believed God actively strikes down bad people and blesses the good people by manipulating secondary forces, from bolts of lightning to imperial armies. But, according to Jesus, it doesn't work that way. God isn't like that. He doesn't micro-manage judgments. When Jesus says, "He *causes* his sun to rise on the evil and the good, and *sends* rain on the righteous and the unrighteous" (Matt. 5:45), he is talking about the *indiscriminate grace* of God as the first cause of all that's good.

On the flipside, God allows (but does not directly cause) the devastations of his created order. Charles Darwin saw this: "God may design the laws of nature, but when lightning strikes, we cannot believe that God designedly kills the person who was struck."[2] A combination of human freedom (a driver's poor choices) and the laws of nature (the physics of an ice on asphalt) can lead to a fatal car accident. Did God cause it? No, God does not *directly* cause car accidents, but he did create the universal conditions that lead to them. So we say, in God's good order, human agency and natural law (the secondary causes) are *necessary* conditions. *Necessity*[3] is established by a good God for our good—thank God we are free to fall in love and able to stand upright on the ground—but necessity can also cause human affliction, from broken hearts to broken bones, from horrific to mundane. In short, God creates and then consents to necessity, for better or for worse, even while we invoke "deliverance from all danger and necessity" (an ancient Christian litany).

Not merely a spectator: God's participation

Thus, God's *consent* is one reality, but another is that he does not and has not stood by as a passive spectator. He consented to *participate* in the human condition. Fully. In love, he saw our predicament and, through the Incarnation, entered into our affliction. He underwent the brunt of these forces with us, in the flesh. Said another way, God-in-Christ *participated fully* in our trauma and calamity as the Lamb slain. He gathered up and suffered every human disaster across time in his Passion; he *consented* to bear the 'gravity' of all sin—past and future—on the Cross.

So now, the Cross of Christ has become far more than the Good Friday crucifixion. The Cross includes and combines God's consent and participation in Christ's Passion to become 'Jacob's ladder,' connecting heaven and earth (Gen. 28:12; John 1:51), containing all of creation and all of history. Fr. John Behr expresses this truth in the loftiest of terms:

> When the apostle Paul speaks of its [the mystery of the Cross] "breadth and length and height and depth" (Eph. 3:18), St. Gregory sees him as inscribing the figure of the cross into the very structure of the universe, created by the God revealed through the cross. The transcendent power

of the eternal, timeless God, manifest in the Passion of Christ, is the same power that upholds all creation, so that the cross is indeed the *axis mundi*, the still, eternal or timeless axis around which the world rotates.[4]

What does the power of the Cross mean for us? Or for those who suffer? It means the same Christ crucified on Good Friday now fills the universe with his cruciform love. He does *not* passively and powerlessly witness the abuse of children or the oppression of the poor and 'do nothing.' Rather, enters the suffering, experiences the anguish, lives the sorrow *for all, with all, for all the time.* The Christlike God drinks our cup of suffering. The Lamb slain bore it all, right down to the foundations of the cosmos. Secondary causes nailed him to the Tree of affliction. And what did Christ do? In love, he *consented* to co-suffer with us in solidarity.

In that sense, I say God is in charge, but he is *not* in control, because he doesn't *do* control. Sometimes I wish he did, but as I scan history and humanity, I don't see him controlling. Sometimes he *seems* and *feels* absent, distant and silent, weak or maybe even dead. Did God simply die and abandon us all to go to 'hell in a hand basket'?

No! Rather than *control* and *coerce*, God-in-Christ *cares* and *consents* to suffer with and for us. We don't concede to the false image of a 'lame duck' dad who sits by silently, watching his kids getting beaten by the bully. Instead, we look to the true image of the *cruciform*—Christ himself—the One who heard our groans and came down to suffer and die with us in order to overcome affliction, defeat death and raise us up to live and reign with him.

Christ's cruciform reign

I know: love can seem as weak as that baby in the manger, as powerless as that Jewish man on the Cross, or as meek as a preacher stoned to death in Jerusalem or in Somalia. We might well ask how the crucified God can be the sovereign King and Lord of Glory. What sort of sovereignty is this? What kind of king is this? Is the Cross how he reigns?

Yes! Christ does reign—he reigns in heaven and in the world, even over secondary causes. There is no question that he reigns; the question is, *how* does he reign? Christ does not reign by arbitrary force or coercion. His reign is not at all like our idea of control. Rather, Christ rules exclusively through the *cruciform* power of love—*not* like worldly powers that rule by force. God's rule is active in the world. But he only rules through the consent of his self-giving Son and through his Son's willing disciples. He makes them into "a kingdom and priests ... who shall reign on the earth" (Rev. 1:6). But their reign, like his, is exclusively through servant love ("by the blood of the Lamb and the word of our testimony" Rev. 12:11) for the restoration of all things in Christ.

The Cross reveals and defines God's kingdom reign—and God's very nature—as *kenotic love*. He rules and reigns through *our* consent, *our* yieldedness, *our* surrender—through our willingness to mediate his self-giving love into the world.

That's a different kind of kingdom! A strange kind of King!

In his book, *Parables of the Kingdom,* Robert Farrar Capon contrasts force as 'right-handed power' with the moral and spiritual power he calls 'left-handed power.' Jesus, he says, consistently eschews worldly force in favor of *kenotic* power. The ultimate example is Christ's willingness to endure the Cross rather than calling ten thousand angels!

One seminary class[5] I visited brainstormed words for these two ways of ruling—control versus consent, or God-like-Constantine versus God-like-Jesus. The results were:

> **Worldly power as force**: authority, recognition, strength, territory, brutality, control, weapons, fear, success,

influence, conquering, fame, bloodshed, wrath, violence, glory, domination, greatness, manipulation, bullying, aggression, striving, insecurity, hegemony.

Cruciform power as love: vulnerability, weakness, obedience, submission, outcast, cursed, ignored, betrayed, risk-taking, wounded, forgiveness, suffering, thirst, dishonor, shame, lonely, empty, bloody, promise, compassionate, dependence, hope, faith, sacrifice, liberation, empathy.

Thus, the slain lamb, like the baby in the manger, reconstitutes every worldly idea of king and kingdom, God and power. The Cross reveals the fullness of the nature of a Christlike God. So because of Jesus, we know:

- God does not 'do control,' so the kingdom of God is without coercion.

- God is not violent, so the kingdom of God has nothing to do with the violence-based power systems of the old age. The sword and the gun are not in its arsenal.

- God wins through love, so the kingdom of God persuades by witness, rhetoric, compassion, Spirit and, if need be, martyrdom, but never by force.

A fellow Canadian theologian, Aaron Riches, brought these themes to a crescendo for me in this beautiful paragraph:

Read Origen: *the Glory of the Lord is the Cross*. What could be more of a scandal? The transfiguration is something any old atheist could understand: "glory" is a body and face shining with supernatural light. This does not unsettle my pagan presuppositions of what "divinity" and the "supernatural" mean. What we need faith to see is this: that the dead Jesus, forgotten and abandoned, naked and hanging on the Cross, is truly the Love of God Incarnate.

In the wounding of his fragile being is the fullness of the divine glory. He is not ashamed to be our God.[6]

Divine Yielding

Kenotic power may seem feeble because it is patient and humble, but in the end, God-as-love—the truly Christlike God—is the overcoming force more powerful because he does what no tyrant can ever do: he wins hearts, restores lives and transforms societies.

The *kenotic* reign I'm referring to is illustrated powerfully (and missed easily) in the Genesis creation story. Rev. Ashley Collishaw showed me what follows and the credit for this insight belongs entirely to him.

To place creation into the hands of humanity at the genesis of the earth is an expression of a *kenotic* God, a yielding and incarnational God. It is a revelation of the *cruciform* God, willing to humbly consent and even bear complicity in the fall of humanity. After all, in that storyworld, God put Adam and Eve in the Garden. God planted the tree of the knowledge of good and evil in the Garden. God apparently created the wily serpent that lured them into sin. And oddly, God allowed the serpent to deceive the couple without interruption or intervention. God is strangely silent and absent at the crucial moment.

And why the tree? Was the tree a demonstration of God's power to reign, his will to establish and enforce his law, to demand obedience and punish disobedience with a curse? Was the tree set there as a trap waiting to be sprung on morally immature innocents? It doesn't seem fair.

But what if the tree had a different purpose? What if it provided a way to enable and maintain the human/divine relationship? What if it was a demonstration of God's divine yielding and a means by which we could legitimately become like God?

Genesis says humanity is created 'in God's image and likeness.'

What if the image we carry is that of *omnipotence laid down*? In other words the image of God within us is intrinsically powerful, but we don't actually become godlike until and unless, like God, we lay it down!

For God's real presence to interact with the world of human and non-human nature—not merely gifting us with being or existence, but actively participating in our world—God willed his image to be enacted (initialized) in and through willing human mediators. If the image of God is perfected in the laying down of inherent power, humanity only perpetuates God's presence in the world by *yielding our will*. To quote Collishaw,

> To enact the yielding image of God within itself humanity requires real power to lay down. The tree and the command not to touch it give humanity genuine choice and therefore genuine potential expression of control and power. By the action of 'choosing,' the reality of humanity's power is brought into being. However, choosing 'not' to eat becomes an act of obedience, which at the same moment lays down that power. The tree is God's simplest mechanism for giving mankind power and the simplest and easiest mechanism for man to lay down that power as a passive ongoing expression of the divine image within. When we do not 'grasp' the power within our reach we *image* God and release his presence.[7]

God could not have set the bar of obedient yielding much lower. We are not even called to do anything! We are simply asked to refrain from something while being filled with innumerable delights ("every other tree in the garden" Gen. 2:16). God's command was not about putting us in our place but, rather, lifting us to the image of the divine. He yields power to us by giving us the dignity of choice. Then by consenting to lay that power down, we become like him! His *kenotic* consent becomes the opportunity for our *kenotic* consent; his glory can become our glory.

Sadly, Adam and Eve blew it. We all have. We are continually being deceived by the enemy, who lies to us and says, "No! You don't become like God by yielding! You become like God by *taking* what is yours. By *grasping* for the power God is withholding. By asserting your freedom and exerting your will to take what is yours by rights."

And so Adam and Eve grasped, just as we do. In their freedom and power and willfulness, far from becoming like God, they (and we) come under the damnation of death and domination of the devil. Humanity became a race of slaves to fear, shame and blame.

Thanks be to God, there was another garden! And another Man—a second Adam—kneels in surrender in that garden and yields his will completely to God the Father. Oh yes, he too had been tempted. That same serpent had come around, attempting to lure Jesus with power, with kingdoms, and with dominion. He tempted Jesus to accomplish his mission, not by yielding but by grasping, just as Adam and Eve had. Satan offered a shortcut to power, bypassing *kenosis* and consent and a cross. But Christ saw through it, passed the test and truly fulfilled what humanity was destined for—the perfection of the divine image—by laying down power, yielding to the Father and mediating God's redeeming love to the whole world.

And now there is another tree. The Cross becomes the fullest expression of an ongoing and coherent pattern of the Christlike God's *kenotic*, incarnational and *cruciform* character. The tree of Christ's *kenotic* death, planted forever in our world, is a perpetual offer of eternal life whereby we too can fulfill human destiny through a response of consent. As in Eden, Christ lays down his power and invites us to lay down ours. By simply yielding as he did, we participate in his *kenotic* death so that we might also become partakers in the divine life. We've now begun the move from consent to participation.

Pausing to think

- Have you ever thought of love as consent before? If love is not consensual—given as a gift and received without coercion—is it really love? Can you think of examples of love-as-consent?

- If God is love and if love includes consent, how might this be manifest within the Trinitarian relationship of Father, Son and Spirit?

- How is God's love-as-consent manifest in creation (natural law)? How is it manifest in human freedom?

- How does God's love allow for sin? And how does it respond to it?

- How does God's love-as-consent play out in the parable of the prodigal son?

- How is God's consent a Cross that God himself had to bear, even prior to Calvary—in the context of God's experiences with his covenant people?

Pausing to pray

God, in your great love for us, you have given us the capacity to love you back ... or not! What a Cross you bear as Father when your children don't reciprocate! What heartbreak you must experience when your Bride is unfaithful! I'm sorry. I'm willing. Open my heart so I won't forget that consent to your love is the life I honestly want most. Lord, make it so!

The Cross as Divine Participation 8

*"For whatever reason, since humankind showed up
on the scene, God does nothing without a human partner."*
– Bishop Desmond Tutu –

If God's *consent* allows *necessity* (the secondary causes of natural law and human freedom) to work—to our joy and sorrow—God's *grace participates* (by the Holy Spirit) in the world wherever willing partners (first and most of all Jesus Christ) actively mediate his reign of love and care into the world.

The Incarnation is God's supreme act of grace—of participation, partnering, sharing—in the world afflicted by secondary causes. In his life and his death, Jesus bears the sins and sorrows, experiences our pain and suffering, endures the tragedies and crimes of the whole race, from Adam forward. On the Cross, Christ participates to the extreme depths of the human condition, even entering death and the grave. For years, I thought Jesus was 'stricken by God.' This very mistake was prophesied in Isaiah 53:4-5, when the prophet says,

> ⁴ Surely he took up our pain
>   and bore our suffering,
>   yet we considered him punished by God,
>   stricken by him, and afflicted.
> ⁵ But he was pierced for our transgressions,
>   he was crushed for our iniquities …

The punishment and affliction, the piercing and the crushing were not at the hands of the Father. *We did that*—people, zealous religious people. Moreover, Jesus was actually bearing (carrying and enduring) the weight of *our* sin, *our* affliction and *our* infirmities. Jesus became a willing victim-participant in the human condition precisely in order to heal humanity of that very condition: the curse of sin and death.

Listen to the theology of participation in the book of Hebrews:

> [14] Since the children have flesh and blood, he too *shared in their humanity* so that by his death he might break the power of him who holds the power of death—that is, the devil— [15] and free those who all their lives were held in slavery by their fear of death. ... [17] For this reason he had to be *made like them, fully human in every way,* in order that he might become a merciful and faithful high priest in service to God, and that he might make atonement for the sins of the people. [18] Because *he himself suffered* when he was tempted, he is able to help those who are being tempted. (Heb. 2:14-15; 17-18)

In other words, by grace God assumes, undergoes and overcomes necessity. He partners with us in and through Jesus, so that he can also save and heal us through Jesus. Christ takes all the afflictions of necessity on and up onto the Cross and, by grafting himself to us, exchanges our curse for his blessing, our death for his life. As he dies for us and we with him (no, we're not off the hook—or cross), the Isaiah 61 grace-exchange occurs in a definitive way. We've read these verses as Jesus' inaugural announcement from Luke 4, but let's read them again as finding their completion in the Cross:

> [1] The Spirit of the Sovereign LORD is on me,
>   because the LORD has anointed me
>   to proclaim good news to the poor.
> He has sent me to bind up the brokenhearted,
>   to proclaim freedom for the captives

and release from darkness for the prisoners,
^{2} to proclaim the year of the LORD's favor
and the day of vengeance of our God,
to comfort all who mourn,
^{3} and provide for those who grieve in Zion—
to bestow on them a crown of beauty instead of ashes,
the oil of joy instead of mourning,
and a garment of praise
instead of a spirit of despair.
They will be called oaks of righteousness,
a planting of the LORD
for the display of his splendor.
(Isa. 61:1-3)

Think in terms of Jesus binding himself to us, to humanity, to you. Becoming fully human, God the Son assumes "the likeness of sinful human flesh" (Rom. 8:3) and infuses it with his divine life. He trades us his riches for our poverty, his wholeness for our wounds, his freedom for our slavery, his light for our darkness, his joy for our grief, his beauty for our ashes, his joy for our mourning, his praise for our despair. Most of all, he takes our tree (the Cross as our curse) and gives us his tree (the Oak of Righteousness). In other words, by consenting to partner with us, Christ is able to take, absorb and overcome the tragedy of our fallenness and impart his glorious inheritance to us.

That message may sound familiar, but take note: he partners with us so we can partner with him. His consent to his Father and to the Cross calls us to consent to his love. He participates in our human nature so we can participate in his divine nature. And his divine nature is what? *Kenosis*! So on the one hand, he empties himself to fill us. But on the other hand, he fills us so we can empty ourselves! And we empty ourselves to be filled with him! Filled with his world-transforming, life-giving, supernatural love. Why? So we can perpetuate his ministry of reconciliation in this mess of a world wracked by the collateral damage of necessity. As Christ laid down his life for us, we too can lay down our lives for others (1 John 3:16).

Participation as God's grace initiative

This participation or partnership is therefore a two-way street. Christ didn't take up his Cross and die so I don't need to, any more than he obeyed his Father so I don't need to. Rather, by grace, Christ empowers us with love, bidding us to take up the Cross and follow him. So Paul can even say, "I have been crucified *with Christ* and I no longer live, but Christ lives in me. The life I now live in the body, I live by faith in the Son of God, who loved me and gave himself for me" (Gal. 2:20). Look closely at that verse: 'crucified' is equated with loving and self-giving. To be 'crucified with Christ' and 'to live by faith' is to have Christ live in us and through us. He loves and gives himself through us. Christ participates in the world and fulfills his mission through us, his partners, by love.

It's crucial (literally[1]) that we see the whole partnership as a grace initiative. God *always* initiates. God initiates by grace and we cooperate by consent. God initiates our redemption by grace, transforms us by grace, empowers us by grace and partners with us by grace to bring about God's purposes in the world. Even our capacity to consent and participate is a grace-gift in the first place.

Furthermore, theologian Lucy Peppiatt[2] reminds us that while the consent and participation are mutual, a fundamental *asymmetry* defines the relationship between God and us. By 'asymmetry,' she simply means that in terms of our salvation and our mission, our relationship is not an equal partnership. Partnering with God's grace is still achieved by Christ alone, by grace alone, but it's Christ's grace at work *in me*. That is, I must live and serve by faith—yet not I, but Christ who lives in me. A free faith response to grace is necessary, but it's a response inspired and capacitated by Christ-in-us.

This is how we participate authentically with grace alone. Our participation is by consent and in cooperation with what Christ has already done in us and what God is doing now to transform the world. There is a synergy at work, but it's a synergy of grace. Our meager but precious contribution (a child's bag lunch) is precisely what grace transforms and multiplies. So while God humbly consents to work in the world through human partners, the whole human-divine collaboration is nevertheless empowered by grace alone. I can think of three ways this is certainly true:

1. God's self-revelation of love is always primary to (comes before) our consent.

Remember, "We love, because he first loved us" (1 John 4:19). First, of course, this initiative includes God's revelation of love through Christ in the Incarnation. While we were still powerless, still ungodly, still sinners and still enemies (Rom. 5:6-10), grace initiated our salvation. Second, God's grace is primary in awakening each of us to our salvation. He must first open our blind eyes and remove the veil that covers our hearts, or we could not and would not believe. He must say, "Let there be light," in our hearts before we can consent and participate in the first place (Gen. 1:3; 2 Cor. 4:3-6).

2. The Holy Spirit's call precedes any particular work in which God seeks (and perhaps even requires) a human partner.

That is, by design, God's reign of love in the world always involves willing participants. But this process also always starts with an invitation by God's Spirit to engage in plans he has been orchestrating well in advance (Eph. 2:10). If God isn't the author, then we may be investing in good human ideas that lead nowhere. "Unless the Lord builds the house, the builders labor in vain" (Ps. 127:1).

On the other hand, any truly good work is first conceived in the heart of God and prompted by his Spirit, regardless of our awareness. In these events, God must take the lead in the partnership, where his empowering grace truly does the work. That's how Jesus served the Father and that's how we must serve Jesus. For example, if God says he wants to feed five thousand people and invites us to participate, we can willingly bring our five loaves and two small fish (whether in action or prayer). We become God's partners. And then, by grace alone, God may move powerfully in the world through us, far beyond what we could ask or imagine (Eph. 3:20). In other words, when God finds a human partner, we find a divine partner. That's when we become 'naturally supernatural,' producing fruit by the Holy Spirit's grace that cannot by squeezed out of the vines of human striving.

My point here is that such ministry comes at God's invitation. We don't force God's hand and use intercession to manage and manipulate God into doing what seems best to us. Rather, we wait on the Lord, watching and listening for his initiatives. I know the old saying, "God doesn't steer a parked car." Fine. Don't lounge idly on the sofa waiting for a lightning bolt from your TV remote. We should probably get off our derrières and 'do something,' as our Salvation Army friends say. At the same time, I notice that God doesn't grab the wheel if I'm steering. He'll let me steer my way all the way into the deepest ditch I can find. The balance seems to have something to do with getting behind the wheel and then asking, "Where do you want me to go?" Sometimes God will seem quite directive: "Head down this road. No, not that road." At other times, he seems to say, "Just drive. And as you drive, pay attention. I'll let you know where to pull over."

3. Mediation serves God as the primary partner.

A mediator participates as the channel—not the source—of God's power. The Holy Spirit is God's empowering presence. This relationship even applied to Christ's mediation! Listen to Peter's sermon on the Day of Pentecost: "Jesus of Nazareth (i) was a man (ii) accredited by God to you by miracles, wonders and signs, (iii) which *God did* among you (iv) *through him*" (Acts 2:22).

When Jesus performed miracles, he didn't turn on his 'God switch' for a few moments, then turned it back off when he went for lunch. Rather, *in his humanity*, he modeled the life of a mediator who emptied himself so that the power of God's love could work through him. It's a little like functioning as a conductor through whom God provides the power. Our involvement (participation) is crucial, but we aren't generating this power of healing, transforming love. Remember the next chapter in Acts, where Peter and John heal a lame man and everyone is aghast? Peter says, "Fellow Israelites, why does this surprise you? Why do you stare at us as if by our own power or godliness we had made this man walk?" (Acts 3:12). They have to admit they did make the man walk, but it wasn't really their power or godliness that did it. They were servant mediators.

Another way to see the difference in God's role and ours is through the image of the porter or gatekeeper (a reference to John 10:1-2). Jesus says in John 10 that the porter's job is to open the door for the Good Shepherd to come. I open a door and Jesus walks through it.

Good, so I'm not the Shepherd; I'm merely the porter and gate-keeper. If we do play those roles, then how do we sign up? Do we need to take a class, do we need to become certified, or can anyone be a gatekeeper? Is just knowing we can fulfill that role enough? I've seen very little children (toddlers) and severely disabled people partner with God, serving as spontaneous porters who opened the door for God's love and grace over a congregation. They are often unselfconscious and seemingly unaware of their role in unleashing something powerful and divine—just like the Gospel child with the loaves and fish.

I've also seen people devote their lives to prayer and study, intentionally pursuing spiritual maturity so they can serve wher-ever and whenever God calls them. Some have grown in their competence and confidence as they play the porter. God bless them! (And he does). But human effort apart from Christ does not bear divine fruit. "Neither the one who plants nor the one who waters is anything, but only God, who makes things grow" (1 Cor. 3:7).

Sometimes, I see a sovereign intersection between the two types that cause me to gasp, "Christ is in our midst!" What they have in common is a humility and willingness, whether natural or sculpted, instinctive or intentional, playful or serene. It's about consenting to participate with an open and sincere heart.

Isn't this the point of the parable of the soil and the seed? My heart can be a bed for the seed of God to sprout, flower and bear fruit. The soil produces nothing of itself, yet nevertheless plays an important role in fruit-bearing. A consenting heart provides the richest soil for seed, and can actually contribute to the size and impact of the harvest. So while there are serious differences between God's role and ours within the partnership, and enormous varieties of people prepared to serve, our surrender (consent) to God's seed initiative is a real and vital factor in spiritual fruitbearing.

Layers of participation

Again, God consents to the free play of secondary causes—that

'Ground of being' is a phrase usually attributed to theologian Paul Tillich. I borrow it here not to identify with his theology so much as to introduce my own—that God is not all, but God is in all—the panentheism of ancient Orthodoxy.

Chrysostom's *Divine Liturgy* has us pray, "O heavenly King, O Comforter, Spirit of truth, who is in all places and fills all things, come dwell in us."

he honors *necessity*—but in no way does this mean his hands are tied. He refuses to coerce or control, but he enters the arena of our lives by grace. His participation is real and it is also layered. The three great arenas of God's involvement include the cosmos, humanity and the Incarnation. I've suggested these three arenas above, but to conclude our chapter, I will summarize these and add two more: our role as kingdom priests and prayer partners.

*1. God participates in the whole cosmos as the 'ground of being.'**

That is, the Creator does not simply stand beside his Creation as one 'thing' standing beside another. Rather, God the Creator holds all things in himself, gives all things their being, and fills all things with his love. God is not a 'Being' among beings; he is the infinite source of all being and in him, all things have their being.[3] Paul describes our belief in, "one God and Father *of* all, who is *over* all and *through* all and *in* all" (Eph. 4:6). "He is *before* all things, and *in* him all things hold together" (Col. 1:17). "*In* him we live and move and have our *being*" (Acts 17:28). 'Creator' does not merely refer to an architect and builder at the beginning of time. Our Creator undergirds, permeates and intimately relates to his beloved creation at all times. God participates in our universe and our universe participates in him, depending on him for its existence. God is the difference between existence and non-existence. Perhaps God is existence itself.

This is a mystery. Trying to explain it is largely ludicrous. But for the sake of a general impression, I'll expose you momentarily to the over-intelligent mind of David Bentley Hart. Please excuse his long words—it helps to treat this subject and his endless syllables as poetry to be wondered at rather than technical jargon to be figured out.

> The whole cosmos—its splendor, its magnificent order, its ever vaster profundities—had been a kind of theophany

[appearance of God], a manifestation of the transcendent God within the very depths and heights of creation. *All of reality participated in* those transcendental perfections that had their infinite consummation in God and that came to utterance in us, in our rational contemplation and coherent articulation and artistic celebration of the beauty and grandeur of existence. The human wakefulness to the mystery of being was thus also already an openness to the divine, because *the world was an image of and participation in the God* who is the wellspring of all being.[4]

Is your head spinning? Try to listen with your heart. Hart is saying that God didn't merely retreat to make space for us. *Kenosis* is more than a self-emptying; it is a pouring out and into. In pouring out his love—in emptying himself (*kenosis*)—the universe comes to be. The energy of divine love poured out gels into all that is. As God fills the universe with his love, the universe participates in God's love in order to exist—in him we find our being.

I'm imagining a baby in a mother's womb—in mom, attached to mom, nourished by mom, every cell of baby invested with mom's DNA, mom's blood coursing through baby's veins. Baby finds life in mom; mom's life courses through baby. Maybe our mutual-participation with God is a little like that. Our life in God, God's life in us.

2. God participates in the world through willing human partners.

In the case of the cosmos, God's participation infuses all that is with 'being,' yet as I've said, God consents entirely to secondary causes without interruption or intervention. To 'mess with' our world (including secondary causes) directly—for his love to be literally 'fleshed out'—God has chosen to participate through the mediation of his crowning achievement: the human race.

This chapter opened with a teaser I once heard the renowned South African human rights activist, Bishop Desmond Tutu, say, "For whatever reason, since humankind showed up on the scene,

God does nothing without a **human partner.***

"For whatever reason." Does this mean God *needs* human partners to work in the world? *Need* is a very strong word to impose on God. Yet if he didn't *need* human partners, why not magically end poverty, feed the starving, heal those dying of disease, and so on? Did he run out of manna?

Tutu's "whatever reason" is his appeal to mystery. I would suggest that the mystery of partnership is not found in any *need* in God, but in his purposeful design for love and fellowship with us, including our God-given ability to embrace or rebuff him.

Tutu then led us on a walk through the Bible, describing the powerful redemptive partnerships that God forged with willing partners such as Moses, the stuttering shepherd who led a nation out of slavery; David, the shepherd boy who became Israel's king; the little boy with a few loaves and fishes, modeling the supernatural possibilities of a sack lunch freely given. And of course, the Bishop himself willingly gave himself to a project bigger than Moses' exodus: the end of apartheid and establishment of the world's first *Truth and Reconciliation Commission*.

Tutu highlighted the story of Mary, the teenage virgin who offered the hospitality of her womb

---

'God's partners'

"Let me put it bluntly, leaving aside some important qualifications and exceptions: It is only in and through people, inwardly developed men and women, that God can exist and act in the world of man on earth. The proof for the existence of God is the existence of people who are inhabited by and who manifest God."
— Jacob Needleman, *What is God?*

as the first home for Jesus Christ. Here is the example par excellence of the way God literally enters the world through the life (and body) of a willing human partner. After the angel announced God's desire to impregnate her with "the Son of the Most High," Mary answered humbly, "I am the Lord's servant. May your word to me be fulfilled" (Luke 1:38).

In our worries (often justified) about Mariolatry (i.e., idolatrous worship of Mary), I believe we overlook and underestimate the enormity of her 'yes' to God. Think of it: God actually came from his heavenly throne into the earthly realm through her body. For nine months, she carried God the Son, the second Person of the Trinity, in her womb. Her own blood passed through the umbilical cord into Christ and coursed through his veins. More than that, when God the Word became flesh, when he assumed our nature to become fully human, 100% of that humanity—all of his human DNA—was contributed by her. The hymns of the ancient church sometimes call Mary 'the gate of heaven.' We do *not* enter heaven through her. Jesus alone is our gateway to God (John 10:9). But Mary submitted to becoming God's gateway, the portal through whom he chose to pass from his dimension into ours.

Mary's example challenges us to likewise say our willing 'yes' to partnership with God. We are to emulate her in welcoming and carrying Christ in our hearts as she did in her womb. Like her, we are to serve the Father, by bearing his Son into the world. And while Christ is our sole mediator before God the Father (1 Tim. 2:5), the Father seems to invite a host of willing partners to mediate his love (i.e., the presence of the Saviour) into this world.

I am not suggesting, of course, that we were partners in Christ's foundational work of salvation. Christ was the only human partner who, because he is also divine, could provide for the redemption of all. Beyond his unique and universal mission, we can ask how God's love transforms the world. How does God feed hungry people, clothe the naked and share the good news of Jesus? These are real works of God in the world, none of which happen magically. God has chosen people like you and me to minister and mediate his love.

In other words, God has established an order of love in which he has consented to use human mediators who bridge heaven and earth. God created Adam and Eve, you and me, to straddle two realms, to be the means and agents by which his kingdom comes, his will is done, on earth as it is in heaven. In singer Bruce Cockburn's lyrics, "That's the burden of the 'angel-beast.'" We live with one foot in the heavenly realm, obliviously mingling with angelic hosts; another firmly on earth's soil, mammals by DNA but crowned with God's glory (Ps. 8:5). It's a humbling honor that God should choose us to mediate his presence in the cosmos, to be the image of God to the world and to steward all creation (Ps. 8:6-8).

Nor is this heavenly realm far off. The kingdom of heaven isn't located in some distant galaxy or illusive dimension. According to Jesus, it's all around us, among us and within us (Matt. 3:2; Luke 17:21)—God's kingdom of love is always at hand, a geyser ready to blow at any moment. But for whatever reason, it manifests in our world and our lives through human representatives—those who consent to mediate God's love. God fills us with this supernatural love and calls us to empty ourselves in love (*kenosis!*). We're designed perfectly for pouring the kindness and generosity of God into the world, nurturing and nourishing all that is. Adam and Eve were to live that role, tending the garden and walking in God's presence. We all are.

Or were. We 'fell.' Whatever that means, it does *not* mean God changed the cosmic order or humanity's vital role in brokering God's participation in the world. The fall was actually inevitable, given our moral immaturity, and God knew that. He knew that the rise of humanity would also require (and receive) his mercy. God foreknew this and thus foreordained that he would take his own participation to the nth degree. From the beginning, he was destined to *become* human.

3. God participates in the world through the Incarnation.

God entered the world (of secondary causes) by uniting with humanity through the Incarnation—through Jesus. God can interact directly with the world if we remember that Jesus of Nazareth was the Word made flesh (John 1:14). That is, the life-giving, order-bringing, intelligent Love that creates and sustains the universe also became the proto-typical human mediator. Christ is the perfect link between heaven and earth because in him, we have the perfect union of God and man. Through Jesus' human and divine nature, God's love is channeled into the world.

Yale theologian, Kathryn Tanner, says,

> The point of Incarnation is … the perfection of humanity. By way of this perfected humanity in union with God, God's gifts are distributed to us – we are saved – just to the extent we are one with Christ in faith and love; unity with Christ the gift-giver is the means of our perfection as human beings, just as the union of humanity and divinity in Christ was the means of his perfect humanity.[5]

Tanner's point is crucial: the Incarnation is the means by which God participates in the world as Saviour and Gift-giver. And we are 'being saved' to the extent that we participate (join, unite) with Christ through faith and love. That is, he offers us the divine dynamic of relationship in Christ, by grace. He unites with us; we unite with him. He participates with us, and we participate with him. The love of God and world of humanity meet and unite in the God-man, Jesus of Nazareth. Again, our participation is mutual but not equal. He is the Gift-giver and we are the recipients. He is the Savior and we are the saved. He is the Lover—we, the beloved.

And here I will use even stronger words than identification

or participation. In the Incarnation, Christ mysteriously and completely *assumes or assimilates* all humankind and the fullness of human nature (fallen Adam) into himself. He takes into himself, bears, suffers all that we suffer—in himself, in his whole life and most especially in his death. He suffers our weaknesses and our wounds, the depth and breadth of the human condition. He bears even our violence and sin, becoming the focal point of all human oppression and aggression. Saint Silouan the Athonite said it this way:

> "The Father judgeth no man, but hath committed all judgment unto the Son ... because he is the Son of man" (John 5:22-27). This Son of man, Great Judge of the world, will say at the Last Judgment that 'one of the least of these' is His very Self. In other words, He *assimilates* every man's existence and *includes* it in His own personal existence. The Son of man has *taken into Himself all mankind* – He has *accepted the 'whole Adam'* and suffered for him.[6]

In human flesh—Incarnation—the Word overcame all that he suffered in real time. He overcame temptation as he faced it; forgave sin as he was confronted with it; and conquered death by passing through it. Because Jesus assimilated all humanity—all who are 'in Adam'—into himself, we participate also in his salvation victory. This salvation is not just theoretical, but 'in Christ,' in real time—a grace-given life-in-Christ that actually overcomes. Through our union with Christ, we become participants of God in his ministry of reconciliation.

4. Christ participates in the world through his kingdom priests.

Having become what Adam failed to be, what mankind and his covenant people failed to do, Christ has restored and has redignified humanity to its place as God's touchpoint in the cosmos. The 'New Adam' has established a New Covenant and chosen a Royal Priesthood, a Holy Nation who, through prayer and action, invites

God's heavenly kingdom into the earthly realm. By the grace and power of the Holy Spirit, we consent, invite and participate in God's active redemption. Tanner continues:

> United with Christ, we are thereby emboldened as ministers of God's beneficence to the world, aligning ourselves with, entering into communion with, those in need as God in Christ was *for us* in our need and as Christ was a man for others, especially those in need.[7]

Like Christ, his servants stand in partnership with the Giver and in solidarity with those who need his gifts. Just as Christ unites (participates) with both God and humanity in order to be a living bridge for the love of God, so his kingdom of priests unite with Jesus (by faith) and with those in need (by compassion) to become channels of the gospel of grace. This ministry of mediation is entirely *kenotic* and *cruciform* in that it involves emptying ourselves of ego and willfulness, consenting to be filled with Christ's own love. And then we emulate the *cruciform* God by pouring out that divine love into the world for the sake of others.

5. Christ participates in the world through prayer.

Prayer is a primary means for partnership with God. Prayer is an act of willing participation in the mediation of God's love. Our prayers somehow play a role in the restoration of all things. Thus, prayer truly matters since God is looking for willing partners who will welcome his healing love into this broken world.

Partnering prayer is also an act of yielding and surrender. In spite of some popular practices of prayer as militant proclamations that 'pull down heaven,' Christlike prayer is *kenotic, cruciform and willing*—not coercive, demanding or manipulative. Partnering prayer listens first to seek God's will, rather than attempting to impose our will in the world in his name. Partnering prayer is founded and funded in the mercies of God, and is therefore best directed at invoking those ever-ready mercies. How or in what form God chooses to deliver his mercies is finally his domain. We can make requests and petitions, but delivering our demands and dictates seems to me out of order.

For example, we are free to humbly ask God for healing, provision and protection, because we are reminded of Christ's ministry, when he revealed the Father's heart and will as healer, provider and protector. So we ask in faith to receive God's faithful care. However, this prayer of faith is *not* psychological posturing, presumption or pretence. We aren't to grasp at our inheritance. Authority in prayer is *not* the loud expression of our own willful demands. Effective prayer is *not* a formula we can or need to master, since the Holy Spirit both reveals and overcomes our ignorance in how we should pray (Rom. 8:26). Far better to seek God's good will than kick at the goads of our own will.

"Thy will be done" is sometimes used as a cop-out for faithless prayer, but it was, after all, how Jesus taught us to pray (Matt. 6:10). It was also the climax of Jesus' own prayer in Gethesemane (Matt. 26:42). There, Jesus perfectly revealed the precondition that opens a channel for God's active grace and supernatural love: self-emptying (*kenotic*) surrender.

In my own prayers, I'm learning to focus on *kenotic* surrender and assume a posture of attentive and receptive openness. When I intercede, I name the person, situation or need, without dictating how God must answer, and then I pray with real expectancy, "Lord, have mercy." If I sense the Spirit leading me to be more specific (as in the Lord's prayer), then I follow, but I do so with open hands.

Historically, I've seen the most positive fruit in prayer when practicing open-handed, contemplative forms of listening prayer, which rest in the type of encounter David had with the Good Shepherd in Psalm 23.

A final caveat

As I was working through this chapter, my friend Greg Albrecht offered this helpful caveat, which opens the way to partnership while avoiding the dangers of Messiah complex.

> The works of God require people, by his own vision and determination. He has, out of his love, consented to involve his own dear children, humbling himself to do so—but woe to the person who begins to think that God *needs* him/her to feed the hungry, etc. He has instead *chosen* and *invited* us to have the blessing of being involved, to pass on his grace which we have been given. Said John the Baptizer to the brood of religious snakes: "Do not think you can say to yourselves, 'We have Abraham as our father.' I tell you that out of these stones God can raise up children for Abraham" (Matt. 3:9).

Let's close this chapter by pondering, without commentary, three passages that describe the self-emptying, gift-giving nature of God in Christ, and the apostles' exhortation to participate in like manner after the pattern of Christ.

2 Corinthians 8:7-9

> [7] But since you excel in everything—in faith, in speech, in knowledge, in complete earnestness and in the love we have kindled in you—*see that you also excel in this grace of giving.* [8] I am not commanding you, but I want to test the sincerity of your love by comparing it with the earnestness of others. [9] For you know the grace of our Lord Jesus Christ, that *though he was rich, yet for your sake he became poor, so that you through his poverty might become rich.*

Philippians 2:5-7

⁵ In your relationships with one another, *have the same mindset* as Christ Jesus: ⁶ Who, being in very nature God, did not consider equality with God something to be used to his own advantage; ⁷ rather, he *made himself nothing by taking the very nature of a servant*, being made in human likeness.

1 John 4:9-11

⁹ This is how God showed his love among us: He sent [gave] his one and only Son into the world that we might live through him. ¹⁰ This is love: not that we loved God, but that he loved us and sent [gave] his Son as an atoning sacrifice for our sins. ¹¹ Dear friends, *since God so loved us, we also ought to love one another.*

Pausing to think

- God's grace participates in the world wherever willing partners mediate his reign of love into the world. Why do you think God chose to work via mediators? Why not prevent or interrupt suffering and evil?

- Think of some biblical faith-partners, either the ones we've mentioned, or other characters you're drawn to. What was the fruit of these partnerships?

- Through even one human partner, God's grace freely blesses so many others. Can you recall some inspiring faith-partners from our era?

- Can someone partner with God unwittingly? What if they aren't Christian believers? Would Gandhi count as a faith-partner with God? How about when Sean Penn serves the poor in Haiti?

- When we partner with God, God partners with us too! God must go with us or our efforts are fruitless. How have you experienced his partnership?

- Partnering with the *cruciform* God means taking up our own cross. What might that look like?

Pausing to pray

God, thank you for pouring your love into the world through willing partners—especially Jesus! I'm encouraged that you would partner with a little boy to multiply his little lunch. If that's the case, sign me up! I am available to help; what would you like to do through me? Lord, let it be!

God is Good & Sh** Happens 9
An Anti-Theodicy of the Cross[1]

*"I am ceaselessly torn between the goodness of God
and the affliction of humankind, and the link between the two."*
– Simone Weil (Seventy Letters) –

*"The theologian of glory says that evil is good and good evil;
the theologian of the Cross says that the thing is as it is."*
– Martin Luther (The Heidelberg Disputation) –

God's goodness and human affliction

So far, our journey together has resulted in three primary assertions when we think about God: we can say God is good, God is
Christlike, and God is *cruciform*—that is, the love of God is revealed
through the Cross of Christ. Now let's pause and ask ourselves with
all honesty: can we affirm these truths with integrity in the face of
the hurt and pain we know and experience in our world?

Simone Weil once said, "When you contemplate God, you
should have in your mind the seventy thousand slaves that Crassus
crucified when he put down the slave rebellion in Rome as a symbol
of the appalling affliction that has occupied human life."[2] It would
be just a few years later that we could add, "and six million Jews just
like Weil."

What are we to make of the gaping abyss between the perfect
goodness and infinite love of God over against the affliction, suffering and evil in the world at large? How do they come together,
if at all? This puzzle has recurred throughout the ages—ever since

people became aware of the reality of both the heights of God and the depths of human misery. When I ask, "What is true about God?" and, "What is the character of the world?" the two realities don't seem to match. The fundamental truth of God's nature (love) seems irreconcilably incompatible with day-to-day life in this world (affliction).

'Theologies of glory'

"A theology of glory calls evil good and good evil. A theology of the cross calls the thing what it actually is. ... He who does not know Christ does not know God hidden in suffering. Therefore he prefers works to suffering, glory to the cross, strength to weakness, wisdom to folly, and, in general, good to evil. These are the people whom the apostle calls 'enemies of the cross of Christ' (Phil. 3:18)."

— Martin Luther

Real life defies our rational attempts to reconcile a God of love with the problem of evil. Myriads of these *theodicies* try in vain to explain why God allows suffering. Martin Luther called these logical attempts to break the tension between a God of love and the fact of evil *'theologies of glory.'** Luther determined that those who try to reason their way out of the problem of evil invariably end up calling evil good. For example, if we say, "God is in control," or "Maybe God is teaching us a lesson," we open the door to justifying all sorts of horrors as if God were to blame. Or, because God is good, we assign his goodness to the heinous evils and senseless tragedies of our world (as we saw earlier in Calvin's system).

I once met a man who had been attending a Bible study at someone else's home. It became apparent that someone was missing—a toddler of one the group members.

With a sickening feeling, they commenced a search that led to the back yard where the child was discovered in the swimming pool. Drowned. Gone. "Well, God is in control." "Maybe God is teaching us a lesson." "God needed another angel."

In truth, any so-called 'answer' offered for such a senseless tragedy would be trite, unsatisfying and spiritually abusive. This unspeakable trauma changed their view of providence—of God and how he works (or doesn't)—permanently.

Another friend of mine, a single mom, was attending another Bible study and leaving her children with a trusted babysitter. Over time, she began to suspect something was wrong. Tragically, when she investigated her fears, she discovered that the person watching her children was also sexually abusing them. "Why God!? Where were you? Was your arm too short to save?" What justification could we offer her in comfort? Any supposedly redemptive suggestion that her children were molested so that would actually paint God's providence as demonic.

Back to Simone Weil. God used her article, "The Love of God and Affliction," at a crisis point in my life when I was tempted to despair. These words struck me powerfully as the truth.

> The grand enigma of human life is not suffering, but affliction. It is not astonishing that innocents should be killed, tortured, flushed from their countries, reduced to misery or slavery, imprisoned in camps and cells—since we know there are criminals who commit these acts. Neither is it astonishing that sickness imposes long periods of suffering that paralyze life and make it an image of death—since nature is subject to the blind play of mechanical necessity. But it is astonishing that God has given affliction the power to take hold of the very souls of innocents and to seize them as their sovereign master.[3]

It *is* astonishing! Astonishing that a God whom we claim to be both all-powerful and all-loving allows affliction such a presence in our lives. It's not just that evils occur, but that they are utterly pervasive around the globe and that God seems powerless to stop them. How do we work out this disparity without abandoning faith?

Beyond reason

Luther concluded we *cannot reason* our way through this mystery—through the contradiction between a God of love and the plain evidence of evil in our world. Reason cannot adequately address this impasse.

Rather, our only hope is that God would give us a revelation that encompasses both realities—God's love and human affliction. Luther believed the only sufficient response to the dilemma is the revelation given through the Cross of Jesus Christ. At the Cross, we see the perfect love of God and the crazy-making affliction of all humanity in one place, one moment, one Man—Jesus Christ, the *cruciform* God.

Rather than dazzling us with a clever answer, the Cross arrests us. It offers an *anti-theodicy*. The love and the anguish—both present in the extreme—are astonishing. The goodness of God and the affliction of mankind is no mere problem, puzzle or paradox. The Cross utterly silences our solutions. God's love (a Cross) and human affliction (a crucifixion) appear as a true contradiction—and in bewilderment we echo Jesus' own cries, "God is good *but* all is *not* well! Where are you?"

Gazing into the darkness of the abyss, we could very well be swallowed by despair, but it is precisely in 'the dark night'[4] that we behold the crucified Christ. His outstretched arms and wounded hands span the infinite chasm between God's perfection and our pain. We hear in his words both anguish and hope, desolation then consolation. From his pierced side, a supernatural river of eternal love flows—blood and water, "sorrow and love flow mingled down."[5]

The life of our Saviour is given and gushing into the world through the torn flesh of that self-same Victim. In the face of the Cross, all of our explanations are flaccid, our rationalizations shallow and our theodicies pathetically empty. In the end, what we are given is a Cross of love that will make all things new. As the old hymn says, "Nothing but the blood of Jesus."

On the Cross, we see that God is neither the triumphant intervener nor the passive non-mover. He has always suffered the sowing and reaping of our sin and violence, but nowhere more so than on the Cross.

But I've been waxing poetic in my stammering way. Let's back up and consider this in somewhat sharper relief so as to really make the point: only a *cruciform* God can account for the human predicament and only he can resolve it.

The problem of evil and theodicy

As I suggested above, numerous formulations of the so-called 'problem of evil' and attempts to solve it have existed since ancient times.[6] Probably the best known statement of the question came from the Enlightenment philosopher, David Hume, in his book *Dialogues Concerning Natural Religion* (published posthumously in 1779). He says, "Is [God] willing to prevent evil, but not able? Then is he impotent? Is he able, but not willing? Then is he malevolent? Is he both able and willing? Whence then is evil?"[7]

If God is, by definition, all-good and all-powerful, then why is there evil in the world? But clearly there is evil in the world. So, God must either not be all-good or God must not be all-powerful and, therefore, not God at all.

Sadly, ignoring Luther's warning against calling evil good has become a regular blunder in recent years. The error arises whenever we attempt to grasp and contain the mysteries of God in the finite compartments of human reason. Examples abound of attributing evil to the retributive hand of God:

- Remember when the terrorist strikes of 9-11 (2001) were cited as proof that God had removed his hedge of protection around the United States because of the nation's moral laxity and tolerance of homosexuality?
- Remember when Hurricane Katrina (Aug. 2005) slammed New Orleans and the popular TV preachers identified it as God's punishment for the promiscuity and hedonism of that modern-day 'Sodom'?
- Remember when the Haitian earthquake (Jan. 2010) was attributed to God's wrath against the nation's supposed voodoo-pacts with the devil (circa 1804)?
- Remember the tsunami that caused the Fukushima Daiichi nuclear meltdown (March 2011)? What caused it? You guessed it: God's anger against the Japanese people for worshiping their emperor a few generations ago.

What did these disasters all have in common?

- They all involved natural disasters.
- They all resulted in mass destruction and death.
- They were all ascribed to sinners (or rather, scapegoats) deserving of divine punishment.
- In many cases, these judgments seemed almost a joyous conclusion—a triumphant verdict that smelled of *schadenfreude*—or literally, 'pain-joy' at someone else's misery.

This rationale for suffering is what Martin Luther meant by calling evil good, and it's nothing new.

The Lisbon earthquake

The problem of evil had already come to a head two decades prior to Hume's formulation when the French philosopher and poet, Voltaire, identified the Lisbon earthquake of 1755 as a fatal, historic blow to any form of providence or theodicy claiming to solve the problem of evil.

On November 1, 1755 an earthquake shattered Lisbon, Portugal, crushing worshippers who were attending All Saints' Day services. Six huge cathedrals collapsed upon them. Survivors fled the building areas to the open harbor, only to face the wrath of a tsunami within the hour. The earthquake triggered fires that would burn for a week, destroying most of the city. Giant waves rolled north to Spain and south to Morocco, engulfing entire coastal towns. The death toll has been estimated from sixty to one hundred thousand souls.

Beyond Voltaire's analysis, the disaster elicited a response across the philosophical and theological spectrum, including John Wesley (who called it divine retribution), Immanuel Kant, Jean-Jacques Rousseau and Voltaire.[8] Ultimately, the theological fallout matched the physical devastation—shaking faith, drowning optimism, and razing theodicies across Europe.

Voltaire's biting response was as logical as it was destructive:

> *'No theodicy has kept its promise.'*
>
> "The result of this trial before the tribunal of philosophy is that no theodicy so far proposed has kept its promise; none has managed to justify the moral wisdom at work in the government of the world against the doubts which arise out of the experience of the world."[9]
>
> — Immanuel Kant

if God is actively involved in history, he is immoral and capricious. For many, therefore, there is no God. One commentator summarized Voltaire's critique this way:

> Voltaire's essay on the earthquake at Cadiz is mainly negative … concerned with ridiculing belief in the providential ordering of the world. How can there be providential ordering of events when evil such as this occurs? The natural evil of an earthquake cannot be blamed on man, as can the moral evil of sin. Its cause is elsewhere. The works of God are condemned in the name of morality, so that the idea of God is killed in man's heart. Belief in God is attacked in the name of a pessimism that cannot reconcile the evil of the world with divine purpose.[10]

Before resorting prematurely to the 'God's mysterious ways' defense, the greater wisdom allows the twinned tremors of Lisbon's calamity and Voltaire's critique to bring all of our brittle assumptions to complete ruin. Many Christians panic when faced with such seemingly incisive and decisive judgments against God or, rather, their *image of God*. However, we should not prematurely scramble to fortify a toppling faith in providence without undergoing the severe truth of our opponent's arguments. Rather than being dismissive or defensive, let's relive the great tragedies of our own era—whether 'Desert Storms' or tropical storms—in the stanzas of Voltaire's haunting poem:

> O unhappy mortals! O deplorable ground!
> O of all the mortals appalling assembly!
> Useless pains eternal maintenance!
> Misled philosophers who shout: "All is well."
> Run, contemplate these dreadful ruins
> These remains, these scraps, these unhappy ashes
> These piled up women,

these children one on the other ...
Lisbon is damaged, and one dances in Paris!
Will you, before this mass of victims, claim that
"God is revenged, their death repays their crimes"?[11]

Does our loss of rational explanations for evil leave us bereft? Absolutely! But embracing this bewildering reality is indispensable. Why?

- First, because this *is* our reality. Awful stuff happens every day all over the world and God does not stop it. To ignore that is to contrive an imaginary god—a useless idol.

- Second, only when the ground is scraped clear of delusional wish-dreams and platitudes is there bedrock for us to discover the actual goodness of God and develop a theology of the Cross that sustains us through disaster.

To hell with our denials, our coping mechanisms and our blame-games—the same foolish mischief exposed and refuted by God so long ago in the Book of Job! If God is good, then really: what the hell? Where do we start? What did we miss? What elements of theological rubble are scraped clear and what truth remains as bedrock?

All-powerful: The errant premise

The first step forward is a return to the key premises in the problem of evil. We can double-check and respond to each as follows:

- *Evil exists.* This is a non-negotiable, irreducible, stubborn fact. The form of evil we call 'affliction' also defies sense or purpose. Any attempt to justify evil beyond 'it is' is offensive in its denial of our experience of the misery that enslaves, oppresses and dehumanizes necessity's victims. Evil is real. Period.

- *God is all-good.* We can never *prove* our way into this statement. From beginning to end, our belief in God's goodness is a revelation, a faith statement, a premise that we either turn toward and experience as true, even in tragedy, or we can "turn our face to the wall" (Isa. 38:2) and finally despair (once our anesthetics wear off). In accepting this premise, we proclaim, "God is good. Period."—the bedrock of our faith.

- *God is all-powerful.* One of the premises must be false, at least in its unqualified form. If evil exists and yet we hold that God is good, then what of his power? Ultimately, the *cruciform* King—the Cross itself— challenges this premise and overthrows our ideas of what it means for God to be all-powerful *in this world.* If by this third premise we mean God is *controlling* history and *causing* all events (good and evil), the implications are impossible, immoral and, in fact, simply pagan. God is Zeus rather than Christ.

A theology of the Cross discovers and admits the obvious: namely, God is truly all-powerful and immovable in his love but also (though not only), surprisingly, we often experience him as *all-powerless* in time, in this world.

'All-powerless'? I only make such a bold statement advisedly, not to diminish God's omnipotent love, but to resist human conceptions of power-as-coercion erroneously imposed them on God.

By 'in time,' I mean, within the system of God's temporal (time-bound) creation, bound by time vis-à-vis the realm of eternity that transcends time and space.

God the all-powerful, all-powerless

Why does God allow particular evils in the world? Why did God allow the mass deaths of Lisbon or Auschwitz? This is a trick question—even a cruel one—in that it implies that God sits as a cosmic regulator, giving or withholding permission for every temporal event, signing off on some and preventing others according to an eternal master plan. Where human freedom cannot be blamed for a particular evil, some theodicies retreat behind mystery to justify God's apparently arbitrary choices. But if God's 'choices' (as willful edicts) are involved, skeptics can reference Lisbon or Auschwitz to make the formidable case that God's choices have been monstrous.

By contrast, a theology of the Cross responds to "why does God allow X?" with "God (obviously and observably) allows everything!" If God is all-powerful, his power is not akin to *control*. As noted earlier, God does not *do* control (employ power as force or coercion). Rather, God's omnipotence is two-fold:

- God is *all-powerful* as the Creator of all that is within a fixed order. God established and set the limits of the universe. Within those limits, God lovingly chose to grant the realm of necessity (free will and natural law) free play without direct interference. Rather than an act of abandonment, the cosmos is an expression of God's plenitude, his hospitality, yielding space for authentic flourishing.

- God is *all-powerful* as the Savior of all that is through his supernatural love and his boundless grace. A chorus I remember singing as a child said, "His steadfast love never ceases; his mercies never come to an end. Great is thy faithfulness, O Lord." But as we've discovered, God's care for the world isn't magical: it is mediated by willing human partners who pray and work for God's kingdom will on earth. Most of all, God's grace has been mediated through Jesus Christ.

Conversely, the *cruciform* One also willing chooses to manifest a certain *powerless* love in time:

- God willingly chose *powerless love* in the *cosmic Cross* of Creation. That is, when God through the Logos (John 1) created the universe, he relinquished control to natural law. From the beginning of time, God has voluntarily refrained ('chained' himself) from violating the order of necessity.

- God willingly chose *powerless love* in the *historic Cross* of the crucifixion. That is, when God in Christ assented and ascended to the Cross, he relinquished control to human autonomy (i.e., freedom as rebellion). He even allowed us to nail his body to that cross-piece of wood, rendered helpless and immobile.

Neither of these Crosses—the cosmic nor the historic—are mere momentary events in Christ's biography. God's *cruciform* love extends beyond the nanoseconds of the Big Bang or hours of Good Friday. In chapter 8, we saw how, in the Incarnation, God-in-Christ entered and experienced our afflictions—drank our 'cup of suffering'—for all people, for all time.

And yet, even after the Cross, our sin and suffering continues, doesn't it? The *cosmic crucifixion* extends through time and space to every so-called 'act of God' (!?)—every natural disaster—that unleashes destruction. And the *historic crucifixion* includes every instance where rational beings (human or angelic) choose to inflict harm in the world. Because our sin and suffering persist, so too, the *cruciform* love of Christ persists. Is there a sense, then, that Christ continues to co-suffer with us even now?

How Christ continues to co-suffer

If God is a Father who loves us, then when we as his children suffer—and so many millions undergo chronic misery on a second-by-second basis—God knows that. He sees us and loves us. And while he is not constrained to move, to feel or to react, he is certainly capable of moving, loving and acting. The movement he willingly chose was this: "For God so loved the world that he sent his only Son" (John 3:16).

The Book of Hebrews makes it clear that the Incarnation enabled God to enter the fullness of our affliction firsthand. Beyond the compassionate empathy of a concerned Father, God Incarnate actually experienced poverty, displacement and refugee status—then later also mockery, humiliation, abuse, torture and violent murder.

So Christ's experience of suffering both reveals God's love and also fulfills it in the Incarnation and at the Cross. Over his whole lifetime, from womb to tomb, the Word became flesh in order to endure the depth and breadth of the entire human condition. And then Jesus' lifelong struggle climaxed at the Cross.

In the Incarnation, Christ assumed "the likeness of sinful flesh" (Rom. 8:3). In taking up our humanity and suffering it in himself—in bearing all our sins and our sorrows (Isa. 53), yet without sin—he overcame them in his death ("It is finished!" John 19:30) and resurrection.

Thus, all suffering before or since the Cross are dealt with definitively there. It's not that we no longer suffer, nor that Christ no longer feels empathy for us now. Rather, all that is suffered (and which Christ co-suffers with us) finds its locus at the Cross, so that all he achieves comes to fruition in his resurrection (and ultimately our resurrection).

Finally, when we speak of God's co-suffering love in Christ, we are not talking about God suffering what we suffer. Rather, his co-suffering refers to the ongoing identification of Christ with his suffering people—a transforming union of Christ's self-giving love and our affliction. His love and our brokenness meet so redemption can occur. So when I say that Christ 'co-suffers' with us, think of Jesus as the 'co-' [God with us] and we as the '-suffering,' uniting for the sake of our redemption.

I believe this. But I also worry about forms of charismatic triumphalism that are in serious denial about the unhealed victims of affliction (now), where redemption is clearly not in play (yet). For our theology to be true, it must work in the worst case scenarios. Only the Cross is capable of that. I think we can honestly say to those in affliction:

- Yes, you are suffering. There's no denying your affliction.
- Jesus *sees* your suffering and *cares* about your suffering.
- Jesus *knows* your suffering intimately and experientially, because he too suffered but also because he dwells in you.
- Jesus suffered too; he completely *identifies* with your pain.
- Jesus is here with you now. He co-suffers with you here, even in your experience of his *absence!*
- His co-suffering love does *not* mean he's in the same helpless state of suffering or despair that you are in.
- Co-suffering means he wants to graft your pain to the resources of his divine love.
- We can welcome his self-giving love to transform your pain and bring redemption, even in the dark night of absence and affliction. Let's meet him at the Cross.

Crucifixion as the absence of God

I am beginning to see how the truth of Christianity is verified *not* by Christ's signs and wonders—perhaps not even in the Resurrection! Yes, I *need* Christ to have risen or else he is not alive to me and for me. Yes, I pray the Nicene Creed that says, "I look for the resurrection of the dead and 'the life of the age to come." But honestly, even if Hitler had been resurrected fifty times, I would still not love and worship him! Nor, in the end, does my faith stand on the profundity of Christ's words of wisdom, truth and love— as beautiful and life-giving as they are for me.

> ### 'Crucifixion and absence'
>
> Christ's crucifixion experience of God's absence is what makes Christianity true to life, true to our lives—to our familiarity with God's felt and practical absence, especially in our brushes with affliction.

Rather, what has gripped me, what alone could redeem my life from the pit, is the authenticity of Christ's experience on the Cross— including God's felt absence—an experience we share and through which we see God for ourselves. Anything less seems like a shallow fairy tale, insufficient for true mediation, for only the crucified God can span and mediate the infinite distance to my own reality. A God who cannot cry out our own anguished "Why?" back to God would fall short of crossing the chasm.

I resonate with George P. Grant, a disciple of Weil and survivor of the London bombings of World War 2, who said,

> Doesn't Jesus' death go more to the heart of what life is than Socrates – the fear, his sweat was these great drops of blood falling to the ground. All this is what convinces me of

Christianity; it seems to me important. This is more what life is like. I mean, it's strange; this is exactly what makes Christianity attractive and necessary. It so expresses the absence of God from God, the absence, the total forsaking of God by God. It is this that holds me to Christianity.[12]

For Grant, Christ's crucifixion experience of God's absence is what makes Christianity true to life, your life—to our familiarity with God's felt and practical absence in our brushes with affliction.

Notice that I refer to God's *felt* and *practical* absence. We might know theologically that God is everywhere and always present, but we don't always feel it. In affliction, God's real presence often makes no practical difference; people still suffer and die in all manner of cruel ways. So in the crucifixion, Jesus shared fully in our experience of absence, assuming it and thereby utterly redeeming it.

Companion contraries

When I say God is both present and absent, or all-powerful and all-powerless in time, I mean that we experience God in both ways, sometimes alternatively but often simultaneously, in a very real way. Thus, we envision and experience a God who is at once:

- near and distant;
- present and absent;
- manifest and hidden;
- personal and impersonal;
- existent (theism) and nonexistent—yes, we as people and societies do have our atheistic periods!

This tension of opposites seems difficult on paper but makes absolute sense in the gravity and grace of real life and real death existence. I love to sing that God is near, present, manifest. But when I cannot sing—or laugh or smile or hope or even stand—I can cling to and cherish the 'old rugged Cross.'

To admit these tensions functions to preserve our sanity in affirming the goodness of God, the reality of affliction and the distance between them. It also begs the question of how God bridges the distance between God's goodness and our suffering. The Cross reveals that Christ experienced that distance, but it also shows us how God-in-Christ spanned it.

God allows everything *and* God is present

This is the tricky part: if God is present *and* God allows everything, then does that mean when evil happens, he merely sits by and watches? What kind of Father, if present, would sit in the corner and passively observe suffering without stepping in to intervene? How could we call such a Father 'good'? Where is Jesus when the child is being molested? When a civilian is being tortured by government forces? When a rocket launcher takes out a passenger jet? When a terrorist literally crucifies a Christian?

God neither controls the situation nor is he found sulking in the corner, passive and idle. Behold: he's there on the Cross. And he takes up all the evil and suffering and sin and sorrow into himself. All the despair and selfishness that leads to suicide; all of the perversion and obsession that leads to sexual assault; all of the powerless and desperation that leads to terrorism; all the pride and power that leads to domination and slavery. Christ takes it all up into himself on the Cross. He felt it all, endured it all, absorbed it and transformed it through self-giving, radically forgiving, co-suffering love.

He doesn't sit in the corner while an adult harms a child; he hangs on a Cross. He doesn't watch and do nothing; he endures and transforms and he will have the last word:

Mercy. Redemption, restoration, reconciliation.

Yes, Christ is *powerless* to save, since he's been crucified to control and coercion. At his temptation he rejected any use of 'the right hand of power' to fulfill his mission.

Yes, Christ is *mighty* to save, since his love is a power far greater than force: the left-handed scepter of enduring mercy.

Bridging the distance

A summary is in order. First, we have stressed the importance of accepting the reality of human suffering—of the real and vast distance between the affliction of humankind and the goodness of God. Only when we thoroughly concede that gap, stare full into the abyss of our misery, we can then ponder the bridges that might cross it.

Second, we have exposed the bankruptcy of our rational arguments, our theodicies. Luther's point, above, is that these explanations can only justify the goodness and the power of God by calling evil good. Like Luther, Simone Weil proposed instead her theology of the Cross. She argued that the Cross reveals a faulty premise in the problem: the *cruciform* God, she said, is obviously *not* all-powerful *in this world*.

Third, we have seen how this distance is bridged by 'Christ alone, and him crucified.' On the Cross, we behold God's goodness and our suffering. Said another way, God has not explained the problem of pain. Rather, he has crossed it through the descent of living Grace, through the Incarnation, through the crucifixion. Weil once said, "The infinity of space and time separates us from God. ... We cannot take one step toward the heavens. *God crosses the universe and comes to us.*"[13] Surprisingly, supernaturally, the gorge of affliction itself becomes a bridge where contact—a real encounter—with the living God becomes a real possibility. Weil recalls her own encounter in these terms,

> In my reasoning on the insolubility of the problem of God, I had not anticipated this possibility: a real contact, person-to-person, here below, between a human being and God. ... Moreover, in Christ's sudden possession of me, neither my senses nor my imagination had any part; through

my suffering I only felt the presence of a love analogous to what one reads in the smile of a beloved face.[14]

At the Cross, by grace alone, our lowly hearts make contact with the supernatural love of God and with the beauty of the gospel. The Cross of Christ becomes our vision of divine descent and human consent. The Cross—affliction *par excellence*—proclaims the vastness of God's distance, but also acts as the mediating bridge for his nearness.

Only in terms of the Cross is any adequate response possible. Only in the *cruciform* God can we truly affirm that God is Love without denying our own capacity for sin, or closing our eyes to the suffering of the world.

Here are our takeaways from this chapter:

- The Cross represents and responds to (not 'solves') the problem of evil.
- The Cross repudiates and replaces failed theodicies.
- The Cross reflects the true, *kenotic* and *cruciform* nature of God.

We leave this chapter with a brief reflection by Fr. Richard Rohr, who beautifully summarizes our 'anti-theodicy' of the Cross as God's consent and participation:

> We live in a finite world where everything is dying, shedding its strength. This is hard to accept, and all our lives we look for exceptions to it. We look for something strong, undying, infinite. Religion tells us that something is God. Great, we say, we'll attach ourselves to this strong God. Then this God comes along and says, "Even I suffer. Even I participate in the finiteness of this world." [This] image of God is not an 'almighty' and overpowering God, but in fact a poor, vulnerable, and humble one like Jesus. ...

The enfleshment and suffering of Jesus is saying that God is not apart from the trials of humanity. God is not aloof. God is not a mere spectator. God is not merely tolerating or even healing all human suffering. Rather, God is participating with us—in *all* of it—the good and the bad! I wonder if people can avoid becoming sad and cynical about the tragedies of history if they do not know this.[15]

Pausing to think

- "God is good, all the time." Do we believe that? Even during calamity? What does God's goodness look like then? What shape does it take?

- "God is in control." Do you believe that? Even in the face of human suffering? Or conflict? Or evil?

- How is it that divine goodness and human affliction co-exist in Christ on the Cross? As you ponder the crucifixion, where do you identify each?

- Recall a time when you felt the presence of God in the midst of personal suffering. How did God comfort you? Have you felt the darkness of God's absence during such a time? How did you endure it?

- Explaining suffering often makes God seem capricious. Have you ever experienced foolish input of poor Job's friends? How might we respond?

Pausing to pray

God, you are good and all that you do is goodness. And yet, when things get dark, sometimes I can't see you or feel you at all. Where did you go? Why have you forsaken me? Come quickly! I need you! Lord, let it be!

Part III

'Unwrathing' God

- In which we revisit our notion of 'wrath' in light of the Christlike and cruciform God.

- Does God have a dark and wrathful side that balances out his goodness and love?

- If not, then how shall we understand the biblical language of wrath?

- How does wrath relate to God's consent?

- If we unwrath God, how do we understand the Cross?

- And how do we present the gospel?

Love and Wrath as Consent **10**

Parable: Wrath as a hammer-throwing contest

We begin this section on 'unwrathing God' with a parable from actual events in my childhood. The 'wrath of God' is like the hammer-throwing contest. My father warned me as a child. "Do not," he said, "throw hammers in the air." Apparently he saw this as a good warning in fatherly love. I saw it as an enticing challenge, an irresistible curiosity and a rule to be broken. My neighbor Dougie and I (perhaps seven at the time) each took our fathers' hammers and had a contest to see who could throw his hammer higher. Straight up. Perhaps I won. Certainly Dougie lost, for my hammer soared skyward, then descended directly onto poor Dougie's skull. Blood everywhere. Screaming followed. Then I found myself running home, locking all the doors and hiding in my room. Shortly, the phone rang (Dougie's mom) and we were flying to the hospital where doctors were already stitching up Dougie's head without the benefit of anesthesia. More screaming.

It did not escape me that 'the wrath' intrinsic to my sin caused both Dougie and I a great deal of suffering, even though my father's response was only love and comfort. The wrath did not involve or require any active punishment. I did not imagine that my father had struck Dougie with the hammer for participating in my rebellion. Even when Doug's father held him down as the surgeon applied sutures, I didn't think they were taking out their vengeance on us.

'Unwrathing'

is the interpretive process by which we recognize wrath as a metaphor for God's consent ('giving over') to the consequences of sin, even when the text describes events as if God was actively provoked into violent retribution (punishing for the sake of punishing).

The wrath of our fathers was a self-inflicted experience of rejecting and receiving their loving care.

It seems to me that making me go to the hospital and hear Dougie's screams was a torment worse than retribution, in that it forced me to look at the pain I had caused and didn't allow me to cower in my room in a sort of self-loathing denial. It was also the most important element in moving forward to not only owning my rebellion (far better than a spank) but also reconciliation with my victim. I wonder if this event might be close to the truth of the 'great and terrible day' of the Lord's final judgment.

A repulsive wrath

The Scriptures frequently describe divine violence and the wrath of God in the extreme—texts so repulsive that many Bible-readers prefer to avoid them and eventually forget they are even there. I think of Lamentations 2, where we find the weeping prophet, Jeremiah, crying out his tears, sick to his stomach (v. 11). He surveys the siege of Jerusalem and sees the bodies of the elderly and wee children strewn throughout the streets—death by starvation and the sword are everywhere. In 2:20 and 4:10, he describes women so desperate to survive that they resort to boiling their own babies and eating them! Who is responsible for these atrocities? Jeremiah tells us: God is. In Jeremiah's Lamentations, we are beholding the wake of the wrath of God in all its fury!

How on earth or in heaven can we reconcile such horrors—this *monster-god*—with the self-giving, radically forgiving, mercy-enduring God revealed in and through the Lord Jesus Christ? Having developed our *cruciform* theology in some detail, we can now begin to apply it creatively throughout this section, which I've entitled *Unwrathing God*.

In this chapter, we'll use the language of God's *consent* to address the problem of wrath. While I'm referring to this interpretive process as **unwrathing**,* I am not at all intending to erase the word 'wrath' from the text from the Bible as if it were not or should not be there. Indeed, it appears over two hundred times in the popular English Standard Version. Rather, the Bible itself takes us on a progressive, cruciform pilgrimage from primitive literal understandings of wrath, where God appears to burn with anger and react violently, to a metaphorical reading of wrath, in which God consents—*gives us over*—to the self-destructive consequences of our own willful defiance. The *cruciform* God will not and cannot, by love's nature, coerce us to obey. God grants us the dignity (and discomfort) of 'finding our own bottom' (to use 12-step recovery terminology), the end of which is willing surrender to the arms of grace. In the Bible, the shorthand for this process is 'wrath.' This is the process laid out poetically in scriptures such as Lamentations.

Lamentations

If we read between the lines of Jeremiah's mournful poem, we can see how the Israelites had brought destruction on themselves.

Willful choices had caused this suffering. Quite literally, the evil empire Babylon—not God per se—had come to annihilate Jerusalem's people and reduce the city to powder. But never mind reading between the lines; read the lines themselves. From Jeremiah's perspective, God had brought this calamity upon them. Scanning the verbs in chapter 2, here is what we see:

Verse 1:

- The Lord in his anger has brought Jerusalem to shame.
- He has thrown down ...
- He did not remember ...

Verse 2:

- The Lord swallowed up without mercy ...
- In his anger, he pulled down ...
- He threw down ...

Verse 3:

- In his anger, he has removed ...
- He took away ...
- He burned against ...
- He burned up ...

Verse 4:

- Like an enemy, he prepared to shoot ...
- Like an enemy, he killed ...
- He poured out his anger ...

Verse 5:

- Like an enemy, he swallowed up ...
- He destroyed ...
- He caused moaning and groaning ...

Verse 6:

- He cut down his temple ...
- He destroyed ...

- He rejected in his great anger …

Verse 7:

- He rejected …
- He abandoned …
- He handed over …

Verse 8:

- The Lord planned to destroy …
- He measured the wall to destroy …
- He made the walls sad …

Verse 9:

- He destroyed the bars and smashed the gates …

Verse 17:

- The Lord has done what he planned …
- He kept his word that he commanded …
- He destroyed without mercy …
- He let your enemies laugh at you …
- He strengthened your enemies …

Verse 20:

- Lord, Lord, see to whom *you* have done this. Women eat their babies …

Verse 21:

- You killed them in the day of your anger …
- You killed them without mercy …

Verse 22:

- You invited terrors to come …
- No one escaped alive on the day of the Lord's anger …

Repulsive. And when these gruesome events are attributed to God in active verbs, they make God seem repulsive, tyrannical.

With heaving dry sobs, Jeremiah proclaims and portrays God as a destroyer, burning with anger, pouring out death. Jeremiah depicts Yahweh as unmerciful and vengeful.

Note the key verbs above: *attribute, proclaim, portray, depict.* Could it be that God is not the culprit at all? Could the real conundrum be rooted in our misperceptions about how God is present and how we should interpret and describe his participation in the tragic consequences of our sin? In fact, are these ancient and fierce portrayals of God consistent with what God has finally disclosed about his nature to us in Christ?

These fiery visions of a volatile God have not only been revolting to civilized moderns with first-world problems, but also posed a serious dilemma for early church disciples, sensitized as they were to the love and nonviolent mercy of Christ. Holding fast to the revelation of the *cruciform* God, our life-giving Saviour and merciful Redeemer, how did early Christian commentators integrate such texts into their vision of a loving God? To read these texts in light of the gospel, they often minimized, allegorized or spiritualized wrath. While their efforts were not without flaws, they did a fantastic job of finding Christ in the mix and emphasizing texts where the Christlike God shines through.

Imagine: Lamentations, same book, next chapter:

> [22] Because of the LORD's great love we are not consumed,
>   for *his compassions never fail.*
> [23] They are new every morning; great is your faithfulness.
>   (Lam. 3:22-23)

Jeremiah! Are you describing the same God? The one who you just told us broke your teeth with gravel and trampled you in the dust (3:16)? How shall we untangle this bipolar image of God? And even if we can, how shall we interpret the manic wrath texts?

Cruciform theology offers us God's love-as-consent as a way forward. It allows for the reality of sin's cruelty without painting God as a moral monster.

If God operates in the world by consent, then we see wrath, not as the retribution of a willful God, but as a *metaphor for the consequences* of God's consent to our non-consent. That is, God's wrath (the metaphor) is that he allows us to resist him, and includes our experience of all the fall-out that ensues. When we understand the way consent relates to wrath, we can use the language of '*cruciform consent*' to 'demetaphorize' wrath—a fancy word for transposing a metaphor back to what it's actually describing. We don't need to deny the metaphor—even the metaphor of wrath—instead, we ask what real-time reality the metaphor is pointing to. We also need to ask ourselves why God is used in the metaphor at all. Sure, the Bible authors use metaphors, but why make God look complicit if he's not really the steamed-up agent of wrath they depict?

Literalizing metaphors

Let's begin by applying our theology of consent to the problem of how we read 'wrath' in Hebrew and Christian Scripture. In an effort take the Bible *seriously*, many faithful believers have fallen into the trap of taking it too *literally*—that is, reading portions of Scripture that the authors meant poetically, figuratively or symbolically as if they were meant to be taken as sterile stainless steel facts. We know intuitively not to believe Jesus is a literal woolly lamb with seven horns, yet many forget that in the same apocalyptic genre, neither should we assume Jesus literally flies across the sky with a sword exploding from his mouth, chopping up his enemies! Odd that we would see the image of peace metaphorically, but the image of wrath literally—a pattern of error evident throughout the ages, I might add.

When the Bible speaks in a metaphor, to understand its message, we must read it and interpret it as metaphor. This sloppy propensity to literalize metaphors is a major reason why so much misunderstanding about 'wrath' (i.e., 'God's wrath') persists. As the church father, John Cassian once said,

> And so, since these things cannot without horrible sacrilege be literally understood of him who is declared by the authority of Holy Scripture to be invisible, ineffable, incomprehensible, simple, and uncomposite, the disturbance of anger (not to mention wrath) cannot be attributed to that immutable nature without monstrous blasphemy.[1]

'Stage 2 faith'

Fowler's stage two or *mythic-literal faith* appeals to black-and-white / either-or thinking appropriate to early childhood. Stage two faith is most likely to read metaphors literally.

This error is often cute in children – but silly and hazardous in adults with religious or political influence.

When biblical metaphors are read as if they were meant literally, the texts where God intervenes with smoldering vengeance are offensive because they portray a God of personal wrath through violent force—the willful *über-Gott* (super-god or over-god) who is far more pagan than Christian. Whenever we literalize metaphors, we end up blaming either the Bible or God for being nasty. But what is the real problem? The issue is neither the so-called 'God of the Old Testament' (which one?), nor the Bible itself but, rather, our own simplistic literalism—a developmental stage that we urgently need to grow beyond.

Beyond stage two faith

James W. Fowler, in *Stages of Faith,* describes spiritual development in a series of steps from 0 to 6. I will summarize them here:[2]

- **Stage 0** – *"Primal or Undifferentiated"* faith (birth to 2 years). Early learning of the safety of their environment (i.e. warmth, safety and security v. hurt, neglect and abuse).

- **Stage 1** – *"Intuitive-Projective"* faith (3 to 7 years). Unprotected exposure to the unconscious. Faith is learned mainly through experiences, stories, images, and other people.

- **Stage 2** – *"Mythic-Literal"* faith (school children). Strong belief in the justice and reciprocity of the universe, and their gods are anthropomorphic. Metaphors and symbolic language are often misunderstood and taken literally.

- **Stage 3** – *"Synthetic Conventional"* faith (adolescence; 12 years to adult). Conformity to religious authority and development of a personal identity. Conflicts with beliefs are ignored out of fear because they threaten inconsistencies.

- **Stage 4** – *"Individuative-Reflective"* faith (mid-20's to late 30's). Angst and struggle. Taking personal responsibility for one's beliefs and feelings. Openness to a new complexity of faith, increased awareness of conflicts in one's belief.

- **Stage 5** – *"Conjunctive"* faith (aka mid-life crisis). Acknowledges paradox and transcendence, reality behind the symbols of inherited systems.

- **Stage 6** – *"Universalizing"* faith, or "enlightenment" (middle to late adulthood). Treats all people with compassion. Views people as part of a universal community, according to principles of love and justice.

What strikes me as very relevant to our understanding of wrath is Fowler's description of stage-two or 'mythic-literal' faith. This faith is found mostly in school children. It includes a strong belief in (retributive) 'justice' and reciprocity (cause-and-effect, eye-for-an-eye). The gods of stage-two faith are almost always *anthropomorphic* (i.e., given human traits, such as emotions—in this case, anger). Notice that during this stage, metaphors and symbolic language are often misunderstood and taken literally.

So there's the rub. When studying the Bible in search of God, we corner ourselves into childish errors whenever we forget that:

1. Many texts were written in stage-two *language*, but the Old Testament authors expected them to be interpreted metaphorically.

2. Even though Old Testament authors sometimes wrote from a stage-two *perspective* (i.e. when Judaism itself was mythic-literal faith), Jesus and the New Testament writers interpret them metaphorically through a *cruciform* lens.

Now imagine this: entire streams of Christendom are not only stuck at stage two faith, but actually train and require their ministers to interpret the Bible through the mythic-literal eyes of school children. Within such a religious culture, growing up and moving forward is rebranded as backsliding; maturing is perceived as falling away. Moreover, this problem is common to both fundamentalist faith and anti-faith alike.

'Freedom'

Debates continue as to whether 'free will' is a reality or a delusion. What we call 'freedom' is often the illusion of autonomy and our own self-will.

Real 'freedom' is:
a. God's loving consent to our authentic otherness; and,

b. the flourishing that results from giving our consent to God's care for our lives.

For example, swaths of ex-Christians and anti-faith activists oppose Christian faith because like their counterpart opponents, they too read and then reject Scripture as immature literalists.

Supertramp's "Logical Song," comes to mind, describing this precise problem. The song was a theme of mine as a child and now seems to have taken on prophetic relevance! The first verse describes the wonder and awe of a childhood filled with beauty and magic. But then,

> They sent me away to teach me how to be sensible,
> logical, responsible, practical.

Things accelerate downward from there—a descent from dependability into clinical sterility, the calcification of imagination, and finally, the death of hope in fashionable cynicism. The end game: politely play your role as a 'vegetable.' And woe to those who buck the system:

> Now watch what you say or they'll be calling you a radical,
> liberal, fanatical, criminal.

The dilemma described in these lyrics emerges when stage two believers and unbelievers alike pound the lectern, the pulpit or the blogosphere! Metaphors become literal, human experiences are deified and our wrath is projected onto God's character. We get stuck there. Yet we can and must grow beyond these immature stages of spiritual development.

By reading the Bible's judgment narratives through the lens of *cruciform* consent—through the Cross—we will begin to understand the wrath metaphor. And we will be equipped to retrieve rather than dismiss the so-called 'toxic texts' of the Bible. In later chapters, we will even see their genius and purpose.

At this point, I want to model how to talk about God's love and wrath in terms of consent and the Cross—I will demonstrate how I would address the problem of wrath to Evangelicals, who tend to be most vulnerable to stage two myth-literalism, and to post-Evangelical skeptics who reject the Bible as repellent because they too continue to read it woodenly. The following bullet points synthesize what we've learned about the *cruciform* God. They describe God's love above and beyond wrath, where "mercy triumphs over judgment" (James. 2:13).

The lens of cruciform consent

- God is good.

- God is love.

- God is not violent, because he never does violence directly.

- In his love, God will *not* bring about his ends through violent means.

- In refusing to exercise violence, God nevertheless consents to our freedom, a gift we abuse through violence.

- His love consents to our **freedom,*** even when used in violence against each other and against God.

- God's consent is *not* complicity.

- But God may *appear* complicit in our violence because God allows it; God consents to it and consents to us. In love, God bears the guilt of maintaining covenant relationships with violent people.

- When God refuses to apply force, might and violence but, instead, consents to the free rein of our rebellion and its bitter and violent fruit, God seems violent in his consent.

- Our blood is on God's hands, just as God's blood was on our hands.

- In love, God consents to undergoing and enduring our wrath on the Cross.
- He consents to allowing our wrath against 'Rome.'
- He consents to allowing Rome's wrath against us.
- *His consent is wrath.*
- *His consent is love.*

What have we seen in Scripture and in our experience? First, that God in his love grants authentic freedom to humanity and to the natural (and supernatural[3]) forces of the world. God in his wrath also consents to permit, and not spare, the powerful consequences of these forces to take their course. And so, in the Bible, where we see or hear of God's wrath, what we actually witness is God's nonviolent, *cruciform* consent—the painful results of God letting us have our way.

Intrinsic wrath

In his books and blogs, Pastor Gregory Boyd describes this severe consent as *organic* or *intrinsic judgment*. These terms correlate well with what I've described as *wrath-as-consent*. Boyd teaches that the judgment of sin is not an externally applied penalty by a divine judge. God doesn't actively investigate, arrest, convict, sentence and punish sinners. There's no need and, in fact, that's not God's heart at all. Here's the bottom line: sin carries its own penalty (or 'wages' in Rom. 6:23) because consequences are built into the fabric of the universe. This is what Boyd means by saying wrath is organic or intrinsic. So there is some truth to stage two, cause-and-effect faith, isn't there? But it's not that my sin literally **causes** God to be angry and provokes God's judgments. Rather, that sin itself is harmful to us and to others. What we need is a Savior-God who rescues us from ourselves, our sin and its consequences

Boyd describes the process this way: God in his patience allows sin to go on and on. His mercy continues until he must finally with-draw it. Finally, God pulls back his mercy and gives us over to our self-destructive stubbornness. Here is where Boyd and I differ.

First, I don't believe 'surd' evil (random and irrational suffer-ing), or third party evil (abuse, assault or killing) continues simply because of the patience of God with a situation he could stop at any time, either by intervention or by withdrawing his mercy from the wicked. Wouldn't that be nice. But if it were so, I think most would agree that God is far too patient. If a loving father could just step in and stop it, then he would. But he doesn't.

Second, I don't believe it is ever God's choice to withdraw mercy. Scripture describes mercy as an everlasting, unfailing attri-bute of God. His open-handed mercies endure forever! Psalm 136 says so twenty-six times in twenty-six verses, even when the phrase describes an act of wrath (such a the plagues of Egypt in v. 10)! It strikes me, then, that our *experience* of divine mercy must therefore also somehow be intrinsic—contingent on our willingness to receive it … or rebuff it. But from God's side, his mercy is not given at times and revoked at others; it is always available.

As I said in the previous chapter, I first learned this truth in the children's chorus, "The steadfast love of the Lord never ceases; his mercies never come to an end." But wait a moment: that song was directly quoting the Book of Lamentations! In both cases—Psalm 136 and Lamentations 3—when we invoke the language of wrath, God's Spirit slips in the message of enduring mercy, not as a contra-diction, but as a counter-narrative (i.e., God's alternative viewpoint). Exactly when the psalmist or the prophet describes an experience of the consequences of sin as God's wrath, they also recall the cov-enant faithfulness of God to the great news promise: the river of God's grace *never* stops flowing. The sun shines and the rain falls generously on both the righteous and unrighteous, including the sunshine and rainfall of God's sweet mercies.

When mercy is hidden and the wrath of self-destruction begins to play out, rather than assuming God's patience has run out as if he's decided, "Okay, enough mercy; now I'm *choosing* to withdraw mercy to release the wrath," what if it is really we who make that choice, consciously or unconsciously? What if the valve that shuts off mercy is intrinsic in the same way wrath is? In fact, what if it's the very same thing?

Cliffs, ditches & an ecstatic Shepherd

If, for example, I come to the edge of a cliff, but nevertheless ignore the warning signs, climb over the fence and slip off into the abyss to my death, at what point did God strike me down in his wrath? Never! And at what point did God withdraw his mercy? Never! But in choosing to step beyond the invitation of grace into the laws of gravity, I experience the consequences of my own defiance. My free agency coupled with cause and effect creates results. And God doesn't directly interfere—people everywhere cross boundaries every day and God grants us that dignity, even if it leads to our demise. God simply doesn't levitate us out of our choices or our world.

Greg Albrecht, who heads up Plain Truth Ministries, once served as Dean of Students at Ambassador

> ### 'Wrath'
>
> Literal human 'wrath' combines emotional anger with violent retribution. We describe the 'wages of sin' (self-destructive consequences) as 'the wrath of God' because we infer sin's consequences as God's reaction. In actuality, biblical wrath is a metaphor. It signifies the intrinsic consequences of our refusal to live in the mercies of God.

College. He had a plaque sitting on his desk, facing two chairs that often contained squirming students who were called into his office. It read, "I have no right to deny you the consequences of your actions." God does have that right, but he laid it down from the beginning, offering instead his enduring mercy to those who willingly receive it. So there is a *law* of consequence (wrath) along with a *gift* of mercy, intrinsic to God's good order.

Thus, God consents, but remember, there is so much more. God also *participates*. This is super-important. Yes, our heavenly Father allows, but he is also truly good and he cares, so the above scenario is incomplete. On its own, that would amount to a life under the law—and that's not the whole story. Beyond gravity there truly is grace. God is continually and mercifully recruiting and sending willing helpers in an attempt to warn, to rescue and to redeem us from our many slips. In my own foolishness, I have known the injuries—to myself and to others—that come with playing beyond the edge of God-given wisdom. I have repeatedly stumbled into self-inflicted gullies of painful thorns. And what did God do? Jesus tells us in the Gospel of Luke:

> [4] What man among you, if he has a hundred sheep and has lost one of them, does not leave the ninety-nine in the open pasture and go after the one which is lost until he finds it? [5] When he has found it, he lays it on his shoulders, rejoicing. [6] And when he comes home, he calls together his friends and his neighbors, saying to them, 'Rejoice with me, for I have found my sheep which was lost!' (Luke 15:4-6 NASB)

During one of my meetings with my spiritual director, we talked about my anxieties—my insecurity and vulnerability, nervousness about whether I could depend on God to keep me from falling (Jude 1:24) back into the dark ditches that once held me. Steve took me to this parable and had me shift my focus away from the spiritual vertigo of hovering at the cliff-top. Steve reminded me that when I had already fallen, Jesus came after me and looked for me until he found me. And having found me, he carried me on his shoulders, rejoicing. And he brought me home, called his friends and neighbors, and he celebrated me! The parable speaks about his motivation: he longs for me and desires me with sheer joy! He has not always prevented my willful disasters, but he has repeatedly welcomed me into the Father's banquet of redemption and mercy.

Waypoint summary

Like hikers who halt briefly at a waypoint to catch their breath, we're now ready to pause and collate these thoughts before a chapter-break recess. We've covered a lot of territory with some steep elevation gain. We can now distill what we've learned into a precise definition of wrath that holds mercy in mind. **Wrath*** *is a metaphor for the intrinsic consequences of our refusal to live in the mercies of God.* To review:

- God's mercies endure forever. He never shuts them off.
- When mercy gives way to wrath, it must be that we ourselves hit the off-switch and rebuffed mercy through our sinful acts. Tragically, our rejection of mercy harms not only ourselves, but others who may wonder why God is punishing them, when in fact it is our sin that hurts them.
- God is never arbitrary about who receives his mercy and who doesn't. He never withdraws his mercy. But the enduring mercy of God can be received or refused.
- This experience is organic, intrinsic to the nature of things, to human freedom and to our capacity to turn toward or away from God's grace.

- Where intrinsic wrath abounds, active mercy abounds all the more! Our happy Shepherd seeks and finds us, carries us and rejoices over his found sheep.

We're now ready for the next leg of the trek, in which we look at how the Bible frames wrath in the language of 'giving over.'

Pausing to think

- When life is difficult, do you imagine that God is displeased with you or even punishing you? How did you come to that conclusion?
- How does the idea of God's intrinsic wrath strike you? What if *sin* is the real punisher, rather than God?
- Why would God 'give us over' to ourselves, to our sins or to our enemies? Is God being aloof? Does he care? How does God's care show up in your life?
- Sin hurts us. This is the law of sowing and reaping. But why do the innocent suffer? If we assume suffering is a sign of reaping consequences, aren't we making the same mistake Job's friends made?
- If mercy—not wrath—endures forever, what are the implications?

Pausing to pray

God, when I blew it and suffered the consequences, I often pointed the finger at you. I blamed you for punishing me. I assumed you were 'wrathing' me. In truth, you've been inexplicably kind—merciful without fail. For those who suffer the 'wrath' of their own choices, grant the same mercy you gave me. Lord, let it be!

Divine Wrath as Giving Over 11

> *"He conquered the wrath*
> *not by strength of body and not by force of arms,*
> *but by his word he subdued the punisher,*
> *appealing to the promises and covenants*
> *given to our fathers."*
> – Wisdom of Solomon 18:22 –

> *"I am Jesus whom thou persecutest:*
> *it is hard for thee to kick against the pricks."*
> – Jesus to Saul of Tarsus (Acts 26:14 KJV) –

What of God's active wrath?

In chapter 11, we discussed God's wrath in terms of consent—a passive wrath in which we're allowed to stumble over the boulders of our own choices. But what about God's *active* wrath? Doesn't the Bible—and even Jesus!—sometimes describe God as an angry and offended King who reacts violently toward sin? Doesn't the Bible explicitly assign active wrath to God's account?

For example, did not God slaughter Egypt's firstborn (Exod. 12)? Did God not massacre the Jewish grumblers in the wilderness (Num. 26)? Did God not incinerate Sodom and Gomorrah (Gen. 19)? Did God not repeatedly reduce Jerusalem to smoking rubble (Jeremiah 52)? And even in the New Testament, did God not strike down Ananias and Sapphira at Peter's feet (Acts 5) or eat Herod alive with worms (Acts 12:23)?

No.

And Yes.

First, no. Were these acts of violent intervention by an angry and punitive God who was reacting to sin? No. When the Bible becomes specific about the immediate causes of death, they are attributed to natural events, such as diseases, earthquakes (the ground), serpents or fire raining from the sky (volcanic eruptions). And who or what are the active agents and spiritual forces behind these disasters? Scripture either says or assumes they reflect the work of 'the Destroyer,' angelic or human agents of violence, or Satan (Gen. 19:13; Exod. 12:23; Jer. 4:7; Acts 5:3; 1 Cor. 10:9–10). God's wrath is metaphorical and passive, but his active participation is directed toward protecting and redeeming his people, mediated through willing partners who consent through repentance, surrender or intercession (e.g., the bartering Abraham does in Gen. 18, or Moses in Exod. 33).

Who incited David?

As God is increasingly unveiled as life-giver rather than death-dealer, the biblical authors reflect this perspective more and more, becoming ever more careful to assert that God is not to blame. A simple example of this shift appears when David counts his armies. In the earlier version of the story, we read, "Again the anger of the Lord burned against Israel, and he incited David against them, saying, 'Go and take a census of Israel and Judah'" (1 Sam. 24:1). As David makes his plans, Joab resists. Something is wrong here! Don't do it, David! (v. 3).

But David overrules Joab and takes the census. Immediately David regrets his decision. Though God had supposedly instigated the census, David felt ashamed, and says, "I have sinned greatly by what I have done. Lord, I beg you to forgive me, your servant, because I have been very foolish" (v. 10). Why is it a sin if the Lord was behind it? At least David repents so the Lord can forgive him. But wait—instead of forgiving David, the Lord gives him three choices: three years of famine in Israel, three months of David having to flee his enemies, or three days of disease on the land (v. 13).

David responds, "I am in great trouble. Let the LORD punish us, because the LORD is *very merciful*. Don't let my punishment come from human beings!" So, we read, "The Lord sent a terrible disease on Israel" (v. 15). Yet oddly, an angel appears and raises his hand to trigger the plague. The angelic plague continues until seventy thousand people are dead from Dan to Beersheba! How was this plague "very merciful"?

At this point, the biblical text says the angel turns to strike Jerusalem, but God starts having regrets. The narrator puts it this way: "The LORD felt *very sorry* about the terrible things that had happened. He said to the angel who was destroying the people, 'That is enough! Put down your arm!'" (v. 16) But it is not until David buys a threshing floor, builds an altar, and offers burnt sacrifices and fellowship offering to the Lord that the disease runs its course.

Does God's judgment seem harsh to you? The 1 Samuel account says that God was angry, so he provokes David to sin and then destroys 70,000 people as punishment. I think that's harsh. Am I balking because I'm too sentimental? If you think it's troubling, you're in good company. The author of 1 Chronicles does too! And in a critique of this perspective, he retells the story with one enormous difference. Who inspires the census? The Lord? No! The chronicler says, "*Satan* rose up against Israel and incited David to take a census of Israel" (1 Chron. 21:1).

While the story still presents us with serious difficulties concerning wrath and punishment, don't miss this worldview-shaking change in perspective. The chronicler rejects the earlier version in 1 Samuel that God incited David, and puts the blame on Satan instead! One thousand years later, the Book of James confirms this correction: "No one should say, 'God is tempting me.' For God cannot be tempted by evil, nor does he tempt anyone; but each person is tempted when they are dragged away by their own evil desire and enticed" (Jms. 1:13-14). God is not to blame.

How Paul reworks wrath

What the chronicler hints at, the Apostle Paul establishes as a principle. More than any other author, he demonstrates how Christians are to read these texts after the revelation of God in Christ.

For example, in Numbers 16, 21 and 25, the children of Israel rebel against Moses' leadership, grumble against the Lord, and then 'play the harlot' with the 'daughters of Moab.' In these stories, the narrator says that plagues of judgment came upon the people, with body-counts in the five-digit range! The author clearly says that *God sent these plagues*. He killed them. This angle on events is a good example of Fowler's stage two mythic-literal storytelling, as mentioned earlier.

However, in 1 Corinthians 10, reflecting on these stories, the Apostle Paul explains,

> [9] Nor let us try the Lord, as some of them did, and were *destroyed by the serpents*. [10] Nor grumble, as some of them did, and were *destroyed by the destroyer*. [11] Now these things happened to them as an example, and they were written for our instruction, upon whom the ends of the ages have come. (1 Cor. 10:9-11)

Paul is careful here to distinguish: yes, the people tested God, but what actually killed them? First of all, sin. And 'the serpents.' And 'the destroyer.' Paul's warning is not, "God will get you," but that the intrinsic consequences of sin opens the door for 'serpents' or 'the destroyer' to lay waste to our lives. Notice that even when citing an Old Testament text that only mentions God as the cause of the plagues, Paul still accredits destruction to the destroyer. To

Paul, where wrath appears, Satan is the destroyer and God is not. God is the redeemer.

Why does Paul assume this? How did this become a general principle in Pauline theology? The easy answer is that Paul had experienced the revelation of God in Christ, including this overarching truth: "The thief comes only to steal and kill and destroy. I have come that they may have life, and have it to the full. I am the good shepherd. The good shepherd lays down his life for the sheep" (John 10:10-11). Since God is manifest perfectly in Christ—the Lord whom Paul met on the road to Damascus—he could read Hebrew Scripture through that abiding lens.

To take this thought one further step, we know that first century Jews were into the book called

'The destroyer'

In some Old Testament stories, there is often little distinction between 'the wrath of God' and the violence of 'the destroyer.' The 'destroyer' is virtually God's 'hitman,' sent on missions to keep God's hands clean.

But Jesus and Paul draw a sharp distinction: God is always a life-giver and redeemer. Satan is the death-dealer and destroyer.

Wisdom of Solomon. We know it was part of the Greek translation of the Hebrew Bible (called the Septuagint, or LXX for short), which New Testament authors such as Luke used and quoted in Jesus' day. We know that it was considered part of the Christian Bible by most churches until the Reformation (and still is by many today).

We can observe Paul's engagement with Wisdom of Solomon throughout the book of Romans, since his opponents were trying to use it against him.[1] Moreover, we know that Paul read Wisdom through the template of the gospel of Jesus.

I say that to emphasize the importance and popularity of the book in first century Judaism and Christianity—and in the mind of Paul—because it makes a clear distinction between the destroyer and God, and sees God's Messiah as the deliverer who overcomes the destroyer. Reading Wisdom of Solomon through Christ; look how beautiful it is:

> [20] Yea, the tasting of death touched the righteous also, and there was a destruction of the multitude in the wilderness: but the wrath endured not long.
>
> [21] For then *the blameless man* made haste, and stood forth to defend them; and bringing the shield of his proper ministry, even prayer, and the propitiation of incense, *set himself against the wrath*, and so brought the calamity to an end, declaring that he was thy servant.
>
> [22] So he *overcame the destroyer*, not with strength of body, nor force of arms, but *with a word subdued him that punished*, alleging the oaths and covenants made with the fathers.
>
> [23] For when the dead were now fallen down by heaps one upon another, standing between, *he stayed the wrath*, and parted the way to the living.
>
> [24] For in the long garment was the whole world, and in the four rows of the stones was the glory of the fathers graven, and thy Majesty upon the diadem of his head.
>
> [25] Unto these *the destroyer gave place, and was afraid* of them: for it was enough that they only tasted of the wrath.
>
> (Wisd. of Sol. 18:20-25 KJV)

Excuse the old English, but in terms of the Messianic promises, it doesn't get much better than that! Look at the parallels in these verses. The Messiah—our Jesus—is:

- the blameless man;
- the defender;
- the overcomer;
- the servant;
- the crowned one.

Look at his victory:

- he stayed the wrath;
- he overcame the destroyer;
- he subdued the punisher.

Notice the identifications: the wrath is equivalent to the destroyer and the punisher. Is Jesus overcoming and subduing God? Of course not! Is God the wrath-spewing, people-destroying punisher? Not in this passage! And not in Paul's mind. So, did God's wrath destroy so many?

No.

But also, yes. Indirectly. These were acts of God's wrath in that God consented to allow natural and supernatural destruction to take its course through events set in motion by human decisions. In that sense, God is seen to have 'sent' the destroyer and 'sent' the destruction. God is perceived as commissioning the destruction and even the destroyer (Gen. 19:14; Exod. 12:29; Num. 21:6). But again, Paul to the rescue!

Wrath as 'giving over'

Paul clarifies throughout Romans 1: what had been described in the narrative as active wrath is in fact a metaphor. He defines 'wrath' three times as the 'giving over' (God's consent) of rebellious people to their own self-destructive trajectories—even when the shrapnel of our actions accrues collateral damage on others. Watch carefully:

[18] For the wrath of God is revealed from heaven against all ungodliness and unrighteousness of men who suppress the truth in unrighteousness, ...

[24] Therefore God *gave them over* in the lusts of their hearts to impurity, ...

[26] For this reason God *gave them over* to degrading passions; ... [28] And just as they did not see fit to acknowledge God any longer, God *gave them over* to a depraved mind, to do those things which are not proper, ...

(Romans 1:18, 24, 26, 28 NASB)

Nor is this only a New Testament discovery. Although Isaiah uses a lot of myth-literal language, he seems fully aware that God's wrath is a metaphor, and clarifies on a number of occasions. In the Book of Isaiah we read, "No one calls on your name or strives to lay hold of you; for you have hidden your face from us and have *given us over* to our sins" (Isa. 64:7). This giving over is played out in the exile, as Jerusalem is *given over* to her enemies.

Now in Romans, Paul wants to make this fact clear in a decisive way. We read in Romans 5:

[8] But God demonstrates His own love toward us, in that while we were yet sinners, Christ died for us. [9] Much more then, having now been justified by His blood, we shall be saved from the wrath *of God* through Him. (Rom. 5:8-9 NASB)

Did you notice the italicized phrase 'of God' inserted there? Yes, *inserted*. By now, readers may have noticed that I use italics for emphasis a lot—C.S. Lewis (and my editor) would say too much. I do this to highlight points I want readers to focus on. All of the italics in this book, including those within quotes, indicate *my* emphasis—I put them there. Except here. The italicized phrase *"of God"* in the New American Standard Bible is the translators' way of letting you know they added the phrase. No manuscript includes those words. The verse literally ends, "we shall be saved through him *from the wrath*." Translators add "God's wrath," or, "wrath from God" or "wrath of God," because, they say, it is *understood.* Other translations, like the New International Version, insert "of God" without any indication that they placed it there, either in italics or a marginal note. They assume it belongs.

God's wrath is *understood?* Really? By whom? And why? The translators' assumption is that they can and should insert the words, 'of God,' though they are not found in the manuscripts, nor implied by the grammar. We are to accept the translators' own interpretation, passed on to readers, that Paul meant Jesus saves us from the wrath of God, even though Paul certainly did *not* say 'wrath *of God.*' Neither, I would suggest, is that his meaning in context.

What Paul actually says is that God through Christ was saving us from the wrath. Period. We are not to believe that Jesus is saving us from God the Father, but from the consequences intrinsic to sin itself, namely death. In the next chapter, the Apostle of Grace could not lay out the contrast more clearly: "For the wages of sin is death, but the free gift of God is eternal life in Christ Jesus our Lord" (Rom. 6:23 NASB). We rattle that verse off from memory too quickly, don't we? Let's double-check:

- Who is rescuing us? God.
- What does God rescue us from? The wages (or consequences) of sin.
- What consequences does God rescue us from? Death.
- What do we receive *not* from God? We do not receive the wages or consequences of sin from God.
- What do we receive from God? We receive a free gift.
- What free gift do we receive? Salvation. Resurrection. Eternal life.
- How? Through Jesus Christ.

So yes, God rescues us from 'the wrath,' from sin, from death. Wrath then, is not the punishment of God but our experience of the intrinsic and fatal consequences of sin—of rejecting God's mercy. Yes, the pigpen was the punishment, the wrath, the consequences. Of what? Of the prodigal son's own selfish choices. And in love, yes, the Father consents and gives him over—gives *us* over until we are done. Then when we're done, we come back like the prodigal son and get what? Punishment? No. Wrath? No. When we come back, God welcomes us and gives us a free gift: eternal life!

In Romans 5, who is the agent of salvation? Whose love is at work? Who is forgiving and reconciling sinners? God! God is the agent of salvation through Christ. And what is God saving us from? Himself? No. In Romans 5, does God say or even imply, "I love you so much that I will save you from myself?" No. God saves us from 'the wrath'—period.

Is God's consent complicity?

Still, what of those who challenge God: "How can you allow this? Is your permission—your giving over—not tantamount to complicity?"

And the answer, at some level, is probably yes. If not complicit, God has accepted ultimate responsibility as the First Cause of it all—such that some biblical authors do use the phrase 'wrath of God' to describe what are technically secondary consequences. Ultimately, this is God's good order and God is finally responsible for all that is, including intrinsic consequences for our abuse of freedom. I have called this wrath as giving over or wrath as *cruciform* consent.

Wrath as consent is the great and terrible price of God's plan and God's *cruciform* nature, but it is not the whole story. God has also chosen to redeem and restore the world through his love. Redeeming the world through love, instead of taking it by violent conquest, means allowing horrible things to happen that, from the our limited human perspective, make God look both wrathful and weak all at once. The cognitive dissonance (i.e., 'brain freeze') we feel cannot be resolved rationally. Instead, we have looked in wonder to the Cross—a tree of love and life, not a tree of keen arguments and answers. On that Cross, we witness God's nonviolent consent.

God's nonviolent consent extends to the whole of natural and spiritual reality. It includes nonviolent consent to human freedom, for good or ill. It includes nonviolent consent to the laws of nature, for beauty or tragedy, creation or destruction. It includes nonviolent consent to spiritual laws of sowing and reaping, blessing and cursing. In this sense, God's consent means that God has renounced the exercise of his Almighty capacities in this world.

The Lamb slain from the foundation of the world died to being all-powerful before Creation. This *kenotic* self-renunciation has made space for creation. For freedom and for violence. For genocide and hurricanes and car accidents and pedophiles.

But also for love.

Intrinsic love

God's nonviolent consent and self-emptying love make space for natural law and human freedom to function freely. These same attributes also convey God's superabundant love into the world, manifest to and through humankind as divine care.

God has woven supernatural love into the very fabric of the world; a love that not only consents to violence but also subverts and overcomes violence. Far from feeble in this nonviolent consent, God's love is powerful—*all*-powerful! In fact, it's the only conceivable power that can make all things right and new. God's love does not need to violate the freedom or the laws of that which exists by suspending natural and spiritual order, because love is the ground of all that exists. Love is part of that order—its essential heart. At the top of that order is humanity, with the created capacity to be like God, that is, to consent to bear and seed God's supernatural love throughout all of creation.

Somehow, though, we know—we see with our own eyes and hear with our own ears—something is broken, has ruptured. All of creation and, most of all, humanity groans under an affliction whereby God's consent to violence seems to enslave us rather than free us. Or perhaps God's loving consent to our freedom has born the fruit of violence rather than love. Our very freedom has become the violent means of our slavery.

From that point of view, God seems cruel, whether through absence or complicity. God seems impotent, for how can God possibly mend a breach that God's love and our freedom ultimately created?

Thanks be to God, at the pinnacle of humanity stands Jesus Christ. His nonviolent consent to the Cross—the intersection of humanity's affliction (our freedom-to-violence) and God's radical forgiveness—becomes the occasion whereby supernatural love flows through God's own wounds into the world. God's love, far from being weak or impotent, will eclipse violence, might and force as the relentless catalyst for the renewal of the world.

The Lordship of Christ (or the Kingdom of God) over the world and the universe is not contradictory to God's nonviolent consent. In fact, consent is precisely (and only) how God's love is released in the world. For example, in the Gospels, Christ did not operate in the power of miraculous interventions (the magical suspension of laws), but in the authority of supernatural love (the application of God's highest law).

God's Kingdom does not advance through violence, freedom-violating force or law-breaking interventions. God's kingdom reign is the expression of supernatural love in and through those who consent to being indwelt and transformed by Christ-mediated love. Here we are not merely talking about enthusiastic activists performing good and loving works. Neither is this consent restricted to card-carrying Christ-followers. Rather, this consent is defined in 1 John 4:7–8: "Dear friends, let us love one another, for love comes from God. Everyone who loves has been born of God and knows God. Whoever does not love does not know God, because God is love."

Through their own nonviolent consent, those who love as Christ did (knowingly or not, cf. Matt. 25:37-40) may appear as torn veils or cracked vessels (2 Cor. 4:7–18), but through their wounds, supernatural love pours its healing light into natural realm, permeating the world.

God consents to our reluctance to consent, resulting in this painfully slow but inexorable transfiguration of our violent world.

Love will have its way, because while it may look like passive consent to extreme violence, it is nevertheless "stronger than death, more jealous than the grave, more vehement than a flame. Many waters cannot quench love, nor floods drown it" (Song of Sol. 8:6–7). The death and resurrection of Christ are the firstfruits of the destiny God's love has arranged for the whole universe.

Is God an angry King?*

Even so, the critics are right: the Kingdom of God in Hebrew Scripture often describes a violent and willful God of wrath. Instead of dismissing the critics or the texts too quickly, a *cruciform* interpretation allows us to investigate three broad possibilities. I will illustrate these with the phrase, "God, the King who is angry," and comment on each approach.

1. God may actually be an angry King.

Maybe God did actively decree that Israel should go to war, obliterate and enslave their enemies, or suffer God's wrath through those enemies. In this view, Jesus comes to introduce a New Covenant, altering how God deals with people in the New Kingdom. But this common Evangelical interpretation falls short of the eternally *cruciform* God who was, is and always will be the perfection of goodness and love. If these texts are taken literally, they fall far short of the image of Christ, really are toxic and ought to be discarded.

But if we read these same texts through Christ's revelation of the *cruciform* God, the biblical passages that describe God's anger and violence could prove supremely valuable as inspired warnings of how God's people continue to worship their own shadows and baptize their own violence, all in the name of God. This thought directs us to a second possibility.

2. God may not be an angry King at all.

Maybe the Old Testament characters and authors infer God's emotions, reactions and destruction through their own cultural and political filters that misrepresent the nature of God. In this view, Jesus calls us to an entirely new way of thinking (a *metanoia*, repentance) about God. Jesus reveals the true nature of the Kingdom of God, not as an overbearing, militant empire but as *shalom*: a culture of harmony, wholeness and peace.

In this view, God has never been a coercive emperor. We must never diminish the Spirit of living Love and our *cruciform* King to an idol of our own anthropomorphisms. That is, we must refuse to attribute imperfect and finite human attributes to a perfect and infinite God as if they were literal descriptions. If so, the question arises: when the Bible describes God as an angry king, should we simply ignore it? Or ought we make an effort to extract divine truth from errant human projections?

Sometimes, Jesus simply made use of such texts by way of contrast, "You have heard that it has been said … but I say to you" (Matt. 5:21, 38). In those passages, he doesn't cleverly work out some hidden meaning: he simply demonstrates the superior authority of his own incarnational revelation. Jesus usually shows us that God is not an angry king at all. He portrays God as a gracious and loving Father.

I say usually because at other times, Jesus is not afraid to use the metaphor of a wrathful king in his parables. One example is the parable of the unmerciful servant in Matt. 18:21-35. The parable ends:

> ³⁴ In anger his master handed him over to the jailers to be tortured, until he should pay back all he owed. ³⁵ "This is how my heavenly Father will treat each of you unless you forgive your brother or sister from your heart."

What's going on here? Is this how Jesus sees God? Is he slipping into the old violent ways of imagining God? I don't believe so. Especially not after just telling Peter that God requires us to forgive seventy times seven! (Matt. 18:21–22)

> ### Is God an angry King?
>
> Even though Jesus employs angry and vengeful kings in some parables, this reflects the nature of kings rather than the nature of God.
>
> On the Cross, Christ trumps the angry king metaphor with a far better and more life-giving picture— the crucified King of enduring love.

More likely, Jesus is intentionally borrowing his listeners' own common misunderstanding of God—God the angry king—and he uses it ironically. He will finally subvert that false image with the truth of the Cross, where as King of Glory, he forgives seventy times seven billion. And as Judge of the World, he delivers a verdict of superabundant pardon rather than never-ending torture.

3. God may be a metaphorically angry King.

Still, when we read the angry King texts, we must concede that sometimes God's so-called wrath is not simply a misunderstanding, but rather, a metaphor. As we've seen, the vocabulary of wrath points to the reality that God's loving rule includes *consent* to our self-destructive ways and their consequences. The cruciform King is not *literally* an angry monarch seething from his heavenly throne, but we do experience wrath as God's passive and indirect consent to the destructive forces of necessity. The wrath texts thus serve as urgent warnings of real and destructive consequences, but are not to be literalized as direct threats from a volatile divine death-dealer.

In this view, like Jeremiah the prophet, Jesus also freely but advisedly uses the metaphor of an angry master in some of his parables—a concession to our conceptions of wrath—because deadly consequences really were in the works. At the end of Matthew 24:50-51, Jesus says,

> [50] The master of that servant will come on a day when he does not expect him and at an hour he is not aware of. [51] He will *cut him to pieces* and assign him a place with the hypocrites, where there will be *weeping and gnashing of teeth*.

Really? Are we to understand that our heavenly Father will do this violence? Or Christ himself? No! But in rejecting Christ, the religious establishment was sealing the fate of Jerusalem. The angry master is again a metaphor for God's heartbroken consent. Their own sin would result in the Roman siege—a repeat of Lamentations. The graphic climax of the parable expresses the desperation of God's warnings. He has come in person to try to avert the wrath they would bring on themselves.

We can hear these desperate appeals from the Author of life, pleading tearfully with us—sometimes loudly—the way a parent cries out to a toddler who is running thoughtlessly into a busy street. If that parent hollers, is that anger? If that parent shouts, "Don't do that or you'll be killed!" is that wrath? If a car hits that child, did the parent cause it? No, but if the child reels into the traffic, weeping and wailing will surely follow, and that by the parents!

Matthew 24:45-51 goes further. The picture is not of a concerned parent, but of a vindictive master. That's disconcerting, but less so when we bear in mind three particulars:

- The wrath of the master in the parable points not to what God will do to them, but what Rome will do to them once they reject their own Messiah-King.

- The master in the parable is not Jesus' image (or this Gospel's image) of God; Jesus himself is.

- The punchline of all Jesus' parables is *not* the wrath of God, but rather the mystery of mercy, grace and forgiveness revealed in the death and resurrection of Christ.

Wrath as love and consent in 'real life'

Before we close this chapter, we need to ask ourselves what the wrath of love and consent looks like in 'real life.' If wrath is a metaphor for intrinsic consequences, what does that look like and how does the Savior enter the picture? To think about this question, let's use two stories—one old and famous, the other contemporary and personal.

1. The conversion of Saul of Tarsus.

When I think about intrinsic wrath, I recall Jesus' statement to Paul, "It's hard for you to kick against the goads." Allow me to recall the incident. In the book of Acts, we hear the testimony of the Apostle Paul's conversion three times, indicating how important that event was to him, to the early church and to us. The most complete version is found in Acts 26, where we read Paul's own recollections:

> [10] On the authority of the chief priests I put many of the Lord's people in prison, and when they were put to death, I cast my vote against them. [11] Many a time I went from one synagogue to another to have them punished, and I tried to force them to blaspheme. I was so obsessed with persecuting them that I even hunted them down in foreign cities.
>
> [12] "On one of these journeys I was going to Damascus with the authority and commission of the chief priests. [13] About noon, King Agrippa, as I was on the road, I saw a light from heaven, brighter than the sun, blazing around me and my companions. [14] We all fell to the ground, and I heard a voice saying to me in Aramaic, *'Saul, Saul, why do you persecute me? It is hard for you to kick against the goads.'*
>
> [15] "Then I asked, 'Who are you, Lord?'
>
> "'I am Jesus, whom you are persecuting,' the Lord replied. [16] 'Now get up and stand on your feet. I have appeared to you to appoint you as a servant and as a witness of what you have seen and will see of me. [17] I will rescue you from your own people and from the Gentiles. I am sending you to them [18] to open their eyes and turn them from darkness to light, and from the power of Satan to God, so that they may receive forgiveness of sins and a place among those who are sanctified by faith in me.'
> (Acts 26:10-18)

That phrase, "It is hard for you to kick against the goads," was common idiom similar to our expression, "Banging your head against the wall." It describes both the futility of one's stubbornness and basically says, "You're just hurting yourself." To kick against the goads ('spurs' or 'pricks' in the KJV) was an expression drawn from the rural image of a tiller's 'goad'—a pointy stick—which kept oxen in line as they worked the fields. Kicking the goad in order to resist the farmer was painful and pointless.

Prior to Paul, the Athenian tragedian Euripedes (480-406 BC) used the same expression to describe the futility of resisting the gods. In his poem, *Bacchae*, we hear Dionysius say, "I would sacrifice to the god rather than kick against his spurs in anger, a mortal against a god."[2] In other words, divine discipline (or wrath) was experienced, not as active retribution by an angry god, but as the hurts caused by our own angry resistance—our 'kicking.'

Let's return to Saul of Tarsus. First, Jesus shows him that persecuting Jesus' church is resisting Jesus. Second, he shows Saul that resisting Jesus is 'kicking against the goads.' In an email correspondence with Sean Davidson[3] (a scholar, minister and theological sparring partner), he compares 'kicking the goads' to wrath as a metaphor:

> "Saul, Saul, why are you persecuting me? It hurts you to kick against the goads." This puts God's wrath in a different frame. Jesus is expressing regret that Saul is hurting himself in his misguided /perverted efforts to practice justice. If there was ever a time for wrath-as-violent-retribution, it would be in this moment when Paul was bent on destroying the church in its vulnerable infancy. There is an intervention, and there is a kind of violence about it, but accompanied by words of almost tender concern: "It hurts you ..."

What hurts him? Who hurts him? Kicking hurts. Kicking hurts the one kicking. This picture is what intrinsic wrath looks like in real time.

Sean continued,

Remember the words given to Ananias? "I myself will show him how much he must suffer for the sake of my name" (Acts 9:16). He eventually takes it as a privilege—even a joy—to suffer for the sake of Jesus' name. It's interesting how even that gets transformed in Paul's theology. This is somehow entirely different from the 'wrath' he was under when violently persecuting the church. In one respect, it's a more troubling kind of suffering, but it would be the sign of blessing given its connection to God's glory.

Indeed. A counter-wrath of martyrdom emerges in Jesus' death and also in the apostles' martyrdom (including Paul's beheading): instead of giving them over to sin, God gives them over to sinners—to the wrath of wicked men—and offers them up as living sacrifices of love to the world.

2. Strapping down Mark.

For our second sampling of wrath as consent, I give you exhibit-B, who I will call Mark. 'Leslie,' a friend of mine, sent an urgent message, concerned for her buddy Mark. She believed his life had spiraled out of control and that he had rejected God. She felt he had become delusional and self-destructive, to the point of driving his truck off a cliff. He did survive and yet no one—neither his local church, nor the hospital, nor even God—seemed to be intervening.

When I suggested we pray for Mark, Leslie expressed her anger at God. She said, "If God was here in front of me, I would scream at him and punch him in the face and kick him in the balls, if he even has any!" Well then! I asked her what she thought God should be doing about Mark. She replied, "He should strap him down and keep him there until he's better. That's what *I* would do."

I suggested that if God really worked that way, what a funny world this would be. Imagine all of the people all over the world strapped down! Where would we put them all? Who would take

care of them? How exactly would they get better? I am pretty sure
I'd be strapped down most of the time as well, completely against
my will.

But God loves us too much to be the Great Warden of a
global super-max penitentiary. He has chosen not to violate our
freedom—our authentic otherness—in this way. He has chosen
instead to reach out in love through caring friends such as Leslie,
inviting Mark to a better way. Who knows—perhaps it may even be
through a loving friend that Mark actually is buckled to a gurney in
a hospital until he gets well. In the meantime, I assured her, God is
not surprised, embarrassed or wounded by her anger. In fact, he has
even provided her with angry prayers to pray—such as Psalms 6 and
13—that allow her to lash out without fear that God will retaliate.
And so Leslie agreed to pray with me for Mark.

Ponder for a moment how wrath is at work in Mark's life. Is
God punishing Mark? No. After taking into account any mental,
emotional or chemical factors (God certainly does), wrath is a metaphor for Mark's own self-inflicted wounds of defiance. At this point,
he couldn't even escape such wrath by himself. The Savior will need
to get involved through loved ones who consent to truly help, rather
than deny the problem or demand to fix it their own way. If Mark is
to survive, love will need to overtake wrath—and it could.

Ponder, also, how wrath is at work in Leslie. Even in her desire
to rescue Mark, she is offended that God works by consent. She
wants God to coerce, to interfere, to 'strap him down' in ways that
she would if she could but would never accept for herself. Her
anger at God's unwillingness to control others will run its course
if she consents to praying it through like David. But if not—if she
remains postured to 'kick God in the balls'—she too will know the
ongoing pain of Paul's kicking at the goads. This too is the wrath of
love and consent.

Summing up

The broader point in this chapter has been that a theology of *cruciform* consent helps us see the metaphor of God's wrath and the reality of God's love, both in the Bible and our experience. It really is all there in the story of the prodigal son: the Father consents to the son's stubborn defiance and selfish recklessness. In love, God lets him leave and gives him over to the wrath of sin. Then, when the son bottoms out, wakes up and heads home—when he consents to the Father's way—the Father welcomes him home with great joy and without shame. The party resumes!

This revelation—God's *cruciform* consent and participation—directs our focus back to the events and significance of Calvary. We are now ready to revisit the Cross for a fresh understanding of its meaning, with a special focus on what Christ decisively achieved.

Pausing to think

- In this chapter, we distinguished between God's passive wrath (giving over) and biblical accounts that describe God's active wrath. Do you think this distinction is actually found in God or could it be in the authors' perspectives?

- Is it fair to interpret stories of God's active wrath as metaphors for natural consequences? What are some examples?

- Even if God didn't directly 'smite' his rebellious people, we read that sometimes 'the destroyer' or 'an evil spirit' brought the destruction. Should we take these descriptions literally or are they sometimes metaphors as well?

- Can you think of some popular modern instances where religious fundamentalism assigned blame for a natural disaster to God? To Satan? To people?

- When you participate in acts of love, do you get a sense of God's partnership? What if you are mediating God's care in the world, alleviating the consequences of sin, just as Jesus did?

- When you partner with God in prayer, how do you deal with unanswered requests? Do you blame God? Do you blame yourself? What if you let go of blame and embrace the mystery of life?

Pausing to pray

God, it's difficult to understand your cruciform love. When you allow us space to live and love, we also find ways to fall and fail. How is it your love leads to life in the pigpen? But I'm starting to see how my own stubborn ego sabotages me. I don't need to be strapped down; I need to be set free! Lord, let it be!

Unwrathing the Cross part I 12
The Gospel Metaphors

"Since the children have flesh and blood, he too shared in their humanity so that by his death he might break the power of him who holds the power of death—that is, the devil—and free those who all their lives were held in slavery by their fear of death."

– Hebrews 2:14-15 –

How did Jesus save us?

Christians, in our sanest moments, believe we cannot and do not save ourselves. We believe Jesus alone saved, saves and is saving us. Though the word *'saved'** has often been reduced to an Evangelical byword, let's redeem it momentarily by recalling its proper New Testament usage. What does 'Jesus saves' mean in New Testament context? We believe God Incarnate did for us what we could not do for ourselves and came in person to rescue us. He has led us out of our alienation and estrangement and has reconciled us to the Father's house. Christ's incarnation, passion and resurrection together comprise 'the finished work of Christ,' through which we receive the gift of *reconciliation*, or what some English Bibles (since the Tyndale Bible in 1534) translated *atonement* —literally 'at-one-ment.' By grace, Jesus Christ restores us to oneness with God, to the unity and harmony intended for us since Eden. Ultimately, this journey of salvation will culminate in our resurrection and glorification for all eternity.

But *how* did this reconciliation or atonement work? *How* did

'Saved'

'Save' or 'saved' are popular but slippery terms. In the New Testament, 'salvation' can refer to redemption, healing or deliverance. It can include a literal rescue, a special conversion event, one's life-long faith journey or even our future resurrection. Readers can normally interpret the word 'save' in this book according to usage. But they should *not* assume the standard narrow Evangelical use that identifies 'getting saved' with the moment we say the 'sinner's prayer.' In my view, salvation is what God has done, is doing and will do—through Christ, in us, on our journey toward union with him.

the life, death and resurrection of Christ save us and reconcile us to God? Was the wrath of God somehow satisfied through the punishment of Christ? Or was the Cross God's grand rejection of wrath as a solution to sin? Theologians have asked, proposed and battled over that 'how' for centuries. We call their proposals *'atonement theories.'**

We need to pause first to address two significant problems that arise with the modern use of this English word, 'atonement.' First, when we think of atonement, we often collapse the whole of Christ's saving work into an economic transaction or legal reparation that took place entirely on Good Friday. While the Cross was truly a definitive event in our salvation, we must not forget or negate all that was accomplished for our salvation through the Incarnation, nor the essential elements yet to happen through Christ's resurrection from the dead, his descent into *hades,* his ascension into heaven and his final return in glory.

Contrary to the pop-slogan, Christ was *not* just born to die. His salvation project is far bigger and broader than the word 'atonement' can express. Our salvation began the instant the eternal Word joined humanity to his divinity, 'without division or confusion.' Through the miraculous union of God and man in one Person—the Incarnation—he could endure creatureliness, including a voluntary death on the Cross, and rise in that same humanity from the dead, winning for it—and for us—sinlessness, incorruptibility and immortality (cf. 1 Cor. 15:42–55)

Here is the boast of the Christlike God: "God became man that man might become a god." This bold affirmation is no mere 'New Age' drivel. It is the inspired revelation of the Psalmist (Ps. 82:6) and of Jesus Christ (John 10:34). The early church theologians, including Irenaeus, Athanasius and Augustine, echoed it unanimously. As a major Christian doctrine, it

'Atonement theories' are *not* the gospel. They are theological interpretations exploring the meaning of the Cross and the mystery of salvation.

Examples include:

Irenaeus (130-202): recapitulation theory.

Origen (182-254): ransom theory.

Anselm (1033-1109): satsifaction theory.

Abelard (1079-1142): moral influence theory.

John Calvin (1509-64): penal substitution.

came to be known as *deification* or *divinization* or *theosis*. Not that we literally become God (as in the Trinity) or equal to God, but rather, as Peter said, "We become partakers of the divine nature" (2 Pet. 1:4) and so receive, by grace, God's gift of immortality.

A second issue with atonement and atonement theories is that some theologians are so attached to their own pet theory that they privilege it and even mistake it for the gospel itself. They might charge those who disagree with their interpretation of abandoning the gospel. Some theorists accuse those who disagree with them of 'heresy.' Others are critical of particular atonement theories,

'The gospel,'

as told in the four Gospels, is the story of Jesus' life, his death and his resurrection. The gospel is not an atonement theory, or four spiritual laws, or five steps or any doctrine of man.

It is the good news about what Christ actually did in history to initiate the restoration of all things.

perceiving something toxic to the gospel embedded within them. So periodically—and again recently—Christian theologians engage in 'atonement wars.' While a discussion of atonement theories could be edifying, these disagreements can get ugly. Consider how bizarre it is that believers come to theological blows and even become cruel toward each other in the name of the Cross?

Let's be clear: atonement theories are not the gospel, nor are they to be confused with the biblical metaphors they claim to interpret:

- *The gospel* is the story of how Jesus came to reveal the love and mercy of God, and how in his life, death and resurrection, Christ decisively accomplished God's saving work.

- *Atonement theories*, by contrast, are human interpretations and working models exploring different aspects of the mystery of how that salvation might have 'worked.' Make no mistake: salvation is a mystery.

- Moreover, atonement theories are often treated as synonymous with the *biblical metaphors* used to describe Christ's work of redemption. For example, Jesus used the word 'ransom' as a metaphor in the Gospels. Later, Origen (185-254 A.D.) develops the 'ransom theory' of the atonement. The *metaphor* and the *theory* are not the same thing.

Confusing atonement theories with the gospel itself, or with the biblical metaphors they strive to interpret, leads to a terrible mistake. The mistake occurs when we want to speak about the meaning of the Cross, but skip the Gospel narratives and New Testament metaphors, and charge straightaway into debatable and polarizing theories. We err when we overlook the gospel story, expounding theories *about* the gospel in its place—interpretations composed by theologians many centuries after 'the faith once delivered' (Jude 1:3) was already finalized. Yet these theories of the Cross are often elevated and even idolized. Congregants are frequently indoctrinated with one totalizing theory as if it is quite literally 'the gospel truth.'

Perhaps even worse, elements of the gospel proper are demoted to the status of theories alongside the rest. For example, the victory of Christ is redubbed *Christus Victor* and labeled 'a theory,' when in fact it's an indisputable New Testament metaphor.

God's saving work through Jesus is so multi-faceted that Christ and the apostles found it necessary and helpful to use a constellation of metaphors to describe its benefits. Each metaphor serves to clarify, but can also obscure. Every metaphor can extend our understanding, but can also be over-extended such that we corner ourselves into error. So our *theories about the metaphors* need to be held very lightly—*no* theory holds a monopoly on the gospel, nor should it lay claim to actually being the gospel. For this reason, in this book, I will give priority to the actual story of salvation and some key biblical metaphors, while intentionally marginalizing the standard theories as tertiary to our understanding of the Cross.

Here is my prayer: that with open hearts, we might be willing to revisit and reform our assumptions about the meaning of the Cross, and thereby make fresh and beautiful discoveries about Christ's glorious gospel. I pray for a new season of pondering the Cross (and the rest of Jesus' saving agenda) that breaks free from religious straightjackets and theoretical nitpicking. I pray we would all learn to nuance our language and make whatever course changes God requires. I pray we would realize with much greater precision what these metaphors mean and what they don't mean. Most of all, I pray we would collectively pause to worship afresh the *cruciform* God.

The story of salvation

I would like to explore some of the salvation metaphors in detail, unpacking key biblical and historical symbols of atonement. Before I do, I must say it again: atonement theories are *not* the gospel. Across the New Testament, while metaphors do appear to hint at the 'how' of atonement, the emphasis is not on these symbolic explanations, but on the story itself. Preaching the gospel never meant theorizing how atonement happens but, rather, proclaiming good news: the events and impacts of Christ's life, death and resurrection. When the evangelists in the Book of Acts went preaching, whether it's Peter or Stephen to the Sanhedrin in Jerusalem, or Paul and Barnabas to pagan Gentiles in Greek and Roman cities, their message is consistent. They usually follow this basic storyline:

- God sent Jesus into the world to announce the good news of peace, to turn us from wickedness and save us (from ourselves).
- Jesus was crucified (and sometimes, "You killed him").
- God raised him from the dead.
- Jesus is Lord and Saviour; he is making all things new.
- Now turn to this Jesus, entrust your life to him, and he will make you new too.

Do you see how this outline follows the Passion story? No theories, no clever analogies. **The gospel*** is what actually happened in space-time history. The facts. I think modern Christians, especially those who self-identify with *the evangel* (literally, the good news announcement), should consider trusting the power of the story—telling the story, sharing the story, showing the story told by Matthew, Mark, Luke and John. Orthodox Churches keep a single gold or wood-bound copy of the four Gospel books. They call that volume 'the Gospel' because the story—the words and works, the life, death and resurrection of Christ—are there to read and hear. No atonement theory, however beautiful or accurate, can or should supplant it. But, in fact, a good metaphor used rightly can serve as a spotlight to illumine the richness of the story. The first apostles and theologians used illuminating metaphors, and so did Jesus. So, we will start with some metaphors drawn straight from the Gospels themselves.

A constellation of Gospel metaphors

Let's begin with a sampling of the biblical metaphors used to describe the meaning of Jesus' mission.

One of the tragedies of the atonement wars is how wound-up many pastors and theologians get about theories composed many centuries after the New Testament, and the great efforts involved in imposing those later theories back onto Scripture. If this weren't already worrisome, the comparative dearth of concern for the breadth and depth of Jesus' own metaphors is pretty appalling. Even here, I'll barely scratch the surface, but hopefully doing so will suggest some places where readers might dig deeper. What metaphors did Jesus use?

1. Lost–and-found.

Jesus clearly saw his mission as finding and rescuing lost people. When he invited himself to Zacchaeus' house, Zacchaeus is so moved that he announces, "I will give half of what I own to the poor, and pay back anyone I've cheated four times over!" Jesus replies, "Today salvation has come to this house, because this man, too, is a son of Abraham. For the Son of Man *came to seek and to save the lost*" (Luke 19:9-10).

This metaphor is important for at least three reasons. First, it means that Jesus' mission was not exclusive to what he did on the Cross. Although the Cross was a decisive climax in many ways, Jesus' mission 'to seek and to save' was already functioning in full force prior to his death. That he 'came' meant God's redemptive plan was already activated during Jesus' life.

Second, the seek-save metaphor used here hints at how we are lost, what we are rescued from and what we are invited to. "Because this man, too, is a son of Abraham," emphasizes the way Zacchaeus had been alienated from God's covenant community. He had been ostracized, treated as an outsider, no longer in fellowship with his community or welcome to worship with them. Jesus takes the initiative to find him, and his love for Zacchaeus initiates the journey of a wholistic at-one-ment, reconciliation not only with God, but also with his community.

Jesus uses the lost-and-found metaphor again in Luke 15, in the parables of the lost sheep, the lost coin and the lost son(s). All three parables are metaphors for something Jesus' grumbling opponents observed: "This man welcomes sinners and eats with them" (v. 2). Jesus' three parables draw an analogy between welcoming 'sinners' to table fellowship and finding something precious that had gone missing for whatever reason.

How does heaven (i.e., God) feel about Jesus' indiscriminate hospitality? Jesus tells us, "There is more rejoicing in heaven over one sinner who repents than over ninety-nine righteous persons who do not need to repent" (v. 7).

If we moderns think about finding a lost coin or wayward sheep, these parables may not hit home, but have you ever felt the frustration of a lost cell-phone or the sickening feeling of a lost wallet, full of ID? How about the panic of a girl who's discovered her diamond ring is missing? Oh, the sense of relief when someone restores that lost item!

Now intensify that feeling. You are on an outing with your family and suddenly realize your toddler is missing! Has the little guy wandered off into the forest? Has someone plucked the little girl away in the crowded department store? What predator might have made off with them? A bear? A cougar? A pervert? And then, at the height of the crazy-making fear, the explosion of emotion—the tears and elation—when the little one is found and returned!

How much more does the Father rejoice over his Son's perilous but successful rescue party! When the lost are found and restored!

In these lost-and-found scenarios, what does Jesus mean by 'repent'? Jesus seems to mean, 'being found'! He appears to mean, 'welcomed in'!

Again, this mission is in full-swing throughout the ministry of Christ. Are not the lost already being found and saved? Yes! How? Through Christ's diligent search party and God's gracious homecoming welcome—with a huge emphasis on the party!

The third reason this metaphor is so important—it 'unwraths' atonement! Oh yes, there is the sacrifice of the Rescuer who must suffer the thorns, nails and Cross to find us. Confused, afraid, angry and in pain, we bite back at our rescuer like any ensnared animal. But where in this metaphor do we find 'the wrath of God was satisfied'? Where do we see an angry God who needs to be appeased? Where is retribution required before sin can be forgiven? It's just not there. Perhaps we will come across it later in another metaphor. We mustn't be hasty or reduce the gospel to one atonement theory, right?

2. The Great Physician.

Encountering a similar objection to eating with tax collectors (such as Zacchaeus) and sinners (such as me), Jesus uses another metaphor. "It is not the healthy who need a doctor, but the sick. I have not come to call the righteous, but sinners" (Mark 2:17). This time, the problem is seen, not in terms of lostness, but of sickness.

What needs to be restored is some kind of spiritual (and apparently social) health. In this case, sin is not seen as guilt to be punished or a debt to forgiven (normally our dominant metaphor) but some sort of disease rooted in the suffering soul that needs to be healed, in this case, through fellowship with Jesus.

When we see sin as a fatal disease that produces ugly symptoms and a sure death-warrant, we see how useless punishment is as a cure. When HIV/AIDS first hit North American shores and communities, do you remember the terror it produced? Here was this new epidemic, seemingly incurable, spreading rapidly and taking many lives. How did we react? First cover-ups and denial, then blame and scapegoating, just like in the first garden! But when has fear or anger ever cured a disease? When has shame and guilt ever restored someone's life? When has punishing the victim ever transformed a heart or life? So it is with sin. As a disease, it cannot be punished out of us! We don't need a punishing Judge, but rather, a great Physician.

But how does eating with Jesus heal the disease of sin? I don't know, but I imagine that the very presence of Jesus is medicinal. I imagine that his gaze, his smile and his kind words wash the stains and shame of sin away. Jesus, then, is both the good doctor and the grace prescription that heals the soul of sin's crippling effects. Again, notice how this metaphor describes how Jesus saves even during his active ministry.

3. The Healing Serpent.

On a similar note, Jesus uses another healing metaphor, this time relating directly to the Cross. In his night-cap dialogue with

Nicodemus ('Israel's teacher', v. 10), Jesus says, "Just as Moses lifted up the snake in the wilderness, so the Son of Man must be lifted up, that everyone who believes may have eternal life in him" (John 3:14-15).

Later in the same Gospel, Jesus adds, "And I, when I am lifted up from the earth, will draw all people to myself." Then John comments, "He said this to show the kind of death he was going to die" (John 12:32-33).

We often see this symbol, the snake on the pole, zooming by on the side of an ambulance, or around a wrist on a medic-alert bracelet. The serpent on the pole has come to represent healing to the broader public. Sometimes the symbol includes two snakes wrapped around the pole, with two wings at the top. It's called the 'caduceus' and is associated with the Greek God Hermes (in Rome, Mercury).

The other version has a single serpent wrapped around the pole, with no wings. This is the *staff of Asclepius*, who was a Greek physician who later became the Greek god of medicine and healing (son of Apollo and Coronis). Asclepius' skills were such that some believed he could bring the dead to life. This image is the symbol of the American Medical Association and the one usually used on the bracelets I mentioned.

Some commentators believe the staff of Asclepius really originated in the story of *Nehushtan*—the same serpent on the pole Jesus referred to in John 3 and 12. In these passages, Jesus borrows a story from Numbers 21, where a plague of snakes had come to torment the people of Israel. Remembering that wrath can be a metaphor for God's consent, this infestation was a consequence, caused and allowed by the people's rebellion. God's heart is never to punish but to heal, so God provided the means for healing. He had Moses put a bronze serpent on a pole so that anyone and all who looked its way would be healed.

Jesus uses this story to intensify the healing metaphor. I say intensify because in this case, sin is more than a crippling chronic sickness; it is fatal venom from the serpent's bite (think of the first garden). It infects and ultimately kills everyone. Furthermore, Jesus intensifies the metaphor because on the Cross, Jesus himself is lifted up and becomes the definitive saving cure. Anyone in the whole world and across all time who looks to the *Cruciform* God will be healed of sin's lethal effects.

In the story, why is it a serpent on the pole? I'm a bit uncomfortable seeing Jesus as a bronze snake. I think of Satan, not Jesus, as a serpent. However, Paul will write a generation later, "Christ redeemed us from the curse of the law by becoming a curse for us, for it is written: 'Cursed is everyone who is hung on a pole'" (Gal. 3:13). This means that in his death, Jesus himself absorbs the curse of sin and death for all of us, sucking the darkness of the world into himself, where his own blood is the all-powerful, spiritual anti-venom that cleanses sin and overcomes death. Assuming the likeness of fallen humanity, he is able to heal it.

Now it's extremely important to remember that the serpent on the pole is a metaphor. The 'venom' is sin's curse and the 'blood' of Christ is his forgiving love even in death. And the 'look' that heals is active trust in the One who hung on that Cross. In this metaphor, it's important that we see who or what we are being saved from. Christ rescues us from the serpent, heals us of the fatal venom and negates the inevitable curse of death.

This imagery recalls God's verdict on the serpent in the original Eden chronicle: "I will put enmity between you and the woman, and between your offspring and hers; he will crush your head, and you will strike his heel" (Gen. 3:15). The serpent strikes the heel of Eve's offspring. This imagery anticipates the crucifixion of Christ. It is what Christ *endures* and *overcomes* on the Cross; he undergoes the venomous bite for us all. Why? Because standing in for us, Christ did what we could not do for ourselves: in his Passion, Jesus overcame the poison of our sin through perfect obedience and total forgiveness. And he overcame death by entering the grave, trampling on death and rising again on the third day. This victory is how the seed of the woman (Christ) 'crushes the serpent's head' once and for all.

4. Atoning Sacrifice.

Jesus is called the 'Lamb of God' only twice, both times by John the Baptist (John 1:29, 36), who says he "takes away the sin of the world." Because "he takes away the sins of the world," some connect this reference to the offering of two goats on the Jewish Day of Atonement:

> [7] [Aaron] is to take the two goats and present them before the Lord at the entrance to the tent of meeting. [8] He is to cast lots for the two goats—one lot for the Lord and the other for the scapegoat. [9] Aaron shall bring the goat whose lot falls to the Lord and sacrifice it for a sin offering. [10] But the goat chosen by lot as the scapegoat shall be presented alive before the Lord to be used for making atonement by sending it into the wilderness as a scapegoat. (Lev. 16:7-10)

In this ceremony, the sins of the people are taken away in two ways. One goat is given to the Lord, its blood sprinkled on 'the mercy seat' of the Ark of the Covenant. It's not being punished for sin and could never be a payment for sin but, rather, this goat is offered as a gift to God in exchange for the mercies freely received. This goat is not about wrath-satisfaction but a renewal of covenant oneness through a shared meal.

The priest later confesses the sins of the people, lays his hands on the second goat, which then symbolically bears those sins outside the city where it will disappear into the wilderness (presumably to die). In this picture, the second goat or 'scapegoat,' though innocent, bears away the sin, never to be seen again. Surely we can see the parallel to Jesus taking our sin away and securing God's mercy as he lays down his life outside the walls of Jerusalem.

This could be what Paul is thinking in Romans when he says,

> 25 God presented Christ as a sacrifice of atonement, through the shedding of his blood—to be received by faith. He did this to demonstrate his righteousness, because in his forbearance he had left the sins committed beforehand unpunished—26 he did it to demonstrate his righteousness at the present time, so as to be just and the one who justifies those who have faith in Jesus (Rom. 3:25-26).

Christ is given as a sacrifice of atonement, perhaps fulfilling the typology of both goats. But Paul, the apostle of grace alone, has reversed everything. Who is presenting the sacrificial offering? God! Who is receiving the sacrifice? We are! Is this a sacrifice of appeasement to placate God's wrath? No! Christ is the sacrificial gift of grace for all. All who receive him by faith (including those sinners and enemies whose judgment God had forestalled) are forgiven and reconciled to God. God did not need to be reconciled to us—he was never our enemy. It is we who had fled and were lost, we who were hostile and rebellious, we who needed reconciliation and atonement. God did not need a sacrificial Lamb, we did. And so God sent his Son for us so that, like the scapegoat, he could carry away our sin, guilt and punishment forever.

John highlights God's grace-given sacrifice for us in his epistles, when he says,

> He is the *atoning sacrifice* for our sins, and not only for

ours but also for the sins of the whole world. (1 John 2:2)

This is love: not that we loved God, but that he loved us and sent his Son as an *atoning sacrifice* for our sins. (1 John 4:10)

5. The Lamb of God.

Even with these obvious parallels, Jesus is never once called 'the goat of God' or 'scapegoat.' Rather, the Gospel of John identifies Jesus with the *Passover lamb*, when it notes that Jesus is crucified on "the day of preparation for the Passover" (John 19:14), that is, when the lambs were being slaughtered. Paul is even more explicit: "For Christ, our *Passover lamb*, has been sacrificed. Therefore let us celebrate the feast" (1 Cor. 5:7-8).

The Passover was established as an annual feast to commemorate the Lord's protection from the tenth plague in Egypt (Exod. 12). In this story, again, the lamb is not punished for their sins. Rather, it is slaughtered for a family meal of roast lamb—or a hospitality meal for the divine presence. Its blood was applied with hyssop to the exterior doorposts as a sign identifying those inside as God's covenant people, under his protection. Because the Exodus story sometimes identifies God as the active agent striking down the first-born in Egypt, one could get the wrong impression that the lamb metaphor has Jesus' death averting God's violence by undergoing it himself. But that interpretation diverges from what the story actually says and means.

Note who the judgment is against: "On that same night I will pass through Egypt and strike down every firstborn of both people and animals, and I will bring judgment on all the gods of Egypt" (Exod. 12:12). The judgment afflicts the defiant oppressors of God's covenant people, along with all their gods. This judgment targets 'the enemy' who has enslaved and brutalized God's children for four hundred years, and only after nine dramatic warnings!

Still, pretty gruesome if you're an Egyptian—especially the firstborn—and the story appears to assign this violence to God.

And yet, while God allows (consents to, yields to) Pharaoh's self-destructive insolence to bear its awful fruit, who is the actual agent of death here? And where are God and the lamb finally located in the story?

> When the LORD goes through the land to strike down the Egyptians, he will see the blood on the top and sides of the doorframe and will pass over that doorway, and *he will not permit the destroyer* to enter your houses and strike you down. (Exod. 12:23)

In our nuanced view of wrath, we recall that in earlier biblical stories, the narrator conflates God's work of deliverance with the destroyer's work of destruction, as if they are in cahoots. But as Christians, we read the story in light of the revelation of Jesus. Jesus offers a straightforward clarification: the 'thief' kills and destroys, while God (in Christ) comes to save, heal and bring life (John 10:10).

Further, a mature Christian reading of the lamb metaphor in Exodus reveals that the blood of the Lamb actually welcomes God's presence and protection from the destroyer, even while the oppressors and their gods face the destroyer's wrath.

6. Redemption and Jubilee.

What does redemption mean to you? Think about day-to-day life. Do you think of redemption as something or someone that's gone wrong being turned for good? Or perhaps you're more practical so redemption is more like cashing in a coupon. What do we mean when we say God *redeemed,* us or that Jesus is our *Redeemer*?

The biblical language of redemption comes into sharper focus as we continue to recall Israel's miraculous exodus from Egypt. Israel is told, "Remember that you were slaves in Egypt and the LORD your

God *redeemed* you" (Deut. 15:15[1]).

God continues to use the Exodus backstory as an abiding arche-type in new circumstances—whether it's redemption from Philistine marauders in Canaan or the refugee camps of Babylonian exile. That metaphor of redemption finally climaxes in Jesus' saving work. In those contexts, the redemption metaphor (and God as *Redeemer*) is largely about rescuing people out of bondage or oppression into which they had somehow fallen.

Originally, though, this deliverance motif was also symbolic, drawn from the Levitical laws of Israel. The laws of *redemption* and *jubilee*, found in Leviticus 25 and so beautifully illustrated in the ultra-romantic Book of Ruth, were ... well, redemptive! These laws address situations where through some hardship or trial, one's debt became so great that they would lose their property, their inheri-tance or even their freedom. Even in the worst-case scenario, under the Mosaic law, all of that would be freely restored to the clan every fifty years, on the year of Jubilee. Why? Because it was God's land and so you couldn't really lose it or sell it—you could only lease it away temporarily. Every Jubilee year, you would return to your land and to your clan for a fresh start—a great system so long as it was observed (which, sadly, it wasn't).

When Jesus announced his ministry in Nazareth (Luke 4), he quotes Isaiah 61, proclaiming "the year of the Lord's favor"—that his arrival signaled the year of Jubilee, a time of freedom (redemption) from debt and bondage, the restoration of all that was lost, and the ingathering of those who were scattered. Jesus becomes our Jubilee. Why? I suppose simply because the time had come. The debt had lasted long enough. To maintain it longer was too great a burden, not only on the individual, but on society.

It's similar to the decision of Canadian lawmakers who saw how long-term student loans were lasting into people's 40's. They saw that these students were not only personally hobbled, but the general economy suffered for it too. In an act of Jubilee, they decided enough was enough. All student loans, however big, are forgiven after fifteen years—ten if there's a diagnosed disability. The students were not only relieved; they were energized to stimulate the economy and invest that money in their dreams.

But recall how I said Jubilee would come as a worst-case scenario? In that system, you didn't have to wait for the worst case to strike. A *'kinsman-redeemer'**—your closest relative or the clan patriarch—could simply buy back your property, your inheritance or your freedom at *any* time. He could restore you to your place in the clan and bring you under his protection and patronage. So redemption includes *freedom from* (bondage, alienation, estrangement), but it also includes *restoration to* (one's family, inheritance).

God takes up this role throughout the Old Testament, saying that he has taken it on himself to be Israel's Redeemer. He redeemed them from Egypt and would redeem them from exile in Babylon. He would restore them to the land he had promised and to the covenant they had broken. This theme is key, especially throughout Isaiah.[2] God would redeem Israel through his special agent, a co-suffering Servant who, like Moses, would participate in their plight, stand in solidarity with them, lead them out of bondage, restore their inheritance and fulfill their original covenant calling to bless the world.

Christ was and is that agent, that Servant, that Redeemer. In the New Testament, we find his redemption is much more expansive than we expected—it is universal in scope! The redemption of Christ is surely from bondage, but not only the bondage of men: we are redeemed from the bondage of sin (freely, by grace; Rom. 3:24; Eph. 1:7) and its consequences, including the decay of death (Rom. 8:23). We are also redeemed back into God's family—a family composed not merely of the twelve tribes Israel but, in fact, of all humankind!

We have three additional common New Testament metaphors

encapsulated within redemption: *adoption* (Rom. 8:23), *inheritance* (Heb. 9:12) and *reconciliation* (Rom. 5:10-11; 2 Cor. 5:17). All of these metaphors are evident in the parable of the prodigal son—the whole gospel in a nutshell—because the Father's redemption includes the restoration of a lost son (adoption), a squandered inheritance and a broken relationship (reconciliation).

I was also surprised to find out that redemption isn't only for us or for what we have lost. God experiences redemption too. Through Christ, he redeems us back to and for himself. We were *his* own possession, lost for a time, and he has bought us back: "the redemption of those who are God's possession—to the praise of his glory" (Eph. 1:14).

'Kinsman Redeemer'

The book of Ruth is a romantic illustration of the *kinsman-redeemer* in action. Boaz buys back (i.e., redeems) Naomi's lost property and marries Ruth, her widowed daughter-in-law, thus restoring their inheritance and securing the family's future. That family tree that will include King David and Jesus.

The price of this redemption, we're told, is Jesus' precious blood—the cost was his life (Eph. 1:7). "You are not your own; you were bought at a price" (1 Cor. 6:19-20). Obviously, there could be no cost greater than the life of Christ. But there's a difficulty with the metaphor—*who* is being paid?

Jesus surely isn't paying the Father, for God isn't holding us in bondage! God is *not* the metaphorical equivalent to Pharaoh or Babylon! In fact, we see that Jesus buys us *for* God, not *from* God: "You are worthy to take the scroll and to open its seals, because you were slain, and with your blood you purchased *for* God persons from every tribe and language and people and nation" (Rev. 5:9).

But who was Christ paying if not God? Let's address that question with our next metaphor.

7. The Ransom.

Jesus once said, "the Son of Man did not come to be served, but to serve, and to give his life as a *ransom* for many"(Mark 10:45). And Paul writes to Timothy that Jesus "gave himself as a ransom for *all* people" (1 Tim. 2:6).

In modern times, we associate ransoms with the demands of a kidnapper who wants payment for someone they hold in bondage. In this case, giving oneself in exchange for a prisoner, like we see in C. S. Lewis' *The Lion, the Witch and the Wardrobe*, when Aslan gives himself over to the witch Jadis to be slain on the stone table in exchange for the life of Edmund. She is able to leverage this deal because under the law, someone must die. Again, seeing it this way can be a bit confusing and in fact, it's actually problematic on three counts. Specifically,

a. Was the ransom paid to God? If Christ's life was given in ransom (or redemption), the church fathers reasoned that the ransom could not be paid to God, because God is not the slaveholder. The Book of Hebrews makes that clear: "by his death he [broke] the power of him who holds the power of death—that is, the devil—and free those who all their lives were held in slavery by their fear of death" (Heb. 2:14-15).

Lewis' tale solves this problem because he doesn't picture God requiring the payment. The witch is the one who demands punishment—a life for a life—leveraging the law of sin and death against Aslan. As in the New Testament, Aslan gives his own life and, in the end, "a deeper magic [self-giving love] from before the dawn of time" resurrects an innocent killed in place of a traitor.

b. Was the ransom paid to Satan? While some of the church fathers dabbled with this theory (i.e., a ransom paid to Satan), they ultimately reject this idea too. The truth, they said, is that God owes the devil—the thief—nothing. The prolific theologian Origen (182-254 AD) starts out with a ransom to Satan, but like Lewis, treats Christ's offering to Satan as a trap, where Jesus' humanity is the bait. The devil takes the bait, but Christ's divine nature and supernatural love overcomes—it's too hot to handle—and Jesus emerges from death along with all those Satan had held in his dungeon.

The truth is that Jesus utterly judged and defeated Satan on the Cross (John 12:31; 16:11; Col. 2:15). There's no deal-making going on here. In another of his metaphors, Jesus said,

> [26] If Satan opposes himself and is divided, he cannot stand; his end has come. [27] In fact, no one can enter a strong man's house without first tying him up. Then he can plunder the strong man's house (Mark 3:26-27).

A ransom?

Christ 'gave his life as a ransom' (Matt. 20:28). But to whom? Not to God, for God is not the slave-holder. Not to Satan, for God owes Satan nothing. Not to the Law, for mercy trumps Law. Jesus ransoms us from *death*, paying with his life. But Christ owed death nothing either, and so conquers it.

In this metaphor, there is no deal on the table, no careful trap being set. Jesus describes his ministry in terms of an overpowering home invasion where he storms Satan's house, immobilizes him, binds him up and *plunders* his goods (namely, all those he had enslaved). This echoes the Exodus backstory, when God *plundered* Pharaoh of his slaves and Egypt's gold (Exod. 12:36). Rather than paying Satan or Pharaoh, quite the reverse is true: he ransacks their territory and leaves them penniless.

c. Was the ransom paid to the Law? Origen and Lewis both hint at a third possibility—that the ransom meets the demands of some law. That is, the leverage the enemy had was an appeal to the rightful requirements of the law. Sometimes passages from Leviticus and Hebrews are quoted as proof-texts:

> For the life of a creature is in the blood, and I have given it to you to make atonement for yourselves on the altar; it is *the blood that makes atonement* for one's life. (Lev. 17:11)

> In fact, the law requires that nearly everything be cleansed with blood, and *without the shedding of blood there is no forgiveness.* (Heb. 9:22)

And yet the Bible also insists on these five points:

- There is no law or principle of justice higher than God to which he is beholden. 'Justice' is not a god to whom Yahweh must bow or appease with blood. Nor is God's 'Law' some retributive principle that binds him. The whole point of the prophetic Book of Hosea is exactly this: that God is utterly free to forgive sinners—to show mercy to the guilty. He is able to respond to legal demands for punishment with a counter-verdict: *complete pardon* based in God's own grace.

- Similarly, there is no judgment or statute that cannot be trumped by mercy, for mercy triumphs over judgment. On the scale of justice, mercy is always an 'older magic' than retribution or sacrifice.

- In fact, even well before the Cross, Israel could testify to the mercy of God. God had not treated them as their sins deserved. They had received superabundant compassion and mercy (Ps. 103:10-12) rather than tit-for-tat, eye-for-an-eye justice.

- Rather than blood sacrifice or burnt offerings, the response God looks for is "a broken heart and a contrite spirit" (Ps. 51:16-17).

- Further, legal provisions existed for a ransom (basically paying a fine) that would cover the debt for some crimes. But the Bible is clear: Under the law, "No one can redeem the life of another or give to God a ransom for them—the ransom for a life is costly, no payment is ever enough—so that they should live on forever and not see decay" (Ps. 49:7-9). You could ransom people from debts and slavery, but who could pay you out of the grave?

Here we have our answer to who or what was paid the ransom in exchange for our lives? When Jesus gave his life for ours, to whom did he give it? The life of Christ was given over to *death itself.* But, as in the case of Satan, Christ did not 'owe' death anything. He did not 'owe' *Hades* (the Greek god of death) a life. Instead, death is the gate by which Jesus entered *hades* (death) and plundered its captives. In Psalm 49 we read, "But God will redeem me from the realm of the dead; he will surely take me to himself" (v. 15). The early church (drawing from texts such as Matt. 27:52-53; Eph. 4:8; 1 Pet. 3:18-20; 4:6), called this victory raid 'the harrowing of hades' and celebrated Christ's posthumous saving work on 'Holy Saturday.'

So, in Christ, the ransom metaphor points to the rescue of those taken by death and held in the grave. The ransom 'price' is Jesus' life—Death (personified) is paid—but 'payment' might be too strong a word because Death can't hold him. And so, in John's Revelation, Jesus announces: "Do not be afraid. I am the First and the Last. I am the Living One; I was dead, and now look, I am alive forever and ever! And I hold the keys of death and hades" (Rev. 1:17-18).

Let me ask you: if Jesus now holds the keys of death and Hades, what do you think he'll do with them? And here we will segue from the Gospels-based metaphors to those expounded in the epistles of Paul the apostle—especially victory and justification.

Pausing to think

- Remember that each of the metaphors above really is symbolic. For what? How do the metaphors point back to Christ in his Incarnation and Passion?

- How does each metaphor relate to your own faith journey? Which one best describes your experience?

- Just as these metaphors recall both the life of Christ and your own faith journey, they also point ahead. What do they say about your future? About death? The final judgment? Your resurrection? Eternity with God?

- Some preachers imply that Jesus saved us from God. But if the Father doesn't need to be appeased or paid, but rather, God-in-Christ incurred the cost, how might that affect your image of God? Your trust in God?

- I'll ask again, if Jesus now holds the keys of death and *hades*, what do you think he'll do with them?

Pausing to pray

God, religion often implied that Jesus had to save me from you, as if you were the divine monster. But if Jesus was actually God incarnate, doing whatever it took to rescue me, that changes everything. I could love you without any lurking suspicions that you might have a bludgeon hidden behind your back! Lord, let it be!

Unwrathing the Cross part II **13**
The Pauline Metaphors

"May I never boast except in the cross of our Lord Jesus Christ,
through which the world has been crucified to me,
and I to the world."

– Paul (Galatians 6:14) –

"For as we lost the sure word of God by means of a tree,
by means of a tree again was it made manifest to all,
showing the height, the length, the breadth, the depth in
itself . . . through the extension of the hands of a divine
person."

– Irenaeus (Against Heresies 5.17.3) –

Paul the apostle: like him or not—and many haven't, from his day to ours—it is not without reason that he's been called 'the founder of Christianity.' Of course, Christ alone is the "pioneer and perfecter of our faith" (Heb. 12:2)—Jesus stands as our only Savior and Lord. But, it is argued, Paul is second to none in importance for what he taught about Christ and the significance of the Cross. He can surely be credited (or blamed) with laying the theological foundations of the Gentile church, among whom he "resolved to know nothing but Jesus Christ and him crucified" (1 Cor. 2:2).

We'll begin this chapter unpacking two of Paul's primary prisms for interpreting the Cross-event: victory and justification.

Victory

In the 1930's, author Gustaf Aulen proposed that Christ's victory (*Christus Victor*[1]) was the dominant theme for the first thousand years of Christian 'gospeling.' I am inclined to agree. Christ's decisive victory over Satan, sin and death is certainly preached across the New Testament, explained by the church fathers and proclaimed in Christian worship. In fact, isn't it also implied in the Christ's own language of 'kingdom'? Jesus proves himself to be the promised Redeemer-King who rides forth to vanquish Satan, sin and death, and bring every principality, power, ruler and authority under his feet. He conquered death by death and reigns over his Kingdom of love by love—not just someday, but already. This kingdom is 'in our midst.'

Let's examine this victory theme a bit further. The victory of Christ is at least three-fold: Jesus conquers at the Cross, through his resurrection and, again, by his love.

1. At the Cross.

Paul writes to the believers in Colossae,

> [13] When you were dead in your sins and in the uncircumcision of your flesh, God made you alive with Christ. [14] He *forgave us* all our sins, having *canceled the charge* of our legal indebtedness, which stood against us and condemned us; he has taken it away, nailing it to the Cross. [15] And having *disarmed* the powers and authorities, he made a public spectacle of them, *triumphing* over them by the Cross. (Col. 2:13-15)

Paul ends the above paragraph with the victory of the Cross. We can reverse engineer the passage, as follows, to see the process:

- Who does Jesus defeat? The powers and authorities.
- How does he defeat them? By disarming them.
- What weapons did he take from them? The legal charges and debts held against us.
- How did he disarm them of these charges and debts? By cancelling them.

- How did he cancel them? By forgiving all our sins.
- The result? God made us alive (raised us) with Christ.

The Cross, especially as it symbolizes forgiveness, is what defeats the enemy, because without those charges, those laws and those debts, the accuser's got nothing on us. When on the Cross, Jesus Christ asks the Father to forgive us, for complete pardon, and he does! And the enemy's armaments and arguments dissolve in his hands.

2. Through the resurrection.

This victory is assured on behalf of both the living and the dead. This victory is especially focused on the utter defeat of death and *hades*. St. John Chrysostom's Paschal homily (fourth century) illustrates the victory metaphor and the historic church's reflection on it. Let's pause to worship with him:

> Let none fear death; for death of the Saviour has set us free.
> He has destroyed death by undergoing death.
> He has despoiled hell by descending into hell.
> He vexed it even as it tasted of His flesh.
> Isaiah foretold this when he cried:
> Hell was filled with bitterness when it met Thee face to face below;
> filled with bitterness, for it was brought to nothing;
> filled with bitterness, for it was mocked;
> filled with bitterness, for it was overthrown;
> filled with bitterness, for it was put in chains.
> Hell received a body, and encountered God.
> It received earth, and confronted heaven.
> O death, where is your sting?
> O hell, where is your victory?
> Christ is risen! And you, o death, are annihilated!
> Christ is risen! And the evil ones are cast down!
> Christ is risen! And the angels rejoice!

Christ is risen! And life is liberated!
Christ is risen! And the tomb is emptied of its dead;
for Christ having risen from the dead,
is become the first-fruits of those who have fallen asleep.
To Him be Glory and Power, now and forever, and from
all ages to all ages.
Amen!

We could stop there, but I can't help adding one further note of victory, proclaimed by Paul, just to underline the point:

> [24] Then the end will come, when [Christ] hands over the kingdom to God the Father after he has destroyed all dominion, authority and power. [25] For he must reign until he has put all his enemies under his feet. [26] The last enemy to be destroyed is death. [27] For he "has put everything under his feet" (1 Cor. 15:24-27).

3. By his love.

This same victory is now ours, with the all-powerful might of God identified clearly as love itself, the very nature of God:

> [35] Who shall separate us from the love of Christ? Shall trouble or hardship or persecution or famine or nakedness or danger or sword? … [37] No! In all these things we are more than conquerors through him who loved us. [38] For I am convinced that neither death nor life, neither angels nor demons, neither the present nor the future, nor any powers, [39] neither height nor depth, nor anything else in all creation, will be able to separate us from the love of God that is in Christ Jesus our Lord (Rom. 8:35, 37-39).

This Cross-shaped love is higher than the heavens are above the earth, wider than east is to west, and deeper than the deepest sea. It brings into willing surrender and worshiping submission every subject in the heavens, earth and under the earth. Look bigger and further than the reach of the Hubble telescope, smaller and closer than the discovery of quantum particles such as the Higgs Boson. His love is there and it reigns, holding all things together in the care of a good and merciful King!

Justification

The climax of our survey of atonement metaphors is the most famous of all in the Protestant tradition and quite evident in the Pauline corpus. It is also at the heart of huge current theological debate as scholars are revisiting this word—*justification*—with fresh eyes.[2] To avoid bogging down in theological minutiae, I will try to stay close to the actual metaphor.

In Greek, the word *dikaios* can be translated *just* or *righteous*. This word can refer either to someone's character (moral purity) or to their legal standing (innocence). In the Bible, it comes to include our standing before God, who is the perfect standard for righteousness. It also anticipates our standing with and before God, the good and merciful Judge—now, every day, and finally on the Day of Judgment. The problem is that by God's perfect standards, no one is righteous or just. No matter how hard we try, the Apostle Paul concludes, "there is none righteous, not even one" (Rom. 3:10). "All have sinned and come short of the glory of God" (Rom. 3:23).

I remember as a child, cowering under those verses as preached by finger-wagging evangelists who spoke in terribly ominous tones. But Paul himself isn't so condemning. He's just pointing out an obvious matter of fact: everyone sins and no one is perfect. This is only news to the self-righteous. God knows very well that no one is justified (righteous) before him. All of us are law-breakers and all of us are both experiencing and facing wrath. But remember, wrath to Paul is not the seething malice of an angry God, but rather, the deadly consequences of our own sin, namely death or perishing, whatever that includes.

But for our loving Father, that just won't do. He knows we can't justify ourselves—we can't 'unwrath' ourselves. We're helpless to do so. So what will God do? Let's pick up the heart of Paul's logic in Romans 3:

> [21] But now apart from the law the righteousness of God has been made known, to which the Law and the Prophets testify. [22] This righteousness is *given* through faith in Jesus Christ [or *'through the faith/fullness of Jesus Christ*] to all who believe. There is no difference between Jew and Gentile, [23] for all have sinned and fall short of the glory of God, [24] *and all are justified freely by his grace* through the redemption that came by Christ Jesus. [25] God presented Christ as a sacrifice of atonement, through the shedding of his blood—to be received by faith. He did this to demonstrate *his righteousness*, because in his forbearance he had left the sins committed beforehand unpunished—[26] he did it to demonstrate *his righteousness* at the present time, so as *to be just* and *the one who justifies* those who have faith in Jesus [or *'faithfulness of Jesus'*] (Rom. 3:21-26).

So before God, we can't attain **righteousness*** by keeping the right law or being born into the right family or joining the right religion. We can't justify ourselves. But God can. He can justify us by grace—that is, *freely declare* us righteous in Jesus, *graciously give* us the righteousness of Jesus, and *practically produce* the actual righteousness of Jesus in us. He can give us right standing on the final day and even make us right in practice by infusing us with the transforming power of the Spirit of Jesus himself. Rather than giving us over to wrath, God gives us over to Jesus. We are justified *by* Jesus and *in* Jesus. The righteousness and the faithfulness of Jesus *unwraths* us—justifies us. And now before a gracious God, Jesus joyfully declares, "They're with me" (1 John 2:1).

Paul adds that God is perfectly just in justifying us (Rom. 3:26). But this confuses retributive religion. If God lets injustice go unpunished, isn't he guilty of injustice? What just judge would let guilty criminals off scot-free? Isn't that what corrupt judges do?

No, God is not corrupt and faithfulness is not unjust. John the Beloved says God is *faithful* and *just* to forgive our sins and cleanse us from unrighteousness (1 John 1:9). He is able to:

> ¹⁷ Cleanse me with hyssop, and I will be clean; wash me, and I will be whiter than snow.
> ¹⁸ Let me hear joy and gladness; let the bones you have crushed rejoice.
> ¹⁹ Hide your face from my sins and blot out all my iniquity.
> (Ps. 51:17-19)

> *'Righteousness'* refers to being in 'right relationship' with God, through trust in God's faithfulness through Christ.
>
> By grace, Christ restores us to covenant faithfulness with God. He also empowers us by grace to covenant faithfulness in this world. That is, righteousness looks like love of God and love of neighbor.

How is God able to freely justify the unjust and still remain just? Because, we are told, *Christ died for us*, "the just for the unjust" (1 Pet. 3:18). What does "Christ died for us" mean? Similarly, we read that *the blood of Christ was shed for us*, "for the forgiveness of sins" (Matt. 26:28; Col. 1:20). What does the 'shed blood' represent? These phrases are as mysterious and elusive as they are powerful. Ask someone to explain them and you're likely to hear a string of clichés or further mixed metaphors that bring you no closer to their meaning.

Christ died for us; his blood shed for us

Let's keep it basic for as long as possible. We can at least say this: *Jesus died.*

Next, *Jesus' blood*—it represents his life (giving it, laying it down, pouring it out) or his death (suffering, dying). Either way, somehow Jesus died *for us.* What does 'for us' mean? In our place, instead of us? On our behalf, as one of us? For our benefit? How we interpret 'for us' depends on one's default atonement theory, but we ought not impose a theological theory onto the gospel message, so let's press on.

Jesus' life, given in death, is an actual sacrifice. I'm not talking about symbolism now—we're beyond the metaphors of sheep and goats and sacred ceremonies. Religious sacrifices may or may not point to Jesus. Sometimes they foreshadow the sacrifice of Christ. At other times, we contrived them from the confused dictates of our own hearts (Jer. 7:21-24). In any case, Christ's self-offering must define the true meaning of sacrifice, as opposed to letting the symbols of sacrifice define the reality of what Jesus did. Reversing these is the quickest path to paganizing the sacrifice of Christ. Christ doesn't get his meaning from the symbols; the symbols derive their meaning from him, even when they predate his own sacrifice.

The meaning Christ attributes to sacrifice is simply this: laying one's life down for someone else (1 John 3:16). Anyone who gives their life to rescue another—whether it's a fireman dying while pulling someone from a flaming building; a policeman who's fatally wounded while rescuing a hostage; or a martyr stoned to death for preaching the good news—is 'paying the ultimate price.' Here, the metaphors are off the table. Here, sacrifice (laying down your life) is raw actuality—the events as they really happened.

Notice that this type of sacrifice has nothing to do with punishment, payment, retribution or appeasement. In every case, a life is given for the sake of the other, not to satisfy someone's wrath or placate their anger, but as a life-giving, life-saving sacrifice.

When God sent his Son to earth to restore the planet, the sacrifice—his life, his death—was the costly offering of self-giving love. But unlike the fireman, policeman or martyr, Jesus' sacrificial death allows him to rescue even the dead as well, because he brings them with him back from the grave!

Evangelists such as Paul and John add that Jesus' death for us not only rescues us from death, but also deals with our sins once and for all, decisively. God-in-Christ is literally *given over* to the wrath, to our sin, to that murderous death. He suffers our defiant, violent rejection. Because that sin is directed against him, he can do one of two things: he can avenge it or he can forgive it. He can either pay us back with wrath or he can forgive us freely with grace—he can react in kind with punishment or respond with mercy. For love's sake, God opts for mercy and forgiveness on Good Friday. God chooses restoration over retribution. He does this for us; he does it for love.

Amazingly, this forgiveness extends beyond the conspirators and agents of his crucifixion—beyond Pilate and Caiaphas and their cronies. He applies forgiveness to all humankind for all time. How? Why is this death, this blood, this forgiveness universal? I suspect it is because the blood shed is the blood of God, who is himself universal, an eternal storehouse of mercy. This God who is universal love empties himself and pours eternal life into the cosmos through the wounds of that first century Jewish Rabbi, Jesus of Nazareth.

And now we're so deep into mystery that we need to pause.

The mystery of redemption

We have come full circle, back to the question of atonement. We have looked at both the metaphors and the actuality of Jesus' redemptive mission. For some, there may still be a niggling question, "How?" Human inclination would reduce the mystery to mechanics or calculate the exchange to economics. We want—even demand—to know *how* the death of Christ removes sin, whereas Paul resists the mechanics of transaction: "The *wages* of sin is death, but the *gift* of God is eternal life in Christ Jesus, our Lord" (Rom. 6:23). Wages, payment, sin, death—that's ledger language, wrath language. But Christ doesn't balance the ledger; he nails it to the Cross (Col. 2:4)! He utterly removes it. God's ways are not bound to the ledger, but free to the boundless way of pure grace and free gift.

How does Jesus save us? Rather than restating the metaphors, rehashing history, or reliving the atonement wars, I will unpack this all-important question means by *defining* and *delineating* five key words, *describing* once more Christ's death for us. As with metaphors, descriptions are *not* the gospel, they are merely words in the mouths of imperfect observers.

1. Cruciform.

To say that Jesus' death was *cruciform* seems redundant, but remember, we are talking about the works of God here. In describing Christ's death for us, we are not merely talking about a perfect man who died in the presence of his God. Nor are we even to stop at God the Son Incarnate, dying in the presence of his Father. No, *all the fullness* of Trinity, through God the Son, in Jesus the man, empties himself, gives himself, pours himself out for our sake. God the Judge is not awaiting appeasement from God the Sacrifice. Rather, Christ's death for us is the apex revelation and act of God's self-giving love.

2. Representation.

Christ dies not only *for* us, but *as* us. I mean that as Adam represented the whole human race in the fall, so Christ represents the whole human race in his victory. He stands on our behalf as our delegate or agent—the new Adam or new human. As Paul says, "For if the many died by the trespass of the one man, how much more did God's grace and the gift that came by the grace of the one man, Jesus Christ, overflow to the many!" (Rom. 5:15). And again, "For since death came through a man, the resurrection of the dead comes also through a man. For as in Adam all die, so in Christ all will be made alive" (1 Cor. 15:21-22).

3. Identification (participation).

Christ can represent us because he completely identified with us. He embraced and assumed every aspect of human nature, inheriting every cell of his humanity from a willing human mother, so that Paul can say God sent "his own Son in the likeness of sinful flesh" (Rom. 5:3). He not only identified with our human nature, but also with the totality of the human condition.

As Hebrews says, "We do not have a high priest who is unable to empathize with our weaknesses, but we have one who has been tempted in every way, just as we are—yet he did not sin" (Heb. 4:15). "Son though he was, he learned obedience from what he suffered and, once made perfect, he became the source of eternal salvation" (Heb. 5:8-9).

The great, first systematic theologian, Irenaeus, described this complete identification—this mutual participation—in this way:

> [Christ] caused man to cleave to and become one with God. For unless man had overcome the enemy of man, the enemy would not have been legitimately vanquished. ... And unless man had been joined to God, he could never have become a partaker of incorruptibility.[3]

In other words, in the one person of Jesus Christ, God identifies with a man and a man identifies with God. Fully God and fully man, in Christ, humanity and divinity come together to restore humanity.

4. Substitution.

Readers familiar with the atonement wars might be surprised that I use this word, for I have elsewhere rejected John Calvin's penal substitution theory (composed in sixteenth century), which insisted that Christ "was made a substitute ... to sustain all the punishments which would have been inflicted on them ... He suffered death which the wrath of God inflicts on transgressors."[4] For Calvin, Christ's substitution is the "incomprehensible vengeance which he suffered from the hand of God." In short, Calvin (and Jonathan Edwards after him) popularized the idea that God punished Jesus in your place so that the fullness of his wrath would be satiated, and only then would he be able to forgive sin.

I would submit that by viewing substitution as mollification or wrath-appeasement by means of violent punishment, we impose a gross projection of our own twisted demands for retribution onto divine justice, reducing it to carnal vengeance. Wrath was what motivated murderous haters to crucify Jesus; vengeance was the very system God's mercy overthrew. Calvin's vision does horrendous violence to Trinitarian dogma, severing the Godhead, which historic Christianity had formally confessed is eternally 'one in essence and undivided' (Chrysostom's 'Divine Liturgy'). Calvin's model rends the Trinity on Good Friday into Father-wrath against Son-mercy.

In his *Institutes* (2.16.10), Calvin also subverts the obvious intent of the Apostles' Creed that says, Christ "was crucified, died and was buried; he descended into hell." Up until the sixteenth century, Christians had always confessed Christ's **'descent into hades'*** as his victory over the grave. Calvin,

---

Christ's 'descent into hades'*⁵

These verses are sometimes cited as pointing to Christ's victory over *hades*.

Psalm 24:7
Ephesians 4:9
Hosea 13:14
Zechariah 9:11
Ecclesiasticus 24:45
Acts 2:24
Colossians 2:15
1 Peter 3:19

on the other hand, swaps out the original meaning, "laying aside all consideration of the creed," (his self-indicting words) for his own novel interpretation. Instead, he says, Christ's descent into hell happened while Jesus was still alive, suffering the torments of hell—God's wrath—on the Cross. "It was requisite," he says, "that he should feel the severity of the Divine vengeance, in order to appease the wrath of God ... necessary for him to contend with the powers of hell and [endure] the horror of eternal death." According to Calvin, even while Christ suffered visibly before men, he also experienced "the invisible and incomprehensible vengeance which he suffered from the hand of God."

My own conviction, and that of the historic church, is that God was not punishing Jesus on the Cross at all. According to the Apostle Paul, God was *in Christ*, giving himself in forgiving love, reconciling the world to himself, *not* counting our sins against us (2 Cor. 5:19). That is one reason I usually shy away from the language of substitution.

While on a hike in the Colorado Rockies with Yale theologian, Miroslav Volf, he observed that substitution is a word many Christians probably won't be able to relinquish, and we won't need to if we define it more carefully and more biblically. We might re-label Calvin's theory 'wrath-satisfaction'⁶ (still popular in neo-Reformed circles). But we can retain a biblical form of 'substitution' *if* we ask simply, "Did Jesus do for us what we could not do for ourselves?" Of course he did. Did he 'step into the ring' as our substitute? Did he go through the battle royal with Satan, sin and death for us? Sure he did. Did Jesus 'take a bullet for us'? Yes! The key is to remember, *God is not the one holding the smoking gun*. We are. And as he bleeds to death, he forgives us and says, "I'll be back—see you in three days."

If we are going to use the language of substitution, we'll need to remember these two limitations:

a. Substitution mustn't be divorced from identification. Jesus didn't exactly suffer death in our place—we still die, remember? In fact, Jesus beckons us to take up *our* cross and follow him. "Die with me," he says in effect. But Christ leads the way. He identifies with us in our death, calling us to die with him in his death ("I am crucified *with* Christ," Gal, 2:20a), so that we might also rise with him ("Nevertheless I live," Gal. 2:20b).

b. Substitution mustn't lapse into appeasement. On that hiking trail with Volf, after he had made his case for a certain breed of substitution, I asked him, "At what point do we cross the line? When does substitution become heretical—even pagan?" He replied, "Appeasement. To say that Christ's death appeases an angry God would be heresy—formally." His perspective reinforced my own views and provided clear language for the problem I've been articulating.

5. Exchange.

Finally, when the *cruciform* God became human—identified with us as our representative and our substitute—he became the locus and mediator of a great exchange. He takes our curse (death) and gives us his blessing (life); he takes our hell and gives us his heaven; he participates in human nature so we can share in his divine nature. As Christ participates in us and we in him, he takes our old, brittle and broken hearts of spiritual stone and gives us new, vibrant hearts of spiritual flesh. My 'Adamic nature' is exchanged for a new glorified 'Christ-nature.' The old is gone, the new has come.

Unwrathing the atonement

This, then, is what I mean by 'unwrathing of the atonement.' Yes, every human being on the planet was destined for wrath (Eph. 2:3). Wrath, not as the vengeance of an angry God, but as the process of perishing under the curse and decay of sin. And what did God do? He *unwrathed* us! He freed us from sin's slavery and *unwrapped* us from death. How? By *wrathing* Jesus in our place? No! By becoming one of us and, as Jesus, overcoming wrath by his great mercy!

We close with Paul's description of Christ's unwrathing work:

> [1] As for you, you were dead in your transgressions and sins, … gratifying the cravings of our flesh and following its desires and thoughts. Like the rest, *we were by nature deserving of wrath.* [4] *But because of his great love for us, God, who is rich in mercy,* [5] *made us alive* with Christ even when we were dead in transgressions—it is *by grace you have been saved.* (Eph. 2:1, 3-5)

Such good news! What a Saviour! What a gospel! Or at least a description of the beautiful gospel we shall now proclaim.

Pausing to think

- Have you ever thought of the Cross as a victory before? The resurrection was obviously a victory, but how does Paul see the Cross itself as the locus of Christ's triumph?

- Have you ever thought about Jesus' descent into *hades* before? How is this descent part of his victory? How is it part of your victory?

- Have you ever thought about what 'justification' means before? When Paul says we are 'justified by faith,' what does that mean to you? Beyond abstract theology, what does it look like in real life?

- Have you thought about the lengths God went in order to identify with you? The almighty Creator of the universe fully participated in the human condition! Are there trials in your life he might understand? Are there some where you doubt that he 'gets it'?

- When God makes an exchange with us, it's always an upgrade: joy for sorrow, comfort for grief, peace for fear. What exchanges do you need to make with him today? Might a trip to the Cross be in order?

Pausing to pray

God, I'm grateful for your victory ... and could use a few victories myself. Please make victory and redemption real to me. I welcome your participation. I would appreciate some exchanges—some upgrades. I think I'm ready for that. Lord, let it be!

A More Christlike Message 14
The Beautiful Gospel

"Praise the LORD, my soul, and forget not all his benefits—
who forgives all your sins and heals all your diseases,
who redeems your life from the pit
and crowns you with love and compassion."
– King David (Psalm 103:2-4) –

The *cruciform* gospel

This entire book has been dedicated to a renewed vision of God—a God both Christlike and *cruciform*. This image of God as all-merciful, incarnate Love calls for a corresponding upgrade of our vision of the gospel, our understanding of the gospel, our telling of the gospel.

Note well! The *gospel* itself does *not* need upgrading; the gospel is perfect. The gospel is the unalterable good news story of Jesus Christ as revealed through the Gospels of Matthew, Mark, Luke and John. On the other hand, as the Spirit of truth continues to guide and illuminate God's people, new light is shed on the wonders of what Jesus has done for us, and the Good News is even better than we thought. We begin to realize that even while the gospel does not change, our vision may improve, our understanding may increase and our presentation may require revisions. Rather than anything novel, what's required may be just the opposite. We probably need to revisit 'the old, old story' with Christ-cleansed lenses in order to do a little 'quality control' on our witness. So again, the gospel doesn't need tweaking—*we* do, in order to restore, ensure and maintain faithfulness to that message.

One project toward that end is a presentation entitled 'The Gospel in Chairs,' or what we now call, 'The Beautiful Gospel.' Originally composed by an Orthodox priest, Father Anthony Carbo (from Colorado Springs), a 9-minute version was then also posted online by Steve Robinson.[1] Brian Zahnd and I discovered it and then recreated our own adaptations.[2] We were both so gripped by 'The Gospel in Chairs' presentation that we've conspired to spur on a 'chair revival.' We've been training others to share this beautiful gospel so that it's now being retold across the US, Canada, the UK, Sweden, the Netherlands, Portugal, Germany, Austria, Switzerland, Kenya and South Africa. Brian led a training weekend in India where over 200 pastors have taken up the challenge and are spreading the word. Another associate presented it to over 400 inmates in a prison, and the prisoners responded with enthusiasm. To them, it was good news indeed! It has also become part of the curriculum for the MA theology program at schools like Westminster Theological Centre (UK), where I now teach.

So what is 'The Gospel in Chairs'—this *Beautiful Gospel?* It is basically a visual presentation of two versions of the gospel, told using two chairs. One chair represents the direction we turn toward or away from God throughout the course of biblical history and, indeed, our own lives. The second chair represents God's corresponding orientation, either toward or away from us, depending on our choices and on which version of the gospel is being preached. You can watch our videos for yourself on the internet, but I hope you'll also ponder and pray about how to improve it, make it your own and share it with others. Consider this your training, your 'course in chairs.' What follows is the basic script describing the two ways the gospel might be shared. It will also repeat and pull together the major strands of this book into a simple summary.

To reiterate, what follows did not originate with me. I am passing on a formulation entrusted to Carbo, shared by Robinson, then retold by Zahnd and I. Many of the phrases are theirs even while I have liberally edited and embellished my version. On the other hand, readers will note that I'm retelling a much more ancient story: the biblical narrative itself in summary form, "the faith once delivered to the saints" (Jude 3).

Two versions of the gospel

Before launching into the two stories, I begin with an introduction, summarizing a few of the basic truths we've covered in this book. I tell the audience I will be using two chairs to compare and contrast two versions of the gospel. The first version represents what Robinson calls 'the Protestant view,' but so many Protestants don't buy into it that we have called it 'the modern Western version' instead. It's the gospel story most familiar to Evangelicals, but originally composed in Geneva circa 1536 by the Reformer we met earlier, John Calvin, when he was perhaps 27 years old. It was made popular in America through the revival preaching of Jonathan Edwards and evangelists ever since. Twentieth century popular adaptations included 'the Four Spiritual Laws' (Campus Crusade) and the 'crusade' preaching of Rev. Billy Graham.

Thus, the first version I illustrate is what most Evangelicals were raised on, and it revolves around that particular theory of the atonement we call the *penal theory* (or the legal, retributive or juridical view). This approach imagines the story of Jesus as a courtroom drama, where sin is law-breaking that needs to be punished and God is the Judge whose justice must be satisfied. Because since our sin is against an eternal God, the punishment must also be eternal (everlasting) *or* an eternal person (Jesus Christ) must step in to be punished or sacrificed in our place. Once the eternal substitute has been punished, the Judge is then free to pardon the repentant sinner since that debt has been paid in full.

I can appreciate this version, because it was my introduction to

Christ and upon hearing it, I responded in faith. That is, I came to Christ after hearing this particular presentation. Over the years as a pastor and evangelist, I shared this version with others, and saw faith spring up—not only faith in a presentation or model, but in Christ himself.

Further, whether or not one is drawn to the courtroom analogy—and in spite of its limitations—some of the legal lingo it leans on does appear in Scripture. In that sense, it's 'biblical.'

I then point out that while the first version is old—at least 500 years old, it's even archaic—it's not actually ancient. I tell them that I believe there is a more ancient, more accurate, more biblical account of the gospel; one established by the apostles and the early church fathers in the first three centuries after Christ. Robinson calls it 'the Orthodox version,' but since other streams of faith (such as Celtic, Anabaptist, etc.) also embrace it, we have taken to calling it the *restorative* theory or *healing gospel* or even the *therapeutic* version. In this version, sin is not merely law-breaking behavior but, rather, a fatal disease. The sin condition is a suffering of the soul that is rooted much deeper than our thoughts and deeds. This disease—this condition—makes us subject to futility and death. In this analogy, more of a hospital or hospice than a courtroom, God comes not as a punishing judge, but as the Great physician who would heal our brokenness and rescue us from the curse of death. While both versions claim to be 'biblical,' it seems to me that the latter is more truly 'apostolic,' if by that we mean aligned with "the faith once for all delivered to the saints" (Jude 1:3).

So, there are our two analogies: criminals versus patients; the courtroom versus the hospital; a Judge versus a Doctor. But also, in sharing the story twice, I will not merely move from one theory of the atonement to another. I will move from a theory (in the first version) back to the actual story of Jesus (in the second version). While the courtroom drama of Calvin's imagination provides us with an analogy for what Christ has done, the hospital comparison can fall away quickly in favor of the actual events of the Bible and especially the four Gospels. In other words, I want to slip out of versions and theories of the gospel into the actual story—the gospel narrative itself.

Now we're ready for the chairs. I'll lay this written script out in bulleted form so you can follow the movements clearly. When I write, *turns from* or *turns to,* readers will know that's when I am turning one chair toward or away from another.

The first telling:
The modern / legal / retributive understanding

- God created humankind (male and female) in his image, to reflect his glory and to have fellowship.
- God placed man in the Garden of Eden to care for the animals, steward the garden and represent him in the world.
- But then the unthinkable happened: Adam and Eve sinned, and in sinning became 'sinners.' They *turn from* God.
- Because God is holy, pure and righteous, he cannot look on sin. So *God turns away* from man. Adam and Eve are expelled from the garden, bearing the curse of sin and passing it on to their offspring.
- Every effort we make to try to please God, to justify ourselves, to be righteous or to rid ourselves of guilt, is as filthy rags. We are 'totally depraved'[1] and deceitfully wicked. Thus, God's disposition toward us is 'enmity'—anger and wrath that needs to be placated.
- Thanks be to God, in his love for humanity, he sends his Son to occupy our place, live in our stead, in perfect obedience and right relationship to God. Unlike us, Jesus continually *turned toward* God and God was always *turned toward* him.

- At end of his life, Jesus is put to death and the Father lays all of our sin and our guilt upon Jesus. Then God, because he is too righteous, holy and pure to look on sin, *turns his face away / turns his back*, forsaking his Son, and pours out the full wrath of God upon him. He sacrifices his Son to appease his own wrath, to satisfy his anger against sin by punishing it perfectly in Jesus.

- Because Jesus endured all of this punishment faithfully and without sin, God raised him from the dead and restored his place at the Father's right hand.

- Now if we *turn to* God, if we believe Jesus did this for us—has borne our sin and endured the full wrath of God in our stead—we are clothed in the righteousness of Christ. Luther says, we are 'snow-covered dung.' R.C. Sproul says, Christ becomes our 'asbestos suit from the white hot wrath of God against sinners.' Because we are hidden in Christ's righteousness, God can finally *turn toward* us.

- But if we don't believe Jesus has done this for us, we remain in our sin, alienated from God. The wrath of God continues to be on us. If we *don't turn* toward God in repentance by the time we die, we sinners are condemned to hell, bearing the wrath of God in ourselves for all eternity. God's favor is forever *turned from* us.

- Therefore, it is urgent that we repent and *turn to* Christ so we can be released from guilt and experience eternal life.

This is essentially the legal or retributive version. It fairly represents the tradition that brought me to faith, that I was trained to share and which I preached for many years.

The overall flow of this gospel is this: when you *turn from* God, God *turns from* you. If you *turn back to* God, God will *turn back to* you. Our choices determine the direction of the God-chair:

1. We turn from God . . .

2. . . . so God turns from us:

3. But if we turn back to God . . .

4. . . . he turns back to us.

Flies in the ointment

Over time, three elements began to trouble me greatly. On many levels—biblical, theological, pastoral and evangelistic—this account drops two nasty 'flies in the ointment' (Eccl. 10:1!).

1. First, it puts salvation in our hands.

Granted, we would have said that salvation is by grace alone, initiated by God and accomplished by Christ. But in the end, your response becomes everything. There is a sense in which this is true, isn't there? We can freely reject or accept grace, right? Then depending on whether we accept or reject the grace of God, there are consequences, right? Even ultimate consequences!

But wait! Is the consequence of turning from God really that God will turn from me? Is God only facing me when I decide to face him? Who seeks whom? Who finds whom? Who saves whom? Is a grace that depends on my capacity to turn the right way really grace at all?

What if, as we've suggested above, the judgment for turning from God is nothing other than turning from God? Turning away is itself the disaster that bears horrid and painful results. What if God's response to our turning away is *not* to turn away also, but to launch the rescue mission that will save us from ourselves?

2. Second, it pits God against you.

How could any Christian teacher possibly conclude that God's "primary disposition is enmity?" How could John 3:16 have been any more clear? "For God so *loved* the world." Thankfully, when I share this message, congregations audibly react with a mixture of obvious disgust and laughter at such a huge mistake. Happily, they can't even relate to the error—at least not once it's spoken aloud, no longer a hidden premise.

But further, where did we ever get the idea that God is too holy, righteous and pure to look on sin? Did it somehow escape our notice that God is everywhere and sees all things? If God was too holy to look on sin, would he know anything about anyone? In fact, did not Jesus walk, talk and eat with sinners every day of his life? Are we saying that Jesus was not God incarnate, fully God and fully man throughout every moment of his life? What Jesus saw, God saw—sin stains and all.

So where did this idea creep in? Let me tell you. It was lifted from half a Bible verse in Habakkuk! In 1:13, Habakkuk is complaining to God about the terrible sins of his nation. He says in the first two lines, "Your eyes are too pure to look on evil; you cannot tolerate wrongdoing." An entire theology was formed around these two phrases, shaming people for being too repulsive for God to look at! If only we had kept reading. The next lines of the verse say, "Why then do you tolerate the treacherous? Why are you silent while the wicked swallow up those more righteous than themselves?"

In other words, Habakkuk's complaint in full goes like this: God, your eyes are too pure to look on sin, *so why do you*? You are too holy to tolerate wickedness, *so why do you*? As the book unfolds, God makes it clear that he does see all of this sin and wickedness, it has not gone unnoticed, and that he will indeed make it right. Habakkuk forecasts the coming of Christ to save his people (3:3-5) and prays prophetically, "in wrath, remember mercy" (1:2).

Some may have also been thrown off by a passage in Isaiah, which says, "But your iniquities have separated you from your God; your sins have hidden his face from you, so that he will not hear" (Isa. 59:2).

Well, that's quite damning, isn't it! Pretty clear, right? The Bible says it, I believe it, that settles it, right? If only we would keep reading! The chapter as a whole goes like this—God *sees* the injustice in the land and how that injustice has broken the flow of blessing and favor he intends. He grieves the situation. So what does God do?

¹⁵ The Lord looked and was displeased that there was no justice.

¹⁶ He saw that there was no one, he was appalled that there was no one to intervene; so *his own arm achieved salvation* for him, and his own righteousness sustained him.

Who or what is this *arm of the Lord?* Keep reading:

²⁰ "*The Redeemer will come* to Zion, to those in Jacob who repent of their sins," declares the Lord.

²¹ "As for me, this is my covenant with them," says the Lord. "*My Spirit,* who is on you, *will not depart from you,* and my words that I have put in your mouth will *always* be on your lips, on the lips of your children and on the lips of their descendants—from this time on and forever," says the Lord.

In other words, when God sees individuals or nations wallowing in sin—personal or social, far from turning his back on us and alienating us, he rolls up his sleeves and stretches out his hand to save. In this case the 'hand' is a metaphor for the Messiah, a prophetic pronouncement of God's remedy, and a promise that he will *not* abandon us.

3. It pits God against Christ.

Just as grievous as the first error—maybe even worse—the penal version pits God the Father against God the Son. That is, even though the Father loves the Son, he is also depicted as turning his face from the Son, forsaking the Son, striking and punishing and tormenting the Son, pouring out all his wrath against sin upon the Son.

I would challenge readers to find one instance in the four Gospels where Jesus casts the Father as the principle conspirator and punisher on Good Friday. Examine every instance of the gospel being preached in Acts (25% of the book!). See if you can spot even a single hint that God the Father was the culprit in the crucifixion. Yet, paradoxically, God did orchestrate our salvation through it. Even the Pauline language of God sending his Son as an 'atoning sacrifice' is a far cry from this picture of an retributive God turning from or lashing out against Jesus in order to fully satiate his wrath.

So where did we get that idea? How did we conclude that God turned his face from Christ? Let me tell you. It is based in an incomplete misread of Psalm 22:1, the verse where David prophesies what theologians call Christ's 'cry of dereliction.' He begins the Psalm, "My God, my God, why have your forsaken me?" And then we do what we always tend to do: we create an entire theology without reading on. You probably know how this goes: Jesus cries out to God in desperation because why?

> **God is for you, not against you.**
>
> Jesus did not come to unwrath you from the Father. God-in-Christ came to unwrath you from the slavery and destruction of Satan, sin and death.

Because God had forsaken him. Why would the Father do that? Because Jesus had 'become sin' (2 Cor. 5:21) and God is too holy, righteous and just to look on sin. So, as one song says, the Father turns his face away. In turning his face away, Christ experiences the very essence of hell—separation from God. It's perfectly biblical and logical. Until it's not.

Let's double-check. When Jesus quotes Psalm 22:1, he's letting us know that on the Cross, this Psalm had come to him. He is not recalling only one verse, but the whole Psalm, which prophetically describes the death and resurrection of Christ from his point of view, even down to what he's thinking. It foretells details such as the mockery and violence of his tormentors, how the soldiers would pierce Jesus' hands and feet, and then divide his garments among them. It looks past the crucifixion to Christ's resurrection and enthronement as ruler of all, and how people from every nation will come to bow before him and worship him.

The Psalm begins on a dark note as Christ co-suffers in solidarity with and for those who have despaired of God's help and could only peer into the darkness of despondency. Their moaning cries become his.

And what happens? Does God abandon him? Turn his face from him? Ignore his cry for help? Let's read:

> ²³ You who fear the LORD, praise him! All you descendants of Jacob, honor him! Revere him, all you descendants of Israel! ²⁴ For he has not despised or scorned the suffering of the afflicted one; *he has not hidden his face from him* but has listened to his cry for help. (Ps. 22:23-24)

Pause and read the italicized phrase again, out loud. *He has not hidden his face from him.* Who is 'he' referring to? God the Father. Who is 'him' referring to? Jesus. According to the Living Word of God, of whom the Psalmist prophetically speaks, and with whom the Lord Jesus identifies during his crucifixion, did God actually forsake him? Does the Father actually turn his face from the Son? What does it say?

He has not hidden his face from him.

And the Son's reply: "Ah, Father, into your hands I commit my spirit!" (Lk. 23:46) Another citation from a Messianic Psalm! These are the words of Psalm 31:5. Again, Jesus knows the whole Psalm by heart. If we keep reading down to verse 22, we hear him testify, "In my alarm I said, 'I am cut off from your sight!' Yet you heard my cry for mercy when I called to you for help." In the darkness of the moment, Christ in his humanity feels cut off—'alarmed'—and cries out for help.

And what does God do? He hears and answers. How? The Book of Hebrews tells us:

> During the days of Jesus' life on earth, he offered up prayers and petitions with *fervent cries and tears* to the one who could save him from death, and *he was heard* because of his reverent submission. (Heb. 5:7)

The Father doesn't pull the Son down from the Cross or save him from dying. Rather, he does something even better: he saves him from death itself and, as so breaks the curse of death for everyone, giving Jesus the keys.

I ask the reader, is there anything in this account that pits the Father against the Son? But we need to go further. 'God' does not refer only to the Father. Christians believe the Bible reveals one God in three persons: Father, Son and Holy Spirit—*undivided*. We believe that one Trinitarian God revealed himself in and through the Lord Jesus Christ—one person in two natures, *fully* human and *fully* divine. In the Incarnation, Jesus of Nazareth was God-in-Christ.

Further, we confess and we believe, with Paul, that *all* the fullness of the Godhead dwelled in Christ in bodily form. We believe that Jesus was fully man *and* fully God at all times, including in his suffering and death. When I share 'The Gospel in Chairs,' I sometimes quote the following biblical texts, asking "Where was God on Good Friday?"

- We believe, "God was *in* Christ, reconciling the world to himself" (2 Cor. 5:19).

- We believe this Yahweh said, "You will look on *me*, the One whom you have pierced" (Zech. 12:1, 10).

- We believe that "the rulers of this age ... crucified the Lord of Glory" (1 Cor. 2:8).

What I don't typically share is how mysterious and complex the doctrine of the Trinity is when it comes to the suffering of Christ. If I dared tread where angels use wings to cover their faces, I'd likely spout some new heresy. For now, I can only offer a taste of sound doctrine from the great theologian and desert father, John Cassian (360-435 AD):

> But when speaking of His Passion, he shows that the Lord of glory was crucified. "For if," he says, "they had known, they would never have crucified the Lord of glory." And so too the Creed speaking of the only and first-begotten Lord Jesus Christ, "Very God of Very God, Being of one substance with the Father, and the Maker of all things," affirms that He was born of the Virgin and crucified and afterwards buried. Thus joining in one body (as it were) the Son of God and of man, and *uniting God and man, so that there can be no severance either in time or at the Passion*, since the Lord Jesus Christ is shown to be one and the same Person, both as God through all eternity, and as man through the endurance of His Passion; and though we cannot say that man is without beginning or that God is passible, yet *in the one Person of the Lord Jesus Christ we can speak of man as eternal, and of God as dead.* You see then that Christ means the whole Person, and that the name represents both natures, for both man and God are born, and so it takes in the whole Person so that when this name is used we see that no part is left out. There was not then before the birth of a Virgin the same eternity belonging in the past to the manhood as to the Divinity, but *because Divinity was united to manhood* in the womb of the Virgin, it follows that *when we use the name of Christ one cannot be spoken of without the other.*[4]

What then are we to make of a gospel that pits the punitive

Father against the victim Son; or the merciful Christ against the wrathful God? When I stopped preaching a retributive gospel, some branded me as a heretic, but a careful examination of the historic Christian faith suggests the real error was in ever preaching that monster-god in the first place. I certainly believed in one God—but undivided? Even on Good Friday? No, I had mistakenly believed in a severed Trinity.

Somehow, we must affirm *both* truths: that Christ entered an authentic experience of our sense of abandonment *and* that he never ceased to be God, nor did the Trinity ever cease to be one. I'll leave the reader to ponder this mystery.

Some eyes will have glazed over and others will have been enlightened, but here is the bottom line: neither the Trinity (Father, Son and Holy Spirit) nor the two natures of Jesus Christ (human and divine) can be divided. *Ever.* Not on the Cross. Not in the grave. Not in *hades. Never.* Any theology that pits the Father against the Son is, according to the fathers and mothers of orthodox Christianity, formally a heresy. We are perfectly free to believe otherwise, but then we should not identify ourselves with their faith.

Nor is this theological hairsplitting. These saints were exiled, tortured and martyred defending the beautiful image of God-in-Christ passed down from the apostles. Some, such as Maximus the Confessor, had their tongues pulled out by the roots and their hands cut off to prevent them from speaking or writing these truths. But speak and write they did, so that you and I might worship this beautiful God rather than an inferior and idolatrous image. This beautiful God was revealed by, in and through Christ—and was *never* pitted against him. But who really even thinks or talks that way? Me. I did. And if I'm the only heretic who needed to repent, marvelous! Mission accomplished!

For those who get impatient with (or too spiritual for) a little sound doctrine, consider the monstrosities conjured by those who abandon it. Think of the blasphemous ways we've slandered God in explaining to our children and others' children around the globe why Jesus died. Blasphemous monstrosities? Too strong?

As I wrote this chapter, a new cinematic remake of *Godzilla* was released in American theatres. Someone tweeted this comment: "Next time someone tells me 'my theology doesn't turn God into a monster,' I'm sending them this." She attached a link to a blog article entitled, "Godzilla and the Salvific Destruction of God,"[5] the moral (?) of which was that "just like the God of Israel, Godzilla brings destruction in order to save." The author continued, "the God of Israel will not hesitate to wreak a little havoc in order to open the eyes of his people to their need."

Or as John Piper explains without flinching,

> *It's right for God to slaughter women and children any time he pleases.* God gives life and he takes life. Everybody who dies, dies because God wills that they die. ... everything he does is just and right and good. God owes us nothing.[6]

All right, enough deconstruction. It's time for the second version, the more ancient and more biblical story—the restorative narrative we call *The Beautiful Gospel*.

The second telling:
The ancient / healing / restorative understanding

At the risk of stealing my own thunder, let's lay out the way in which the second telling differs from the first. When we use the chairs to illustrate God's radically different response to sin, we see a message truly worthy of the name *evangel, gospel, good news.*

The most important element is the direction of the God-chair. Over and over, we'll ask, *'And what did God do?'* That's our signal to move the God-chair. Here is what we'll see God do:

1. No matter how often we turn from God . . .

2. . . . God turns toward us. He forgives us, he seeks us, he finds us, he welcomes us in grace.

3. Even if we turn away from God again . . .

4. . . . God turns back to us again and again and again! He never stops turning to you God is always toward you!

"The Beautiful Gospel" — full version

As you can see, the second version of our gospel presentation has a similar beginning to the first.

- God created humankind (male and female) in his image, to reflect his glory and to have fellowship with him.

- God placed mankind in the Garden of Eden to care for the animals, steward the garden and represent him in the world.

- But then the unthinkable happened: Adam and Eve *turn from* God in sin. In sinning, they (and all of creation) became subject to futility and death. The great problem the gospel addresses is not primarily your guilt or God's need to punish it. Rather, it is about saving us from death and the fear of death through which the devil held us in bondage all our lives (Heb. 2:15).

- Enslaved by fear, the couple turned from God—they fled into the shadows of the garden and tried to hide.

   And what does God do? He comes looking for them!

   "Adam. Eve. Where are you?"

   "Hiding. From you."

   "I see. And what's that on your genitals?"

   "Fig leaves."

   "What are you wearing that for?"

   "To cover our nakedness."

   "Who told you that you were naked?"

   Then the blaming starts, and has never stopped:

   "She did it!" "He did it!" "It told me!"

   And what does God do?

   In his compassion, he sends them from the Garden to protect them from eating of the Tree of Life—to prevent them from remaining in this state of shame forever.

But God not only sends them from paradise—*he goes with them.* And he clothes them. He covers their shame.

"Here folks, try these furs. They'll keep you warmer."

- Adam and Eve have sons—Cain and Abel. And Cain doesn't care much for Abel's worship style. Call it jealousy. He starts plotting.

  And what does God do? He comes looking for him.

  "Cain, what's on your mind?"

  "Nothing!"

  "Cain, be careful. Sin is crouching at the door. It'll eat you alive!"

  But Cain turns from God and murders his brother.

  And what does God do? He goes looking for him.

  "Cain, have you seen Abel around?"

  "Am I my brother's keeper?"

  "Cain, I know what you did."

  Off Cain goes, east of Eden, where he will found civilization as we know it on lies and murder. So it is to this very day.

  And what does God do? He protects him.

  He gives him a mark—a sign of God's covenant protection, warning others not to touch this son of his.

- Here is a man who finds God's favor and receives God's promise.

  "Abraham, I will give you and Sarah a miracle child and through his seed will come a mighty nation."

  But Abraham is impatient. He takes matters into his own hands. Maybe he doesn't believe. Or maybe he notices that Sarah's slave Hagar is less wrinkled, has a better complexion, a little perkier. He takes her. And really, how consensual was this arrangement? She bears a son, Ishmael, the false promise. Talk about a modern, blended family. Or talk about 'monster-in-law,' bullying and dysfunction!

And what does God do? He honors the promise!

Not only does he honor his promise and give Abraham the child of promise, Isaac—but he also establishes a covenant with Ishmael who will father twelve princes of his own! (Gen. 17:20)

• Here is a man who finds God's favor and receives God's promise.

"Moses, I will make of you a mighty deliverer, and you will lead your people out of slavery in Egypt."

But Moses is impatient. Maybe he has some anger and rage issues. He takes matters into his own hands and, seeing an Egyptian taskmaster abusing a Jewish slave, murders him. Things go sideways and he becomes a fugitive, lying low as a shepherd in the wilderness for the next forty years.

And what does God do? He comes looking for him!

He shows up in shrubbery, actually. It's time to set God's people free. He gives him some pretty amazing powers, a magical staff and a spokes-brother to cover the stuttering problem. Good to go and, sure enough, ten plagues later they are crossing the Red Sea, homeward bound.

• Here is a man who finds God's favor and receives God's promises.

"David, I will make you a great king over a mighty empire. We'll call it 'the kingdom of God.' And from your seed will come a royal line whose throne will never pass away."

But David is a bit of a voyeur. He likes hot tubs. And fancies an especially striking woman who enjoys rooftop bathing.

Since the dancing-in-his-underwear incident, he regards his own wife as a bit of a hag (or was it wives, plural, by now?) and takes Bathsheba for himself. He gets her pregnant, botches the cover-up, and ends up having her husband sent to certain death on the front lines of battle.

And what does God do? He honors the promise.

After their baby dies (no, God didn't kill the baby!), God gives that same woman a second son, Solomon, who will be the first installment of God's royal promise. Even better, Jesus of Nazareth, descendent of David and Bathsheba, will carry the royal Davidic bloodline into eternity!

- Here is a nation, chosen by God to enjoy his favor and reflect his glory for the world to see.

But instead, they've become corrupt and unjust. They exploit the poor and oppress the marginalized. God sees their moral and spiritual decline and confronts it through a scandalous act of performance art—'the prophet and the prostitute.'

God tells the prophet Hosea, "Go, take yourself a wife of harlotry And children of harlotry, For the land has committed great harlotry By departing from the Lord" (Hos. 1:2 NKJV). He indicts the nation of its crimes and describes the national destruction they deserve.

And what does God do? He remembers.

Hosea 11 goes something like this:

"Oh Israel, my heart is turned within me. I remember when you were just a baby and I first spoon-fed you. You were adorable! And then you were barely a toddler and you took those first steps, right into my arms! Listen, I can't do it. I won't do it. Here's the deal: if you won't repent (turn), *I will.* For I am God—I'm not a man—I *won't* come in wrath! And then you *will* follow me!"

- This drama is repeated again and again throughout the Old Testament. God makes a promise, someone *turns from* him, they experience the tragic results, *but God comes to find them.*

  Finally, because he loves humanity and doesn't want creation to be spoiled by sin and subject to death, God becomes human, that he might *find* and *heal* humanity.

- Here is a woman, whose heart has been broken again and again. A marriage, a divorce. A second marriage, it doesn't work out. A third, a fourth, a fifth—by now we're getting the picture. "Damaged goods," they mutter behind her back. And now the man she's with isn't *her* husband. She is never able to find the love she's looking for.

  And what does God do?

  God comes and sits with her beside a well and says, "I know who you are, what you've done and why. Your problem is not promiscuity; your problem is that your soul is withering of thirst for real love. Well, I'm the water of life and I will love you and I will install a fountain of life and love in your spirit that will gush up and you will never thirst again." And she didn't! Saint Photini ('enlightened one') became an evangelist that day and shared the beautiful gospel for the rest of her life.[7]

- Here is a man, who for the sake of greed and ambition—and probably a good dose of 'short man syndrome'—became a tax collector, colluding with the Roman occupiers, participating in the system as an oppressor of his own people, ostracized, rejected, without friends.

  And what does God do?

  God walks beneath a tree, looks up and says, "Zacchaeus, come down from there. I will do what no one else will do. I'm going to come to your house, eat at your table and become your friend." That day, Jesus says, "Salvation has come to this house."

Zacchaeus was so touched that he paid back anyone he had defrauded 400%, and of his remaining wealth, 50% went to the poor. Jesus had not only restored him to his family and his community, but had broken the chains of obsessive greed that had ruined his life. He was transformed into the most generous man in town!

- Here is a woman caught in the act of adultery, dragged to the Temple where the religious leadership has condemned her and wants to stone her.

By the way, where's the man? Why only her? Oh, there's probably some 'legal' reason he's not there, but I'm more interested in the *illegal* reason: this was a set-up. John 8 tells us that it was a trap. She was trapped so that the leaders could set a trap for Jesus. Okay, Jesus, shall we stone her or not? Will you even defy the Law of Moses for the sake of your love message?

And what does God do?

God kneels beside her and begins scribbling in the dust. One by one, from oldest to youngest, the accusers disperse. Jesus asks,

"Where are your accusers?"

The woman replies, "They're gone my Lord."

And Jesus answers, "Neither do I condemn you. Go and sin no more." And then, I add with a sinister voice, "… or I really *will* condemn you!"

No! Jesus did *not* say that. But haven't we implied it with our tone, subtly wagging the finger, "Go and sin no more … *or else!*"

No! This was not at all Jesus' tone. I hear him saying,

"Listen daughter, today the slate is clean. You get a fresh start. You're completely forgiven—even the adultery you were just caught in, don't give it another thought! In fact, whatever pain or loneliness or addiction was in your heart that drove you there. All that pain goes now too. Welcome to your new life!"

- Here is a man who has lost his mind and been so captured by the powers of darkness—possessed by a legion of demons—that he seems no longer human. He's a madman living chained in a graveyard, his clothes torn off, his body covered in scars from self-mutilation.

  And what does God do?

  He comes looking for the demoniac. He climbs into a sailboat and crosses the Sea of Galilee. The moment his foot touches dry land, the principalities and powers throughout the region shake in their boots. "Oh sh*t! The Son of God has arrived!"

  I hear this God saying, "I will come to you. I will set you free. I will give you your mind back, your clothes back, your family back." And he does! The man is so grateful that he wants to follow Jesus and become a disciple. And to our surprise, Jesus says "No. Instead, I want you to fill the whole region with the beautiful gospel." And he did just that!

- Here is a man, because of the randomness of broken human nature subject to death, who has either contracted a disease or been born a paralytic, unable to walk.

  In that culture, you know what such a disability means: he is considered cursed by God, punished for some sin committed by either himself or his parents, perhaps up to ten generations previously. Regardless of whose fault it was, the curse was on him and that meant exclusion from community worship. He could never enter the Temple to worship God.

  But what does God do?

  He is telling parables of the Kingdom in the crowded living room of a packed house. Plaster falls into his hair and he looks up. Ceiling tiles are being pulled back. In peek four men who've perhaps heard tell of this beautiful gospel—of the God who removes curses rather than inflicting them. They begin to lower the mat that's holding their friend.

And what does God do?

First, he clears the air of this curse business. "Son," he says, "your sins are forgiven." Then, seeing the skeptics' raised eyebrows, he adds, "Take up your pallet and walk." And so he does. The legs straighten, the muscles strengthen and the man slowly stands. He stretches, gives a little hop, then grabs his cot and marches out, right through the crowd—no doubt breaking into a run long before he arrives home!

- Here is a woman who, through childhood trauma and family dysfunction, struggled with alcoholism from her early teens.

  By her early twenties she had to be rescued from a drug-house by a friend who would become her husband. Now, into her thirties, she could not break the habit and was unable to stay sober for more than three months.

  And what did God do?

  He saw the real thirst in her heart and drew her into his family. She joined our faith community and learned to pray. She discovered how to treat prayer as a face-to-face meeting with a Living Friend. She became a powerful intercessor and taught others to meet Christ in the same way. She had two children and brought them to our local church as well, although her husband tended to remain more on the margins.

  Still, she struggled with alcohol, sometimes showing up at her home Bible study quite loaded, as if to test her acceptance. She tried with all her might to stay clean and sober, only to stumble yet again. Eventually, she fell completely off the wagon and left her family. Over the months, she ended up on the streets, sometimes finding a cardboard box for shelter or living with her new boyfriend in his vehicle. Even then—even while stoned—she would pray and teach other addicts to meet Jesus.

Things got worse. Her marriage ended in divorce, she began injecting drugs and contracted Hepatitis C. Her mental health was ailing, she was having run-ins with the police and barely survived a series of overdoses.

And what did God do?

He came looking for her. Like the Shepherd looking for the lost, entangled lamb, he pursued her. He began his quest from inside her heart, for he had never really left her.

First, God inspired her ex-husband to welcome her and her boyfriend into his home, where he and the kids detoxed the couple for several weeks. Then they were admitted into recovery homes for drug addicts.

During the recovery phase, one day she sat down and had a heart-to-heart with Jesus. In effect, she said, "I'm so sorry. You gave me a faith, a family, a home and a church family. And I lost it all. I've lost my husband, my children, my house and my health. I ruined it. I'm not even asking you to fix this. I just want you to know that I'm so, so sorry."

And what did God do?

In her heart, she saw Jesus take her needle kit, fill the syringe with drugs, tie off his arm and empty the contents into his own veins! What?! Jesus can't do that! And so she told him! But is this not exactly what Christ has done for every one of us? On the Cross, has he not drawn all our sin and sorrow and sickness into himself, assuming the entirety of the human condition precisely in order to heal it?

She heard him ask, "Do you feel the grief as I do this? That's what I felt for you every time you used." Not anger. Not disgust or disdain. No shaming or guilt-tripping. Only his grief. And something amazing happened: the cravings left. The need to self-medicate was gone. He gave her the gift of sobriety, gave her a path to recovery and, without going into another full chapter, healed her hepatitis! The doctors cancelled her interferon treatments and signed off her file with the words, "Healed by the power of faith." Over ten years later, she is still clean and sober.

Still, she had lost her husband, her home and her family.

And what did God do?

Fasten your seatbelts, he's about to pull a Hosea on us! First, her new boyfriend also met Christ in recovery. He too was given the gift of sobriety. He asked her to marry him—and she asked her ex to give away the bride! Is that allowed? Can grace be that kind? Could her ex be that forgiving? His faith is not complex or theological. It boils down to this cardinal concept: if Christianity means anything, it is the call to forgiveness.

Missing her children, she would phone them every night to pray with them before they went to bed. They would pray that, somehow, God would make a way for them to be together again, even though it was impossible.

And what did God do?

He inspired the ex to invite the new couple to move into the first floor of his home and raise the children with him! The two men began doing morning devotions together out on the deck. Unreal! Eventually, the first husband sold his half of the home to them, moved out and was remarried himself. The two couples love each other and often come together for family events. The new husband started a landscaping business that hires and trains addicts in a new trade. He just passed the ten-year mark of sobriety. The young woman went back to school. You won't even believe this, but it's true: As I write this, she's already completed her MA in marriage and family counseling and is now hard at work in that field! Together, the couple serves meals to the homeless and ministers hope to addicts who need to hear their story of redemption.

This is truly the God who *never* turns from us, *never* abandons us and will walk with us through the mess of life. I know it because I witnessed the whole thing!

• Finally, here is the whole human race, chosen and dearly loved by the God who is *always* for us, *always* toward us and *always* in pursuit of us.

Driven by fear and pride, our need to maintain our systems of power, enforced by violence—we arrest, and condemn, torture and crucify this God. The best mankind had to offer—the world's premier religious system and political empire—conspired to murder the Lord of Glory, who had only come to seek and to save and to love the world.

And what does God do?

He says, "I forgive you. While you hated me, I loved. You who took my life, I give you my life. While you were my enemies, I made you my friends."

• Some will resist and reject God's love and forgiveness to the bitter end. And when humanity experiences the penalty of its own sin, when it falls away into death to be forever separated from God, what does God do?

• God says, "My love is stronger than the grave!" (Song of Sol. 8:6). "Even if you make your bed in *sheol*, I am there" (Psalm 139:8). God in Christ pursues us in his wild love all the way into death.

• He also says, "I am the resurrection and the life" (John 11:25), and he conquers death. "I am he that lives, and was dead and behold, am alive forevermore. *I* hold the keys to death and *hades*" (Revelation 1:18). "And *all* who are in the grave shall hear the voice of the son of man and come out of their tombs" (John 5:28).

- Now there is no place where God is not. He is in all places and fills all things with his love,[8] for he is love and from the heart of God's throne of grace flows a river of fire (Dan. 7:10). This love is *always toward* you; this love *never turns from* you.

- To those who respond to God's love with love, they experience this river of fire as warmth, as comfort, as eternal joy and peace. To those who respond to God's love with hatred, they experience this river of love as a consuming fire (Isa. 33:14; Heb. 12:29), 'the scourge of love.'[9]

- Even in this life, we know that love 'burns' for those who make themselves its enemy: "If your enemy is hungry, feed him, give him drink, continue to love him, it will be like burning coals on his head as long as he hates" (Rom. 12:20). But all they must do is *turn and receive that love as love* and, becoming friends, the former enemy no longer experiences torment but, rather, the joy of a shared meal.

This second telling is the restorative version—the *beautiful gospel* of God's healing love.

The grandest of finales!

Whenever we teach the beautiful gospel, we remind audiences of two cardinal Christian truths:

1. God does not change.

2. God is perfectly revealed in Christ.

The basic script[10] of *The Beautiful Gospel* summarizes so well the arc of this entire book:

Christ did not come to change the Father, or to appease the wrath of an angry judge, but to reveal the Father.

God is like Jesus, exactly like Jesus. God has always been like Jesus. We did not know that, but now we do.

Paul said God was in Christ, reconciling the world to himself. It's not the Father that needed to be reconciled to the world. It's the world that needed to be reconciled to the Father. Jesus, perfectly revealing the heart of the Father, confronts the sin of the world this way: I forgive you.

Even when we *turn away* from God, he is always there, confronting us with his love. God is always *toward* us. *Always* for us. He comes, not as a condemning judge, but as a great physician.

Jesus was saving us from Satan, sin and death; not saving us from God.

God *never* turns away from humanity. God is perfectly revealed in Jesus. When did Jesus ever turn away from sinful humanity and say, "I am too holy and perfect to look on your sin?" Did Jesus ever do anything like that? No. The Pharisees did that. They were too holy and turned away. God is like Jesus, not like a Pharisee.

The gospel is this: when we turn away, he turns toward us. When we run away, he confronts us with his love. When we murder God, he confronts us with his mercy and forgiveness.

Is this not your experience?

As a young Evangelical, I inferred that if I was being 'bad,' God would not listen to me or speak to me. My parents did not tell me this; my Sunday School teachers did not tell me this. But somehow, in my own religious 'performance orientation,' I inferred it.

But has that been my experience? Part of me thinks, "If only it were!"

"Hey Brad, what are you doing?"

"Nothing!" And I turn from him.

And what does God do?

"You sure?" He's actually closer. Louder. More intrusive!

"Can I get back to you in twenty minutes?"

"Why is that, son? What are you into?"

And if God is quiet at all, it's because I've jammed fingers into the ears of my heart. Yet somehow, I still can't shake the feeling that God is there, watching, waiting, perhaps grieved, but if he ever seems 'mad' or 'absent', again and again I find the real blockage is my own filters or projections—my pride or shame—distorting the presence of Love.

The truth is, God is always there. And *here*. And *now*. The pure fire of divine Love is longing for you, my friend, his beloved—not merely waiting, watching or even following, but in vigorous, stalking pursuit. This God sold all he had to buy the field of the world to obtain the pearl of great price. You are that pearl. Wild pursuit indeed! One poet called him, "the Hound of Heaven."[11]

Yes, God is all of that. But I hope also that in these pages, you've learned to call him, "the *Christlike God of the beautiful gospel*."

The Love of God
Frederick Lehman

> The love of God is greater far
> Than tongue or pen can ever tell;
> It goes beyond the highest star,
> And reaches to the lowest hell;
> The guilty pair, bowed down with care,

God gave His Son to win;
His erring child He reconciled,
And pardoned from his sin.

    O love of God, how rich and pure!
    How measureless and strong!
    It shall forevermore endure
    The saints' and angels' song.

When years of time shall pass away,
And earthly thrones and kingdoms fall,
When men, who here refuse to pray,
On rocks and hills and mountains call,
God's love so sure, shall still endure,
All measureless and strong;
Redeeming grace to Adam's race—
The saints' and angels' song.

    O love of God, how rich and pure!
    How measureless and strong!
    It shall forevermore endure
    The saints' and angels' song.

Could we with ink the ocean fill,
And were the skies of parchment made,
Were every stalk on earth a quill,
And every man a scribe by trade,
To write the love of God above,
Would drain the ocean dry.
Nor could the scroll contain the whole,
Though stretched from sky to sky.

    O love of God, how rich and pure!
    How measureless and strong!
    It shall forevermore endure
    The saints' and angels' song.

Pausing to think

- What's your story? Does God have a track record of seeking you out? When has he found you?

- In which chapter of the story do you find yourself today? Running? Waiting? Frustration? Enjoyment? Or is there a better word for this chapter? Where is God in your story?

- Can you step back and see the big story of your life? If the book of your life to date had a title, what would it be? What would you like it to be? What needs to happen to see a shift?

- Remember, the chapter you are in is likely not the finale. More trials await us. There are more triumphs ahead too. What is the best 'posture' you could take as you face the future?

- Do the following statements feel true? God is good—period. God loves me—period. Life can be hard—a cross—but redemption will have the last word. When you can't feel it, can you still believe it?

- In your life, learn to ask, "And what did God do?" Then watch. What do you see?

Pausing to pray

God, thanks for never giving up on me. Thanks for pursuing me. Talk about faithful! Thanks for the fresh mercy every day. I need some of that mercy today. And I'll need it again tomorrow, without fail. It's good that it never runs out! Lord, let it be!

A More Christlike Way 15
Epilogue: For Further Exploration

"Human nature is so constituted that any desire of the soul in so far as it has not passed through the flesh by means of actions and attitudes which correspond to it, has no reality in the soul."
– Simone Weil (Gravity and Grace) –

If taken seriously, our vision of a more Christlike God and a more beautiful gospel should raise a host of additional 'what about this' questions. It certainly has for me! I'm especially concerned that we so embrace the Christlike God of grace that Christ-in-us transforms our lives to become more Christlike ourselves. I pray that a clearer vision of the God of enduring mercies would move beyond doctrine, passing through our flesh into action, as it did for the Son of God. Along these lines, the following questions await further exploration:

1. In light of the *cruciform* God revealed through Jesus of Nazareth, how might his character transfigure those who worship him (through the grace of the Holy Spirit)? If we become like the God we worship, could we anticipate becoming a more Christlike people? Is there a God-given pattern for empowered *cruciform* discipleship? I could imagine a study of the Beatitudes, or the whole Sermon on the Mount, as a step in that direction. I could imagine a healthy theology and practice of transformation (what the ancients called '*theosis*') revolving around this Christlike notion of God.

2. In view of the *cruciform* God revealed in Christ, how might we employ a Christ-focused lens when reading Scripture? Perhaps the Bible itself would seem like a more Christlike book if our interpretation reflected the self-revelation of the living God who came in the flesh. We might call this approach 'cruciform hermeneutics.'

3. A *cruciform* understanding of biblical interpretation could help us further unwrath the God associated with violence, especially some of the gruesome texts invoking Yahweh for divinely sanctioned genocide (e.g., 1 Samuel; Joshua). It might also help us see our way through God's own apparent direct acts of mass slaughter (e.g., the Genesis flood, Sodom and Gomorrah, the plagues of Egypt or the death of 185,000 Assyrians, etc.).

4. A *cruciform* cypher may also help us untangle some of the interpretive chaos around the Book of Revelation, beginning with the enigmatic 'wrath of the Lamb' in chapter 6, through to the Battle of Armageddon and the final, more hopeful chapters that conclude John's visions.

While we work at these and related questions, I would encourage readers to explore proposals as they arise through our cadre of authors in CWR magazine and the CWR blog. These resources are accessible through our website at www.ptm.org. You are also welcome to contact the author via email at *bradjersak@gmail.com* with questions, comments and ideas of your own, or visit my website at www.bradjersak.com. Meanwhile, I'll pause one last time to pray, with Paul, for you, the reader.

Pausing to pray

[17] I keep asking that the God of our Lord Jesus Christ, the glorious Father, may give you the Spirit of wisdom and revelation, so that you may know him better. [18] I pray that the eyes of your heart may be enlightened in order that you may know the hope to which he has called you, the riches of

his glorious inheritance in his holy people, [19] and his incomparably great power for us who believe. (Eph. 1:17-19).

[14] For this reason I kneel before the Father, [15] from whom every family in heaven and on earth derives its name. [16] I pray that out of his glorious riches he may strengthen you with power through his Spirit in your inner being, [17] so that Christ may dwell in your hearts through faith. And I pray that you, being rooted and established in love, [18] may have power, together with all the Lord's holy people, to grasp how wide and long and high and deep is the love of Christ, [19] and to know this love that surpasses knowledge—that you may be filled to the measure of all the fullness of God.

[20] Now to him who is able to do immeasurably more than all we ask or imagine, according to his power that is at work within us, [21] to him be glory in the church and in Christ Jesus throughout all generations, for ever and ever! Amen. (Eph. 3:14-21)

Some More Christlike Voices
Appendix: Select Gems on *Kenosis*

Origen

For we must dare say that the goodness of Christ appeared greater and more divine and truly in accordance with the image of the Father when "he humbled himself and became obedient to death, even death on a cross," ... than if ... he had not been willing to become a servant for the salvation of the world.[1]

Gregory of Nyssa

God's transcendent power is not so much displayed in the vastness of the heavens, or the luster of the stars, or the orderly arrangement of the universe or his perpetual oversight of it, as it is in his condescension to our weak nature. We marvel at the way the sublime entered a state of lowliness and, while actually seen in it, did not leave the heights. We marvel at the way the Godhead was entwined in human nature, and while becoming man, did not cease to be God...

We have shown that God's goodness, wisdom, justice, power and incorruptible nature are all to be seen in his plan for us. His goodness is evident in his choosing to save one who was lost. His wisdom and justice are to be seen in the way he saved us. His power is clear in this: that he came in the likeness of man and in the lowly form of our nature, inspiring the hope that, like man, he could be overcome by death and yet, having come, he acted entirely accord to his nature. Now it belongs to light to dispel darkness, and to life, to destroy death.

He united himself with our nature, in order that by its union with the divine it might become divine, being rescued from death and freed from the tyranny of the adversary. For with his return from death, our mortal race begins its return to mortal life.[2]

Gregory of Nazianzus

What He was, He continued to be; what He was not, He took to Himself. In the beginning He was uncaused – for what causes God? But afterwards He was born for a cause – and that cause was, that you might be saved, you who insult Him and despise His divinity because He took upon Him your coarseness and, having united himself with flesh by means of the soul, became human, the earthly God.

Our humanity was joined to and made one with God – the higher nature having prevailed – in order that I too might be made God as truly as He is made human.[3]

In the same category are texts where He is called the servant who serves the good of many and say that it is a great thing for Him to be called the child of God. For in truth He was in servitude to flesh and to birth and to the passions which belong to us with a view to our liberation and that of all those whom He has saved, who were imprisoned by sin. What can be greater for the lowliness of humanity than to be intermingled with God, and by this intermingling to be deified, and that the Dayspring from on high should so break upon us, that the holy one who is to be born should be called the Son of the Most High, and that the name that is above every name should be bestowed upon Him – and what else can this name be but God? – and that every knee should bow to Him who emptied himself for us and mingled the form of God with the form of a slave, and that the entire house of Israel should know that God has made him both Lord and Messiah? For all this was done by the action of the One who has been begotten, and by the good pleasure of the One who begot Him.[4]

But in the form of a slave, He bows down to the level of His fellow slaves – or rather, He bows down to His slaves – and takes upon Him a form not His own, bearing in Himself all that I am and all that is mine in order that He might consume in Himself whatever is bad as fire consumes wax or as the sun disperses the mists of earth, and in order that I may partake of His nature by the blending This is how He honours obedience by what he does, and He proves it in action by His sufferings. For it is not enough to possess the interior disposition, just as it would not be enough for us, unless we also proved it by our acts; for action is the proof of a disposition.[5]

Isaac of Nineveh (Isaac the Syrian)

Far be it, that vengeance could ever be found in that Fountain of love and Ocean brimming with goodness![6]

God chastises us with love, not for the sake of revenge—far be it!—but seeking to make whole His image ... Love's chastisement is for correction, but it does not aim at retribution.[7]

God is not one who requites evil, but He sets aright evil. The Kingdom and Gehenna are matters belonging to mercy.[8]

Even if such words as *wrath*, *anger*, *hatred*, and many meager others are pressed into speaking of the Creator, we should not suppose that He ever does anything in anger or hatred or zeal. Many such figures are employed in the roiling span of Scripture, provisional terms far removed from Who He Is. Even as our own, relatively rational persons have already been tweaked, increasingly if slowly made more competent in holy understanding of the Mystery namely, that we should not take things quite so literally, but should suspect (concealed within the corporal surface of unlikely narratives) a hidden providence and eternal knowledge guiding all so too we shall in future come to see the sweep of many things to be quite contrary to what our current, puerile processes afford us.[9]

Gregory Palamis

He gave himself to us for our sake. Emptying the riches of the Godhead into our lowest depths, he took our nature and, becoming a man like us, was called our teacher. He himself teaches us about his great love for mankind, demonstrating it by word and deed, while at the same time leading his followers to imitate his compassion and turn away from hardness of heart." ("On the Parable of the Prodigal").[10]

Hans Urs Von Balthasar

It is possible to say, with Bulgakov, that the Father's self-utterance in the generation of the Son is an initial 'kenosis' within the Godhead that underpins all subsequent *kenosis*. For the Father strips himself, without remainder, of his Godhead and hands it over to the Son; he 'imparts' to the Son all that is his. 'All that is thine is mine' (Jn 17:10). The Father must not be thought to exist 'prior' to this self-surrender (in the Arian sense): he is this movement of self-giving that holds nothing back. This divine act that brings forth the Son, that is, the second way of participating in (and of being) the identical Godhead, involves the positing of an absolute, infinite 'distance' that can contain and embrace all the other distances that are possible within the world of finitude, including the distance of sin. Inherent in the Father's love is an absolute renunciation: he will not be God for himself alone. He lets go of his divinity and, in this sense, manifests a (divine) God-lessness (of love, of course).[11]

Kallistos Ware

While Philippians 2 speaks of Christ emptying himself, it would be incorrect to say he laid aside his 'Godhead.' As the Vespers hymn for Christmas Eve says, "What he was, remained; what he was not, he took on, for himself, out of love for mankind."

In *kenosis*, the Word was not deprived of anything. Christ remains in union with the Father. They are not separated, but takes on humanity in addition. Therefore, the most we can ascribe to kenosis is a voluntary, self-limitation. For example, he accepts human limitations such as weariness and pain, even ignorance, for Christ said, 'As to when the end of the ages will come, no one knows the day or hour, not even the Son of man. Only the Father knows.'

Perhaps rather than 'emptied himself,' it would be better to say that he poured out himself in love, and that love is his nature. And in this way, *kenosis* is *plerosis*. The supreme manifestation of this love, this glory, is the Cross. "God is never so powerful as when he is most weak."

As Christ said to Paul, "My strength is made perfect in weakness," and this applies to *kenosis*. We could say this at the very least: that kenosis *reflects* something of the eternal Being of God as self-giving love.[12]

Andrew Louth

In the Trinity, there is a kind of *kenosis* in the sense of them making way for one another and, therefore, when Christ empties himself, he actually shows what it is to be God, rather than disguising what it is to be God. *Kenosis* in the modern sense of the Lutheran kenoticists since the 18th century are concerned with what is being taking away, what it is for Christ to be human, with showing why God isn't there. Whereas I think in the fathers, *kenosis* means God coming down alongside us, his 'condescension' to live among us. For the Cappadocians and Maximus, *kenosis* is God's self-emptying love. Sometimes you get the impression of the self-emptying so as to make it possible for us to see him, rather than God disguising himself. And sometimes *kenosis* is bound up with the nature divine being, that love is not concerned with power or force, but love is essentially letting others be and become what they're created to be. And in that sense, kenosis is bound with the nature of love.

In Maximus' treatise on the Lord's prayer, we empty ourselves in response to God's kenosis. We empty ourselves of the passions in order to receive him. In his treatise on the Lord's prayer, he sees the *kenosis* of God as something inspired by love and the response is love.[13]

As the Son involved his self-emptying (*kenosis*), so our deification involves our kenosis, the self-emptying of the passions. The way up is the way down: the *kenosis* of the Son demands the *kenosis* of the adopted sons; the manifestation of the One 'more beautiful than the sons of men' calls for the 'cultivation of the beauty given to them by grace...'[14]

John Behr

It is a mistake to think of *kenosis* as laying aside divine attributes. It is much better to think in terms of humility/self-effacing/self-sacrificial love, so that it is indeed in weakness that the power of God is made manifest, opening up a path for us also to enter into divine life. If Christ had put aside divine attributes to become human, we would not be able to share in his divinity; he would not be a mediator, etc.

In some ways, thinking along such lines results from starting off from an already conceived humanity and divinity—as other than each other. Surely, rather, the fundamental truth of Christianity is that the two are shown together, in and through each other; conceptually distinct (God creates, we are created, etc.), but only ever seen in one *prosopon*, one *hypostasis*.

The difficulty of holding this together results in the many divergences over the centuries, but the creeds always bring us back to this fundamental point of the Gospel.[15]

Christ's taking upon himself the role of a servant, voluntarily going to the Passion, does not diminish our perception of what we might otherwise have considered to be his divinity, but actually manifests his true divinity. The transcendent power of God is manifest in this world in the flesh, in darkness and in death, as a servant. But this manifestation of divine power, in weakness, is simultaneously a transformation: Christ, in the form of a servant, shows us the image of God; darkness and death become light and life; and the flesh assumed by the Word, becomes flesh of the Word—and becomes Word. Or, as St. Gregory put it, "even the body in which he underwent his Passion , by being mingled with the divine nature, was made by that commixture to be that which the assuming nature is." Through the Passion, the body in which the Son suffered comes itself to share in the very divinity of God. Not that it is any the less human, but it is no longer subject to the density, opaqueness, and weight, together with the temporal and spatial limitations that characterize our own experience of our bodies: though Christ was once known after the flesh, he is known so no longer (cf. 2 Cor 5.16). The Passion remains the locus for contemplating the transforming power of God, the "God revealed through the Cross."[16]

Conor Cunningham

We can read Philippians 2:6 to say, "*Because* he was God," rather than, "Although he was God," and so realize that *kenosis* reveals the divine and what it is to be divine. *Since* he is God, he therefore empties himself. This God diffuses himself (Aquinas) for the creation of the cosmos, and then in the Incarnation, repeats and recapitulates creation.

The omnipotence of God is only revealed in his ability to sacrifice. His power is revealed in *kenosis*.

Yet the Incarnation was not just a self-giving diffusion, but an *effusion*, which is why it's *kenotic*. Effusion speaks of the Word pouring himself into the world through the limits of a womb—in Bethlehem, in time—it speaks of specificity. Yet he takes everything—carries the scars, carries history—back up to the Father and into eternity. The Son lifted earth into heaven because what he did was eternal.

In so doing, Christ not only reveals what it is to be God, but what and how it is to be truly human. Christology is anthropology: "Behold the man" said Pilate. And this is our *telos*. To become like gods is our anthropology.[17]

Simon Oliver

Kenosis is not suffering per se, but the eternal reality of God's self-donation. The Cross reveals what is eternally true in the Godhead (the Trinity) and God's creation.

What is important to note is that the Cross is not a response to human evil. Rather, the Cross is the means by which God's eternal love keeps flowing into creation despite human sin. The Cross is God's eternal love, *refracted* through human sin. What God's love looks like now, refracted through human sin, is a crucified Jewish man.

But not as God's plan-B, as if the Cross were God's love were reactive or contingent. Rather, what you see is the eternal flow of God's love. But the violence belongs to humanity, not to God.

For the Eastern Church and patristic fathers, impassibility and ineffability are non-negotiables. This is because the big question is how one defines the difference between God and creation, so that unlike all of creation, God doesn't change. And second, to safeguard the truth that Christ is not just a man (even one filled by the Spirit) or just an angel.

Rather, the Word becomes/was made flesh is rendered 'assumes to himself' a human nature, which changes human nature but doesn't change God.

The radical implication of the Incarnation is that God has been made manifest in the material life of a man. Once materiality has been seen to reveal God, there are no longer any limits to what material reality can reveal, because it's already revealed God in Christ.[18]

Aaron Riches

The Glory of the Lord is the Cross. What could be more of a scandal? The transfiguration is something any old atheist could understand: "glory" is a body and face shining with supernatural light. This does not unsettle my pagan presuppositions of what "divinity" and the "supernatural" mean. What we need faith to see is this: that the dead Jesus, forgotten and abandoned, naked and hanging on the Cross, is truly the Love of God Incarnate. He is not ashamed to be our God.

The resurrection is how we get to proclaim the Cross, which is the true center (and not the resurrection, which like the transfiguration conforms to our preconceived ideas of what is "supernatural").

The victory is all in the failure: the death and the suffering (inhuman as they were), now caught up into his perfect divine filiation ... trampling down death by death.[19]

David Goa

It is a mistake to assume that God is the ruler of the world rather than the measure of the world. The ubiquitous pagan idea is that the gods are in control and all you have to do is propitiate them, know their name and control them. The keystone that holds it all together is not power or force, but God's faithfulness to covenant love.

The problem is more than a theology of God. Christology is anthropology. What we say about God is what we say about ourselves (a projection) until you meet Christ. Theology then shifts from projection to unfolding.[20]

Endnotes

Chapter 1 - What is God Really Like?

1. *'Faith statement'* – refers to a premise that we believe with confidence but cannot prove in a court or test in a lab. But proof is neither necessary nor sufficient for faith. We may have plenty of warrant or reasons for this confidence and, in fact, we may even truthfully say, "We know." Cf. the works of Alvin Plantinga, such as *Warrant and Proper Function*.

2. Meister Eckhart, "Sermon 52: "Beati paupers spiritu," *Meister Eckhart's Sermons*. Ed. Harry Plantinga (Grand Rapids, MI: Christian Classics Ethereal Library, 1999). <http://www.ccel.org/e/eckhart/sermons/>.

3. "New Rules," HBO Real Time with Bill Maher. <http://www.hbo.com/real-time-with-bill-maher/episodes/0/213-episode/article/new-rules.html>.

4. Charles R. Darwin to John Fordyce, 7 May 1879. Darwin Correspondence Project. <https://www.darwinproject.ac.uk/letter/entry-12041>. When Darwin refers to a *'theist,'* he refers to those who believe in God. Hence, a monotheist believes in one god, a polytheist in multiple gods and an atheist in no gods.

5. *'Special creation'* – In Creationism, special creation is defined as the supernatural creation of independent, complex life forms (or at least humans) by God without any evolutionary development. This version of special creation interprets Genesis literally, so that the whole universe came to be in six 24-hour days less than 10,000 years ago.

Chapter 2 - Un-Christlike Images of God

1. Sadhguru, "What is God?"
   <http://www.youtube.com/watch?v=tZ0e8JRu_9U>.

2. St. Gregory the Theologian, *Theological Orations*, 2.4.
   <http://www.ccel.org/ccel/schaff/npnf207.iii.xiv.html>.

3. Soulstream. <http://www.soulstream.org>.

4. "The Serenity Prayer," Reinhold Niebuhr, *World Prayers*.
   <http://www.worldprayers.org/archive/prayers/invocations/god_give_us_grace_to.html>.

5. Ming Tea, "Daddy wasn't there." ©EMI Music Publishing, Warner/Chappell Music Inc., Universal Music Publishing Group, 2005.

6. Many approaches to prayer ministry and inner healing exist: Sozo, the

Immanuel Approach, Elijah House and Theophostic are all effective examples, but depend greatly on the gifts, training and ability of the minister.

7. Jeff Sharlet, "Through a Glass, Darkly," *Harpers,* Dec. 2006.

8. Pope Francis, "The Way of the Cross," *Catholic Insight.* <http://catholicinsight.com/the-way-of-the-cross>.

9. Rev. 13:8; 21:27.

Chapter 3 - Freedom or Love?

1. Charlton Heston, "NRA speech," May 20, 2000. <https://www.youtube.com/watch?v=bOJQFNOQqCY>.

2. Miroslav Volf, "Did 9/11 Make Us Morally 'Better'?" *Huffington Post,* 09/07/2011. <https://www.huffingtompost.com/miroslav-volf/christianity-911_b_944153.html>.

3. Linda Woolverton, Screenplay: *Alice in Wonderland* (film 2010). Ironically, Alice escapes the tyranny of Victorian classism/sexism only to embark upon the adventures of colonial capitalist conquest.

4. Tanya Brothen, "Obama Gives Second Annual Back-to-School Speech," *Obama Today* (2010).

    <http://blogs.america.gov/blog/2010/09/16/obama-gives-second-back-to-school-speech/>.

5. David Foster Wallace, Interview. <http://www.youtube.com/watch?v=E0uQM_qbOEk>.

Chapter 4 - God of Will or God of Love?

1. When I say 'we believe,' I mean either individuals or a culture. 'Once believed in' refers to how the ethics of an atheist may still be a reflection of or reaction to the God they or their culture once believed in.

2. "To the praise of his glory," a phrase used in Eph. 1:6, 12, 14 is specific to the generosity of God's purposes in grace, yet has often been employed as the mysterious reason for the negation of grace.

3. Augustine of Hippo, *Confessions of Saint Augustine,* (Minneapolis, MN: Filiquarian Publishing, LLC., 2008), 7.

4. Ron Dart, "Biblical Judaism, Western Christianity & Liberalism," *George Grant: Spiders and Bees* (Abbotsford, BC: Fresh Wind Press, 2008), 151.

5. David Bentley Hart, "Nihilism and Freedom," (lecture, University of Minnesota, Minneapolis, MN, Mar. 22, 2007).

6. Hart, "Nihilism and Freedom."

7. John Calvin, *Calvin's Institutes,* trans. John Allen (Philadelphia: Presbyterian Board of Christian Education) 3.23.6.

8. John Calvin, *Calvin's Institutes,* 3.17.5.

9. John Calvin, *Calvin's Institutes,* 3.17.11.

10. Adamson, John. "Oliver Cromwell and the Long Parliament," *Oliver Cromwell and the English Revolution* (London: Longman, 1990), 76–84.

11. David Van Biema, "The New Calvinism," *Time* (Mar. 12, 2009). <http://content.time.com/time/specials/packages/article/0,28804, 1884779_1884782_1884760,00.html>.

12. John Piper, "How Can Evil Ever Have a Good Purpose," *Desiring God* (Nov. 2008). <http://www.desiringgod.org/interviews/how-can-evil-have-a-good-purpose>.

13. John Piper, "Putting My Daughter to Bed Two Hours After the Bridge Collapsed," *Desiring God* (Aug. 1, 2007). < http://www.desiringgod.org/interviews/how-can-evil-have-a-good-purpose>.

14. From a famous quote attributed to political thinker, Edmund Burke.

15. An example of cynical reading is *The Brick Testament,* <http://www.thebricktestament.com>, which illustrates numerous brutal biblical narratives with Lego accompanied only by the words of Scripture. They portray graphic events of the Bible in order to mock Christianity. They serve to highlight the problem of a literalist read of the willful God.

16. Mark Driscoll, "7 Big Questions" *Relevant Magazine,* 24 (Jan/Feb 2007). <http://www.relevantmagazine.com/god/church/features/1344-from-the-mag-7-big-questions>.

Chapter 5 – Word Made Flesh

1. Adapted from Brad Jersak, "Christ Almighty: God With Skin," *The Plain Truth* (Winter 2013). <http://www.ptm.org/13PT/winter/index. html#/19/>.

2. *The Nicene Creed* (325 A.D.)

3. 'The Gospel in Chairs' was composed by Fr. Anthony Carbo. Brian Zahnd retitled it 'The Beautiful Gospel.' My version of the message can be heard at www.ptm.org. <http://www.ptm.org/video/chairs/>.

4. A thought inspired by Fr. Michael Gillis of Holy Nativity Orthodox Church, Langley, BC.

5. So says Brian Zahnd in most of his works, especially *Beauty Will Save the World.* He added (via email), "I'm trying to say, we (humanity) haven't always known what God is like; i.e., that the nature of God is

characterized by the kind of mercy and compassion we see in Jesus ... We used to think that God ordered the killing of Canaanites, etc., but now we know better."

6. My thoughts on this have been informed by Roger H. Mitchell, *Church, Gospel & Empire: How the Politics of Sovereignty Impregnated the West* (Eugene, OR: Wipf and Stock Publishers, 2011).

7. Eusebius, *Oration in Praise of Constantine,* 3.3, 5.

8. Derek Flood, "The More I Follow Jesus, the Less I Like His Teaching," *The Rebel God.* <http://www.therebelgod.com/2011/09/more-i-follow-jesus-less-i-like-his.html>.

Chapter 6 – Of Lions, Lambs and Donkeys

1. Note that Paul is quoting from Isa. 45:22-24, identifying Jesus with Yahweh himself, the one and only Saviour of the world.

2. Cf. Kathryn Tanner, *Jesus, Humanity and the Trinity: A Brief Systematic Theology* (Minneapolis, MN: Fortress Press, 2001).

3. Hans Urs Von Balthasar, *Mysterium Paschale,* viii-ix.

4. Thanks to Dr. Lucy Peppiatt for warning me "not to throw the glory baby out with the crappy right-wing bathwater."

5. George Grant, "St. Augustine," *Collected Works of George Grant,* ed. Arthur Davis (Toronto, ON: University of Toronto Press, 2002), 2: 484.

6. Julia Ward Howe, "Battle Hymn of the Republic" (1862). There's nothing quite as compelling as an end times hymn to inspire soldiers for battle— in this case, the carnage of the American Civil War.

7. Fr. Alexandre Turnicev, "Une approche de l'eschatologie orthodoxe," *Contacts* 18, no. 54 (1966): 102-103. My translation.

8. John Cassian, *Institutes* 8.4. *Nicene and Post-Nicene Fathers, Second Series,* Vol. 11. Ed. by Philip Schaff and Henry Wace. Trans. by C.S. Gibson. Buffalo, NY: Christian Literature Pub. Co., 1894. <http://www.newadvent.org/fathers/350708.htm>.

9. Brad Jersak, "I Saw a Lamb," in Michael Hardin, *The Jesus-Driven Life,* 2nd edition (Lancaster, PA: JDL Press, 2013).

10. George Grant, "Good Friday," *United Church Observer,* May 15, 1951, 16.

11. The word here is *bema* seat, or judgment seat, which Paul uses for 'the judgment seat of Christ' in 2 Cor. 5:10.

Chapter 7 – The Cross as Divine Consent

1. We could add supernatural law and angelic freedom, though these are not empirically observable and can only be inferred (often wrongly).

2. David Pleins, "Is God Unjust: The Tsunami and the Book of Job." <http://www.scu.edu/ethics/publications/submitted/DeCosse/Tsunami.html>.

3. Cf. Simone Weil, *On Science, Necessity and the Love of God* (London: Oxford University Press, 1968).

4. John Behr, *The Mystery of Christ: Life in Death* (New York: St. Vladimir's Seminary Press, 2006), 37.

5. Lucy Peppiatt, "Systematic Theology" (lecture, Westminster Theological Centre, Cheltenham, UK, 2013).

6. See also Aaron Riches, *Ecco Homo: On the Divine Unity of Christ* (Grand Rapids: Eerdmans, 2015), 26.

7. Ashley Collishaw, "The self-emptying God and the Necessity of Human Yielding in Engaging Salvation" (unpublished manuscript, Aug. 2013).

Chapter 8 – The Cross as Divine Participation

1. Literally, for the root word of 'crucial' is from the Latin, crux, i.e. cross!

2. Dr. Peppiatt is the principal at Westminster Theological Centre (Cheltenham, UK), where I serve on faculty.

3. David Bentley Hart, *The Experience of God: Being, Consciousness, Bliss* (London: Yale University Press, 2013), 30.

4. David Bentley Hart, *Experience of God*, 58.

5. Kathryn Tanner, *Jesus, Humanity and the Trinity*, 9.

6. Archimandrite Sophrony, *St. Silouan the Athonite* (New York: St. Vladimir's Seminary Press, 1999), 47.

7. Kathryn Tanner, *Jesus, Humanity and the Trinity*, 9.

Chapter 9 – God is Good and Sh** Happens

1. Adapted from chapter 5 of my PhD thesis, *"We are not our own": The Platonic Christianity of George P. Grant: From the Cave to the Cross and Back with Simone Weil* (Bangor University, Wales, 2012), 176-244.

2. David Cayley, *George Grant in Conversation* (Concord, ON: House of Anansi Press, 1995), 178.

3. Simone Weil, "The Love of God and Affliction," *Awaiting God* (Abbotsford, BC: Fresh Wind Press, 2013), 32-33.

4. Cf. the classic poem of St. John of the Cross, "Dark Night of the Soul."

5. Isaac Watts, "When I survey the wondrous Cross."

6. Cf. Gottfried W. Leibniz, *Theodicy: Essays on the Goodness of God, the Freedom of Man, and the Origin of Evil* (1710; Project Gutenberg, 2005). <http://www.gutenberg.org/files/17147/17147-h/17147-h.htm>.

7. David Hume, *Dialogues Concerning Natural Religion*, ed. Dorothy Coleman (Cambridge: Cambridge University Press, 2007), 74.

8. Cf. John Wesley in 1756: *Serious Thoughts Occasioned by the Earthquake at Lisbon* (1755; repro., Gale ECCO, 2010); Immanuel Kant in 1755: *Universal Natural History and Theory of the Heavens*, trans. Ian Johnson (1755; repro., Arlington, VA: Richer Resources Publications, 2009) and "The Analytic of the Sublime," *Critique of Judgment*, ed. Allen W. Wood, (New York: Modern Library, 2001), 306–8; J.–J. Rousseau, "Letter to Voltaire on Optimism," *Candide and Related Texts*, trans. David Wootton, (Indianapolis: Hacket Pub. Co. Ltd, 2000.), 108–22.

9. Immanuel Kant, "On the Failure of All Philosophical Theodicies," Michael Despland, *Kant on History and Religion* (Montreal: McGill–Queen's University Press, 1973), 290.

10. George Grant, *Philosophy in the Modern Age*, 46.

11. Voltaire, "Poem on the Lisbon Disaster or Examination of this Axiom 'All is Well,'" *Selected Poems by Voltaire* (1911).

12. Grant, "George Grant and Religion," *Collected Works* 4: 760-1.

13. Simone Weil, *On Science, Necessity, and the Love of God* (London, New York, Toronto: Oxford University Press, 1968), 181.

14. Brad Jersak, "Simone Weil: Grant's Diotima," *Red Tory, Red Virgin* (Abbotsford, BC: Fresh Wind Press, 2013), 7.

15. Adapted Richard Rohr, *Job and the Mystery of Suffering* (New York: The Crossword Publishing Company, 1998), 25.

Chapter 10 – Love and Wrath as Consent

1. John Cassian, *Institutes* 8.4.

2. Cf. James Fowler, *Stages of Faith* (Harper & Row, 1981). A caveat is in order. As Walter Thiessen (of St. Stephen's University) points out in "The Mosaic of Maturing Spirituality" (unpublished draft), we all have an underlying need to grow through multiple stages simultaneously. For example, parts of our heart may need an anchor that requires a stage 2 season, while in other areas we might already be working other stages. We may also need to revisit various stages as we continue to develop.

3. I say natural and supernatural, because (i) God's order (secondary causes) extends beyond our empirical or rational categories, and (ii) the natural and supernatural realms interrelate beyond our observation or comprehension. Mysteriously, we too interrelate with God's order through our own power of consent to 'bind and loose' (Matt. 16:19) through love and prayer, to intercede in ways that might spare someone the consequences of these 'laws.' This is a great mystery!

Chapter 11 – Divine Wrath as Giving Over

1. Cf. Douglas Campbell, *The Deliverance of God: An Apocalyptic Rereading of Justification in Paul* (Grand Rapids, MI: Eerdmans, 2009).

2. Euripedes, *Bacchae*, line 795, ed. T. A. Buckley. <http://www.perseus.tufts.edu/>.

3. Sean, ever the good Anglican, says, "Agonistic struggle is what we engage in – and then go for a pint." Email exchange in Feb. 2104.

Chapter 12 – Unwrathing the Cross part 1

1. See also Deut. 7:8; 9:26; 13:5; 24:18; 2 Sam. 7:23; 1 Chron. 17:21; Neh. 1:10; Ps. 74:2; 77:15; 78:42; 106:10; 107:2).

2. Isa. 41:14; 43:14; 44:6, 24; 47:4; 48:17; 49:7; 49:26; 54:5, 8; 59:20; 60:16; 63:16.

Chapter 13 – Unwrathing the Cross part 2

1. Gustav Aulen, *Christus Victor: An Historical Study of the Three Main Types of the Idea of Atonement*, trans. A. G. Herbert (London: SPCK, 1931). It has remained the Eastern view from the beginning and finds fresh voices in the West, esp. among Anabaptists. Cf. J. Denny Weaver, *The Nonviolent Atonement: Human Violence, Discipleship and God* (Grand Rapids, MI: Eerdmans, 2007); ed. Brad Jersak and Michael Hardin, *Stricken by God? Nonviolent Identification and the Victory of Christ* (Grand Rapids, MI: Eerdmans, 2008).

2. Readers can sample the debate via the dialogue between John Piper and N.T. Wright on *justification* in their respective books on the subject.

3. Irenaeus, *Against Heresies*, 3.18.7.

4. John Calvin, *Calvin's Institutes*, 2.16.10.

5. Dr. Taylor Marshall "8 Bible Verses on Christ's Descent into Hell." <http://taylormarshall.com/2012/04/8-bible-verses-on-christs-descent-into.html>.

6. See Morgan Guyton, "Isaiah 7 and 53: Should Prophecies by Prooftexts," *Mercy Not Sacrifice* (blog), Patheos, October 18, 2013. <http://morgan-guyton.us/2013/10/18/isaiah-7-53-should-prophecies-be-prooftexts>.

Chapter 14 – A More Christlike Message

1. Steve Robinson, "The Gospel According to Chairs," <https://www.youtube.com/watch?v=TZrsbCK5Hrg>.

2. Brian's Zahnd, "The Gospel in Chairs." <https://www.youtube.com/watch?v=Wnj52gaauBs>.

Brad Jersak, "The Gospel in Chairs," with an introductory interview with Lucy Smith, who presents it in the UK. <http://vimeo.com/57271733>.

3. *Totally depraved* is a phrase commonly used by Reformers like Luther and Calvin. See glossary for definition.

4. John Cassian, Against Nestorius, on the Passion 6.22, trans. Edgar C. S. Gibson. <http://www.ccel.org/ccel/schaff/npnf211.iv.vii.vii.xxii.html>.

5. Derek Rishmawy, "Godzilla and the Salvific Destruction of God," TGC, <http://www.thegospelcoalition.org/article/godzilla-and-the-salvific-destruction-of-god>.

6. John Piper, "Who made it okay for God to kill women and children in the Old Testament?" *Desiring God Interviews* (Desiring God Foundation, 2015). In the copyright notices at the bottom of the webpage, readers are encouraged to 'Share the Joy.' <http://www.desiringgod.org/interviews/what-made-it-ok-for-god-to-kill-women-and-children-in-the-old-testament>.

7. Tradition says she and her family were eventually martyred by Nero (in about 66 AD) for refusing to deny their Savior. Ironically, after torturing her, Nero had her thrown down a well, where she surrendered her soul to God. Cf. "St. Photini, the Samaritan Woman," The Self-Ruled Antiochian Orthodox Christian Archdiocese of North America.<http://www.antiochian.org/node/17560. <http://www.antiochian.org/node/17560>.

8. From the Orthodox 'Trisagion Prayers.'

9. "So it is in Gehenna: the contrition that comes from love is the harsh torment; but in the case of the sons of heaven, delight in this love inebriates their souls." St. Isaac the Syrian, *Daily Readings with St. Isaac of Syria*, Daily Readings Series (Templegate Publishing, 1988), 83.

10. I'm using Brian's Zahnd's script here, because of its essential 'tightness.'

11. Francis Thompson, "The Hound of Heaven," *The Oxford Book of English Mystical Verse*, eds. D. H. S. Nicholson and A. H. E. Lee (Oxford University Press, 1917). <http://www.bartleby.com/236/239.html>.

Appendix – Some More Christlike Voices

1. Origen, *Commentary on the Gospel According to John, Books 1-10*, Book 1.231, trans. Ronald E. Heine, *Fathers of the Christian Church: A New Translation*, Vol. 80 (Washington, DC: Catholic University of America Press, 1989), 80.

2. Gregory of Nyssa, "Address on Religious Instruction," *Christology of the Later Fathers*, ed. Edward R. Hardy (Philadelphia, PA: Westminster Press, 1954), 301-2.

3. Gregory of Nazianzus, *Five Theological Orations*, Oration 3, *On the Son 1*, §19, trans. Stephen Reynolds (Estate of Stephen Reynolds, 2011), 65. <https://tspace.library.utoronto.ca/bitstream/1807/36303/1/Gregory%20of%20Nazianzus%20Theological%20Orations.pdf>.

4. Gregory of Nazianzus, *Orations*, Oration 4, *On the Son 2* §3, 72-3.

5. Gregory of Nazianzus, *Orations*, Oration 4, *On the Son 2* §6, 76-7.

6. Isaac of Nineveh, *Homily* 39.6. Cited in Kalliston Ware, *The Inner Kingdom* (Crestwood, NY: St. Vladimir's Seminary Press, 2000), 209.

7. Isaac of Nineveh, *Homily* 45(48). Ibid, 209.

8. Isaac of Nineveh, *Homily* 39.15, 22. Ibid, 209.

9. Isaac of Nineveh, cited in Scott Cairns (ed.), *Love's Immensity, Mystics on the Endless Life* (Brewster, MA: Paraclete Press, 2007), n.p.

10. Gregory Palamas, "On the Parable of the Prodigal," *The Homilies*, trans. Christopher Veniamin (Dalton, PA: Mount Thabor Pub, 2014), 17.

11. Hans Urs Von Balthasar, *Theo-Drama: Theological Dramatic Theory*, Vol. 4: The Action, trans. Graham Harrison (San Francisco, CA: Ignatius Press), 1994, 323.

12. Kallistos Ware, personal interview, Oct. 16, 2014, Oxford.

13. Andrew Louth, personal interview, Oct. 21, 2014, Darlington.

14. Andrew Louth, *Maximus the Confessor* (London, Routledge, 1996), 34.

15. John Behr, personal correspondence, Oct. 20, 2014.

16. John Behr, *The Mystery of Christ: Life in Death* (Crestwood, NY: St. Vladimir's Seminary Press, 2006), 35.

17. Conor Cunningham, personal interview, Sept. 11, 2014, Nottingham. Cf. Conor Cunningham, *Darwin's Pious Idea* (Wm. B. Eerdmans Pub. Co., 2010), 165; Pope Paul VI, *Gaudium Et Spes* 22. Vatican II. <http://www.vatican.va/archive/hist_councils/ii_vatican_council/documents/vat-ii_const_19651207_gaudium-et-spes_en.html>.

18. Simon Oliver, personal interview, Sept. 8, 2014, Nottingham.

19. Aaron Riches, personal correspondence, Nov. 19, 2014.

20. David Goa, personal correspondence, n.d.

Glossary

'*Anthropomorphism*' – is a description of something not human (like a tree) or more than human (God) using personal human characteristics. Bible authors speak of God's 'anger' to describe their experiences of the consequences of sin. But with God, reactive emotions such as 'anger' are anthropomorphic, to be understood figuratively, not literally. Anthropomorphisms read literally reduce God into a human projection—an idol—whereas the Incarnation of Christ truly unveiled God.

'*Apologetics*' – is not apologizing for something. It is the study of how to defend the faith in the face of objections. As the Apostle Peter wrote, "Always be prepared to give an answer to everyone who asks you to give the reason for the hope that you have. But do this with gentleness and respect" (1 Pet. 3:15). Sadly, when we don't trust the power of the gospel to generate faith, we may lapse into apologetics to try to argue people into belief.

'*Atonement*' – is a synonym for reconciliation. Through the ministry of Christ, we are reconciled with God. We are drawn from estrangement back into relationship with the God who has always loved us. Some English Bibles (since the Tyndale Bible in 1534) translate words meaning reconciliation as '*atonement*'—literally "at-one-ment." By grace, Jesus restores us to *oneness* with God—to the unity and harmony God intended since Eden.

'*Atonement theories*' - The atonement is a mystery, but various 'atonement theories' have been proposed to explore the 'how' of atonement. Sometimes 'atonement theories' become so dominant that they take on 'gospel' status and displace the actual gospel story and the biblical metaphors. For example, 'penal substitution' has been such a dominant theory of the atonement that those who don't hold it have been called 'enemies of the Cross' by some who do.

'Biblical literalism' – is a theory of interpretation that privileges a literal reading of any Scripture unless to do so is impossible. In practice, biblical literalism often imposes literal meanings onto the text where they were neither intended by the author, nor advisable given the genre, nor possible in light of the revelation of Christ.

'Biblicism' – is an ideology that so emphasizes the exclusive authority and all-sufficiency of Scripture it makes the Bible, rather than Christ, "the Word of God" and our "final authority for faith and practice." Biblicism is committed to infallibility and inerrancy. That is, by supernatural guidance, biblical authors were incapable of error; every word was factually true. Thus, biblicism is prone to forcing contradictory passages to harmonize where they are not meant to. The Bible is flattened so all texts have equal authority with the words of Christ—even when the image of God they portray conflicts with the revelation of God in Christ.

'Bibliolatry' – is a reverence for Scripture that becomes worship of the book itself, where the Bible is described in terms only attributable to God himself, and loyalty to one's interpretation of the Bible trumps faithfulness to the Gospel.

'Christendom' – is the sum total of Christian culture, especially where Christianity or the church institution forms a kingdom of sorts. Christendom has historically included actual geopolitical kingdoms, but also any cultural dominance that Christians enjoy or impose when they are strong enough to hold sway as a majority or powerful minority.

'Church' – can be interpreted as (i) a vague universal idea; (ii) a general organization, institution or movement; (iii) particular local fellowships or trans-local communities; (iv) brick-and-mortar buildings and/or their worship activities. I normally use the term to refer to (i) the whole 'people of God' (1 Pet. 2:10) 'in Christ' (2 Cor. 5:17), redeemed by grace 'through faith in his name' (John 1:12, Eph. 2:8), throughout time. I will also allude to specific *forms* of church using adjectives such as 'ancient,' 'western,' 'local,' and 'visible' when referring to particular fellowships or institutions.

The church is more than an institution. It is the *race of Christ* in the place of the race of Adam. Paul saw the church as *Christ's body*, in which we are included through baptism (1 Cor. 12:13. The church is also a *faith family*, in which we are adopted or reborn as beloved children of God. The church is also the Lord's *banqueting table*, where we are united by sharing his supper (Christ's body and blood) together.

'Contemplative prayer' – consists of silent listening, expectant waiting, openness and surrender.

'Cruciform' – literally means cross-shaped, as in the form of the crucifixion. A *cruciform* God would be the God whose nature (love) is revealed through 'Christ and him crucified' (1 Cor. 2:2).

'Divine Energies' – are God himself at work. They are not merely attributes of God, but rather, God himself in his actions, in his activity, in his self-revelation to us. We'll never penetrate the infinite depths of God's *essence*, but God's *energies* do penetrate our lives and our world. Another phrase we use for these energies is 'the grace of the Holy Spirit.'

'Evangelical' – I have capitalized 'Evangelical' when referring to the movement within Western, Protestant Christianity, especially in its conservative and revivalist forms. Lower-case 'evangelical' refers in general to Christian faith in the 'evangel' or gospel of Jesus as Savior of the world.

'Faith statement' – is a premise we believe with confidence but cannot prove in a court or test in a lab. But empirical proof or airtight logic is neither necessary nor sufficient for faith. Instead, we may have sufficient *warrant* for our confidence (vis-à-vis certitude) that we might even truthfully say, 'We know.' Cf. Alvin Plantinga, *Warrant and Proper Function* (Oxford: Oxford University Press, 1993).

'Freedom' – is often the illusion of autonomy and our own self-will. Debates continue as to whether 'free will' is a reality or a delusion. What we call 'freedom' is often the illusion of autonomy and our own self-will.

I would define true 'freedom' as (i) God's loving consent to our authentic otherness, and (ii) the human flourishing that results from our loving consent to God's care.

'Fundamentalism' – is an ever-shifting term that has now become a pejorative synonym for extremism. As I use it here, it refers to the branch of any religion, ideology or movement that has become dogmatic, militant and set in its resolve to purge their movement or society of the perceived heresies of their opponents. Fundamentalism can surface in any group, from left or right on the religious or political spectrum, including Christian or atheist extremes.

'Ground of Being' – is a phrase usually attributed to the theologian, Paul Tillich. I borrow it here not to identify with his theology so much as to introduce my own—the 'panentheism' of ancient Orthodoxy (God is not all, but God is in all). Chrysostom's Divine Liturgy has us pray, "O heavenly King, O Comforter, the Spirit of truth, *who art in all places and fillest all things, come dwell in us.*"

'Identification (participation)' – Christ can represent us because he completely identified with us. He embraced and assumed every aspect of human nature, inheriting every cell of his humanity from a willing human mother, so that Paul can say, God sent "his own Son in the likeness of sinful flesh" (Rom. 5:3). He not only identified with our human nature, but also with the totality of the human condition.

'Incarnation' – is the great truth that in Christ, God became human. As John 1:14 says, "the Word became flesh." When we use the word 'Incarnation,' some mistakenly reduce this to the initial event, the birth of Jesus. But the Incarnation refers to both the whole life of Jesus and to Jesus himself. Jesus is the Incarnation of God.

'Justify,' 'Justification' – In Greek, the word (*dikaios*) can be translated 'just' or 'righteous.' This word can refer either to someone's character (moral purity) or to their legal standing (innocence). In the Bible, it includes our standing with and before God, the good and merciful Judge, both now and finally on the Day of Judgment.

'Kenosis,' 'kenotic theology' – is Greek for emptying, used by Paul in Phil. 2 to describe Christ's self-emptying power, self-giving love and radical servanthood, especially revealed in the Passion. *Kenotic theology* refers to the spectrum of theologies—from orthodox to heretical—that identify *kenosis* as an attribute of Trinitarian glory, rather than a departure from it. Thus, Jesus' *kenosis* reflects the Father's own self-giving, cruciform love.

'Kinsman-redeemer' – Under Jewish law, if someone lost their property, freedom or inheritance, their closest relative or the clan patriarch could buy it back for them at *any* time. He could restore their place in the clan under his protection and patronage.

'Literalism' – here refers to insisting on interpreting the whole Bible literally, as if that were the only way to acknowledge it as true. The reality is that the authors of Scripture also use genres such as poetry, parable and hyperbole, and thus often intend and require their words to be read symbolically if we want to understand their true meaning.

'Negative theology' – is also known as the via negativa (the negative way) or apophatic theology. 'Apophatic' comes from the Greek word for 'deny.' It defines God by denying our definitions of God as being able to encompass or pigeonhole God.

'The New Atheists' – are a particular stream of scientists, writers and media voices who directly attack religious faith (and especially Christianity) considering it a dangerous and violent delusion that needs to be actively repressed and destroyed. The New Atheists include scientists and writers such as Richard Dawkins (*The God Delusion*), Daniel Dennett (*Breaking the Spell: Religion as a Natural Phenomena*), Sam Harris (*The End of Faith*), and the late Christopher Hitchens (*God is Not Good*).

'Neo-Reformed' or *'New Calvinist'* – is the current iteration of classic *Calvinism* (the theology of John Calvin), and typically retains the five major Reformed 'doctrines of grace' under the acronym TULIP: 1. total depravity, 2. unconditional election, 3. limited

atonement, 4. irresistible grace and 5. the perseverance of the saints.
<http://www.reformedreader.org/t.u.l.i.p.htm>.

'Orthodox' – is theology or doctrine that conforms to the plumbline of the 'faith once delivered' (Jude 3) by Christ through the apostles and defined by the early church fathers in the creeds and councils of the ancient church.

'The Passion' of Christ – refers to the events and accounts of Jesus' suffering and death.

'Prayer ministers' – can range from licensed counselors to volunteer laypeople who have been trained to pray with people through spiritual and emotional wounds (sometimes called 'inner healing'). Many approaches to inner healing exist. *The Immanuel Approach, Elijah House* and *Theophostic* are all effective examples, but depend greatly on the gifts, training and availability of the minister. The final chapter of my first book, *Can You Hear Me?*, is a widely used prayer manual that I've developed.

'Ransom' – is a biblical metaphor, based in the Exodus story (ransom from slavery to Pharaoh) that points to Jesus' rescue of those taken by death and held in the grave. The ransom 'price' is Jesus' life—Death (personified) is paid, but 'payment' might be too strong a word because Death can't hold him.

'Redemption' – like *ransom*, the redemption metaphor (and God as *Redeemer*) originates with the Exodus narrative and is largely about rescuing people out of some bondage or oppression into which they had somehow fallen. God-in-Christ redeems us from the bondage of Satan, sin and death.

'Revivalism' – begins with the promise of 2 Chron. 7:14, which says, "If my people, who are called by my name, will humble themselves and pray and seek my face and turn from their wicked ways, then I will hear from heaven, and I will forgive their sin and will heal their land." Revivalism refers to the Evangelical pursuit of that promise through 'revival meetings,' such that revival became its own religious culture and system.

'**Righteousness**' – is being in 'right relationship' with God through trust in God's faithfulness through Christ. By grace, Christ restores us to covenant faithfulness with God and restores us to covenant faithfulness in this world. Practically, we are empowered by grace to love God and neighbor. We err by attempting to attain personal righteousness without grace, just as we err when we don't allow grace to empower us for personal righteousness.

'**Save**' – is a popular but slippery term. In the New Testament, it can refer to redemption, healing or deliverance. It can point to a literal rescue, a particular conversion event, a life-long faith journey or even our future resurrection. In this book, readers will normally be able to interpret the word 'save' according to usage. However, they should not assume the standard narrow evangelical use that identifies 'getting saved' with the moment we say the 'Sinner's Prayer.' In my view, salvation is (i) what God did through Christ (ii) and does in us (iii) in our journey towards union with him.

'**Secondary causes**' – are when God allows natural law and human freedom to do their thing. God is ultimately responsible for all that is—for natural law and for human freedom—but we would say he doesn't directly cause or control human actions or natural events.

'**Spiritual director**' – is when one person assists another's spiritual development. Ironically, the best directors are very *non-directive* companions. They listen well and ask insightful questions that lead the 'directee' to self-discovery, contemplative awareness and clarity about their life journey.

'**Special creation**' – is defined by Creationists as the supernatural creation of independent, complex life forms (or at least humans) by God without any evolutionary development. This version of special creation interprets Genesis literally, so that the whole universe came to be in six 24-hour days less than 10,000 years ago.

'**Theist**' – is a believer in God. Hence, a monotheist believes in one god, a polytheist in multiple gods and an atheist in no gods. Christian *theists* believe in one God in three persons (the Trinity).

'*Total depravity*' – is a doctrine that says that all humanity is born in a state of radical and pervasive corruption due to 'original sin,' thought to infect every part of human nature and to make the natural man unable to know or obey God. In this state, we are dead in our transgressions and sins, and only able to come to spiritual life by unconditional grace. If this were exactly the case, then the universal salvation of all people would be in order, but Calvinists usually believe that God sovereignly elects only some for regeneration, leaving the rest to condemnation.

'*Triumphalist*' or '*triumphalism*' – is a narrow focus or boastful pride in the superiority, dominance and victory of one's faith or one's God, to the exclusion of the realities of weakness and denial of suffering. When our faith is triumphalistic, those who suffer (e.g., Job) may infer or even be accused of failing God or being weak in faith.

Unwrathing – is the interpretive process by which we recognize wrath as a metaphor for God's consent ('giving over') to the consequences of sin, even when the text describes events as if God were actively provoked into violently punishing people.

'*Voluntarism*' – is the primacy of freedom of the will in God or people—it is prior even to love as the primary attribute of God. Thus, voluntarism believes that whatever God wills is good rather than God only willing what is good. For people, it means that freedom, not love, is the highest moral obligation.

'*Wrath*' – Literal human wrath combines emotional anger with violent action. Divine wrath is so called because when we suffer the self-destructive consequences (the wages) of sin, we infer that we're experiencing God's anger and violence. In actuality, biblical 'wrath' is a metaphor for the intrinsic consequences of our refusal to live in the mercies of God.

Shout-outs

It's a joy for me to give 'shout-outs' to key contributors who've shaped my thought and paved the way for this book. Initially, I got carried away and included scores of names over three pages. You were probably one of them. Here's the drastically reduced shortlist.

First, many thanks to my colleagues at Plain Truth Ministries. Their journey includes the courageous story of how God freed them from the bondage of legalistic religion to embrace, as my friend Greg Albrecht says, "Faith alone, grace alone and Christ alone." Their beautiful gospel of the Christlike God helps so many spiritual refugees. What wonderful providence that we would become co-laborers in the kingdom of grace! Greg's Albrecht's hospitality and friendship was emulated by the rest of the staff; so thanks, Laura Urista, Marv Wegner and Dennis Warkentin for your work on this book. Thank you for your generous provision and remarkable trust as I put the good news of *A More Christlike God* into words.

Second, to the faith communities, academic colleagues and spiritual leaders who came alongside me to model and minister the Christlike God to me, my deepest thanks. I think especially of my intercessors, Fresh Wind, All Saints of NA Monastery, Westminster Theological Centre, Soulstream and my 12-step recovery friends.

Third, to those who worked on the book itself, thanks for your laborious line-editing (Greg, Laura and Adria Vizzi Holub), theological corrections (Greg, Dr. Lucy Peppiatt and Fr. Michael Azkoul) and generous endorsements (and great suggestions). Thanks, Brian Zahnd, for the foreword and your help in developing this message.

Finally, thanks to my family: Lloyd and Irene Jersak, for preserving me from so many un-Christlike images of God through my childhood. And most of all, to Eden, Stephen, Justice and Dominic Jersak, for your patience and willingness to support, engage and indulge this nerdy theologian.

Author Bio

Bradley Jersak

Bradley Jersak is married to Eden Jersak and father to Stephen, Justice and Dominic. They currently live in Abbotsford, BC Canada.

After serving twenty years as an ordained pastor (Bethel Mennonite Church, Aldergrove) and church planter (Fresh Wind, Abbotsford), Brad was chrismated into the Orthodox Church (OCA) and ordained, 'Reader Irenaeus.'

After leaving the pastorate, he completed a PhD in theology at Bangor University (Wales) and some post-doc research (in *kenotic* theology) at the University of Nottingham.

Today, Brad serves as the senior editor of Plain Truth Ministries (Pasadena) and writes for *CWRm* (Christianity Without the Religion Magazine). He manages the *CWRblog* (www.christianity-without-the-religion.blogspot.ca) and www.clarion-journal.com as well.

Brad is also on the faculty of Westminster Theological Centre (Cheltenham, UK), where he teaches New Testament and Patristics. He is adjunct faculty at St. Stephen's University (St. Stephen, New Brunswick).

A More Christlike God is Brad's tenth book (author, co-author or editor). He is also available for seminars on this topic. You can contact the author via www.ptm.org or www.bradjersak.com. Or you can email him at bradjersak@gmail.com.

CPSIA information can be obtained at www.ICGtesting.com
Printed in the USA
LVOW04s1501180815

450590LV00023BA/497/P